THE SERPENTS
AMONG US

THE SERPENTS AMONG US

How to Protect Your Children
From Sexual Predators
A Police Investigator's Perspective

Investigator
PATRICK CROUGH

Millstone Justice
www.millstonejustice.org

**IT IS OUR SINCERE DESIRE TO OFFER THIS BOOK
TO ALL PARENTS AT NO CHARGE**

If you feel led to support the printing and distribution of additional books, as well
as the promotion of the book's message, please send a gift of any amount to:

Millstone Justice Children's Advocacy Organization

P.O. Box 277 • Webster, New York 14580

Or visit our web site: www.millstonejustice.org

Millstone Justice is a not-for-profit organization.

Published for the author by

Millstone Justice Children's Advocacy Organization

www.millstonejustice.org

Printed in the United States of America

"Speak up for those who cannot speak for themselves; ensure justice for those being crushed."
PROVERBS 31:8 (NLT)

DEDICATION

"...Trampled like a rose..."

This book is dedicated to the memory of
KALI ANN POULTON,
CARMEN COLON, WANDA WALKOWICZ AND
MICHELLE MAENZA,
as well as to the surviving unnamed children,
who have fallen victim to child predators.

Their tragic stories have been included in this book for the
sole purpose of protecting other children.

TABLE *of* CONTENTS

PREFACE

*T*he evil specter of child abuse is enormously present in our society, afflicting children of all ages, races and gender. Since 1990, and due to national attention, reported incidents of child abuse and molestation have risen alarmingly, with tens of thousands of cases investigated each year.

In order to better address this tragedy, more must be done by authoritative agencies and institutions to raise awareness within our population. Children must be understood to be under-protected, visibly vulnerable, and at times void of human rights considerations. The compassion which must be given to children cannot be limited to parents and to family: it must become the consciousness of the entire community.

To violate the innocence of a child goes far beyond despicability. It is a heinous, ruthless crime that demands the most stringent punishment that the law will allow.

Patrick Crough has provided a compassionate and insightful document based on his many years of dealing with these crimes as a criminal investigator. This will not be comfortable fireside reading. This is a direct, graphic and lurid study of crimes against children. Some will read part of it but will lack the heart to continue, while others will read it over their tears, roll up their sleeves and come out fighting.

JOHN S. WALKER
Facilitator of Child Abuse Network
Rochester, New York

INTODUCTION

This book's content represents my personal perspective and is intended to offer a practical, simple presentation of how child predators operate in today's society. It will educate any concerned parent or guardian about how to recognize when a child predator is in their midst; how to protect their child from that predator; how to recognize if their child has already been offended by a predator; and what to do if their child discloses that they have been offended by a predator. For the adult reader who was sexually molested as a child, it is my hope that this resource may assist you in making some sense out of what happened to you, and help you understand that it wasn't your fault.

First, we will lay a framework to help parents understand the common tactics that predators use to gain access to, seduce, and maintain control of a child. We will discuss specific defensive countermeasures against these tactics. We will study a dozen specific cases that will allow you to apply the principles that you are learning to real-life scenarios that unfold every day all around you. Along the way you will hear my opinion on matters that many parents wrestle with, such as a child's right to privacy versus a parent's right to know, children's cell phone and Internet usage, whether victims should fight back against violent attackers, and how to get your teenagers to open up to you. While you may not agree with every opinion I present here, one thing is certain: when you have finished reading this book, you will be far better equipped to protect your children. If you choose to fully educate yourself on this dark and difficult topic, you will be able to have more peace of mind as your children grow and navigate through many potential dangers.

PATRICK CROUGH - *Author*

SECTION I

—⁓—

UNDERSTANDING
THE SERPENT

CHAPTER 1

—∿—

"MOTHER'S INTUITION"

God has blessed all mothers with two special gifts: the privilege of bringing a new life into the world, and the gift that we often call "mother's intuition" or "woman's intuition." They can pick their child's cry out of a crowded room and know whether they are hungry, angry or hurt. Or without even turning around, they know that their child is up to something. Doubtless, any mother will tell you that sometimes they get it wrong. But they share a special bond with their children that men sometimes can not comprehend. Aside from observing the miracle of this gift at work in my wife with our three children, I have never witnessed a more obvious testament to a mother's intuition than the tragic case of Kali Ann Poulton. Kali was a beautiful, blond four-year-old, full of life and promise before she was kidnapped and brutally murdered by someone that Kali and her mother knew. I share this story with the utmost respect for the woman who lost her beloved child to an undetected child predator.

On the warm spring night of May 23, 1994, Kali begged her mom, Judy Gifford, to allow her to go outside to play on her Big Wheel tricycle. The apartment complex, a quaint and well-kept cluster of two-story buildings nestled in a forest of large maple and oak trees, was teeming with activity thanks to the beautiful weather. Judy was preparing magazines that she was to deliver that evening. The small amount of money that this single mother made from her second job was to pay for a family trip to Disney World the following summer. As Judy put the flyers together, Kali became more and more anxious to go outside. She was looking forward to going to McDonald's after the deliveries were completed. Her mom had promised her a snack and time to play in its outdoor children's play area.

Spring fever was getting the best of both of them, so Judy finally relented and allowed little Kali to go outside and sit on her Big Wheel. She instructed Kali to stay right in front of their apartment door so that she could keep a watchful eye on her as she hastily finished her task. Within minutes, Judy was ready to load up the car and begin her deliveries. When she called out to Kali, there was no response. Judy found no sign of her daughter when she checked outside their apartment. The panic-stricken mother immediately began calling out her daughter's name and scanning the apartment complex grounds. Concerned neighbors began to assist with the frantic search, but still there was no sign of the young child or her tricycle.

About twenty minutes into the search, Judy spotted her neighbor Mark, who had moved into the complex approximately six weeks earlier with his girlfriend and their eighteen-month-old son. Mark was carrying his son to the playground area. Judy noticed that his high-top sneakers were untied. She asked him if he had seen Kali. Mark responded "no," and continued walking. Soon the police were called, and the first of two nightmares that every parent fears crystallized: a beloved child was missing, and no one had any clue where she was.

Patrol deputies and command officers coordinated a physical search throughout the night for the missing girl, while detectives from the Monroe County Sheriff Zone A Substation interviewed the girl's parents, their friends, and family members for additional information. At 4:00 AM the incident was re-classified from a missing person investigation to a kidnapping investigation. This triggered an escalation to the Monroe County Sheriff's Major Crimes Unit, which consisted of three investigators: Investigator Thomas Passmore, me and our supervisor, Investigator Sergeant Gary Caiola. I remember Sergeant Caiola's words from his phone call that morning. "A four-year-old girl has been missing all night," he said. "And it doesn't look good."

Shortly after our arrival, Investigator Passmore and I interviewed Kali's mother. I asked Judy who she thought we should consider as a potential suspect, but she couldn't think of anyone. Then I asked her if anyone had recently moved into the apartment complex who had shown an open affection for Kali. She responded, "There's this guy named Mark who just moved in about six weeks ago. He gives me the creeps." She shared that she and Kali had first met Mark and his son at the apartment complex playground several weeks before. On two or three different occasions, Mark had complimented her on how beautiful Kali was. During one of those encounters, Mark asked Judy if she thought that Kali would tell her if someone tried to touch her in an inappropriate way. Judy responded, "Yes," and felt very unsettled by his odd question. Within the next few days, Investigator Passmore and I made contact with Mark. Mark Christie had a criminal record, but nothing related to crimes against children. He grew up in the village of Hilton, New York. As a youth, he was considered to be a bit of a punk who walked around with a chip on his shoulder. Based upon our initial contact with him, that chip was still firmly in place. We interviewed Mark with the assistance of another colleague, Investigator Bill Connell, for several long hours one evening, but he maintained his innocence, denying any involvement with Kali's disappearance. All three of us felt that he was lying, but we didn't want to spook him into seeking an attorney, which would make us lose the opportunity for a second interview. A second interview would be critical if Mark had kidnapped or murdered Kali, but a defense attorney would never allow his client to help the police locate a victim's body unless the prosecution granted very serious concessions or total immunity. It was excruciatingly painful to let him go.

Mark maintained his silence for approximately two and one-half years. Except for Investigator Passmore and me, nearly everyone discounted Mark as a viable suspect because Judy had seen him near the play area with his son so shortly after her daughter went missing. Thousands of calls, none of which I ever considered a workable lead, were investigated by an army-sized task force of detectives and federal agents. Many potential suspects were interviewed. Many were interrogated in vain. Not one witness or lead was ever produced. I never lost hope, believing relentlessly that every case is just one phone call away from being solved, no matter how bleak the circumstances. We knew that we just had to be patient and prepared to recognize and act on a pertinent phone call if it ever came. Investigator Passmore and I maintained a low-key, casual relationship with Mark. Mark knew that he was our suspect, because we told him that we were ready to talk about getting Kali back to her parents whenever he was ready.

Mark and his family eventually moved from that apartment complex to one located in Wayne County, which borders Monroe County on the east. On August 9th, 1996, our break came: we learned that during an argument with his wife the night before, Mark had blurted out that he killed Kali. This admission sprung from a desperate attempt to gain sympathy from his wife, who had decided to leave him due to his strange behavior. Thanks be to God, Mark's wife immediately left with their son and drove to her father's house, where she promptly called 911. As promising as this lead was, it did not guarantee a conviction at trial that would send Mark to prison. Mark had not given his wife specific details of what had occurred. Her testimony would be challenged in a pretrial hearing, because in New York State, such an admission to one's spouse is considered protected and privileged. It was critical to interview him before an attorney became involved and closed the door on us.

On that particular day, I was working alone. After I learned that Mark might still be at his residence, I immediately drove across half the county to speak with him. Upon my arrival I was met at Mark's front door by his mother. She was infuriated by my presence, shouting that Mark was going to see his attorney, not going with me. Mark appeared dejected, as if he was already resolved to his fate. In spite of his mother's objections, Mark agreed to get a cup of coffee with me, provided that I transport him to his attorney's office afterward. Mark sat in the front seat of my unmarked police car beside me, un-handcuffed. He said that he would tell me everything I wanted to know after he spoke with his attorney. I replied that any lawyer worth their salt would not allow him to speak with me about what happened with Kali, and that meant that her parents would never find out exactly what happened to their baby, or if she had suffered.

"She didn't suffer." Mark responded.

"I hope not." I said.

As we drove back towards Rochester, I suggested that we get some lunch. Mark liked that idea, saying that he was "starving." We settled on an Italian restaurant on Lyell Avenue in the city named Roncone's. Once seated, Mark ordered Chicken Parmesan with spaghetti, while I ordered linguini in red sauce with sausage. As we waited for our food to arrive, Mark and I sipped our Cokes and ate freshly-baked Italian bread. There is something about the casual, comfortable atmosphere of a family-style Italian restaurant that puts people at ease. The smell of a good pasta sauce and the sharing of fresh bread can make would-be adversaries become friends.

Mark stated that he felt bad for what he had done to Kali. He said that he had been living a nightmare ever since, haunted by Kali's face on missing child posters all over the country. Over the two and one-half years that Kali had been missing, the case had featured prominently on local and national news and talk shows, including *America's Most Wanted* and *The Oprah Winfrey Show*. Knowing Mark to be a person who liked to feel in control, I attempted to appeal to his pride. I told him that he had beaten the police, fair and square. Mark opened up to this praise just as I had hoped: he said that he didn't want to sound like he was bragging, but thought that the way he eluded us by getting rid of the Big Wheel was "pretty ingenious." I feigned agreement and told him that I thought it was an amazing feat. A short time later, he asked me if I wanted to know how he "pulled it off." His ego was getting the best of him. Keeping a sober tone and a casual expression, I responded, "Sure."

Mark warned me that he would only discuss the Big Wheel, not what happened to Kali. I reassured him that he didn't have to tell me anything that he wasn't comfortable discussing. Mark informed me that the Big Wheel was in his apartment for three days after he killed Kali, and the police had missed it when they searched his apartment. I asked him how that was possible. He explained that he had cut the Big Wheel into tiny pieces and hid it in various places that he knew the police would not have legal grounds to search for such small items. Because time was of the essence to locate the missing little girl, Mark knew that the police were attempting to search every apartment under the "exigent circumstances exception" without a search warrant. The exception allowed the police to look for a missing child to preserve their life, but not for evidence of a crime. The search of each apartment thus had to be limited to spaces that a child's body could be concealed in, but nothing smaller. This equated to searching rooms, closets, underneath beds, storage bins and crawl spaces. Most of the apartment searches were completed with the occupant's consent. If the occupant was unavailable, the search teams were accompanied by an apartment complex manager.

Mark said that he hid the pieces of Kali's Big Wheel in articles of clothing which were stored in drawers and cabinets, concealing them so well that even his wife never found a single piece. Remarkably, Mark accomplished this before his wife returned home from work the very same night that he murdered Kali. When he needed to sneak the Big Wheel through the police roadblock at the apartment complex entrance, Mark placed the tiny pieces in several small duffel bags and put them in the passenger compartment of his vehicle. Mark said that seven New York State Troopers were at the roadblock when he passed through with Kali's Big Wheel. He thought that his heart was going to jump out of his chest when he handed the keys over to one of the troopers, thinking that they were going to search his entire vehicle and everything in it. However, they never asked to see what was inside the duffel bags. Once through the roadblock, Mark drove to each of the four corners of the county and got rid of the pieces.

Our food was delivered to us, and Mark and I continued to talk as we ate our lunch. It was surreal. Here we were, sitting among sixty other patrons eating their lunch, talking about one of the most brutal crimes anyone could ever commit—the rape and murder of a young child.

Mark told me that he had read a "big book" on police interrogation and was impressed with Investigator Passmore and me after he read it, since we did everything that the book said that we should do when we interviewed him the first time. I asked Mark if he was close to confessing to us that first night. He said no, because he had too much to lose with his wife and young son. I noted that we could see his obvious affection for Kali, and were surprised that he was so open about it at the time. Mark explained that he "owed Kali that much."

"What a warped sense of logic," I thought to myself. Mark acknowledged that he felt bad for making the police work so hard over the past few years. Playing along with his attempt to display his sense of honor, I thanked him for having the courage to come forward and relieve us of this enormous burden. I sensed that he was in an emotionally vulnerable moment, so I asked him if I could tell him what I thought happened with Kali. He knew that my partner and I always suspected him, but lacked proof. Mark welcomed my theory, so I began:

"Mark, I believe that Kali ended up riding her Big Wheel up to your apartment, probably hoping to play with your son. You must have been outside and happily invited her inside your apartment. While she was inside, something must have happened that wasn't supposed to happen. So, you grabbed your son and ran outside to collect your thoughts and figure out what to do. While you were in the play area with your son, Judy Gifford found you while she was searching for Kali. The encounter with Judy provided you with a solid alibi. You returned to your apartment and retrieved Kali's body, placing it in some type of bag or suitcase. You then quietly carried her to your car and drove out of the complex with your son at your side before the first sheriff's deputy was even on the scene."

Mark looked across the table at me and smiled slightly as we sat in silence for a moment. "You're very close," he acquiesced. I assured Mark that Judy and David, Kali's father, would be very grateful if he could share at least some details about Kali's death. I asked him if there was any other person who could provide us with those details, but he said no, he was the only one.

I remarked that I was baffled that no one observed him leaving his apartment with such a big bag or suitcase. Mark explained that there were a lot of people around at the time, but he was insignificant to them and had thus gone unnoticed. Appealing to his pride again, I commended Mark for keeping a cool head, thinking so clearly and quickly under such pressure. He admitted that Investigator Passmore and I were very close to getting him when we had paid a visit to him that past March at the department store where he worked, but he had quickly realized that we possessed nothing new on him. He shared that he thought about Kali every day and had been trying to think of a way to retrieve her body from where he had placed it after the murder – a cooling tank in the building where he worked as a security guard at the time. Mark had feared that Kali's body would eventually be discovered and the police would be able to connect him to it.

Allowing him to stay in control, I patiently told Mark that it was his decision and his alone whether he wanted to tell me what happened. I encouraged him to consider that although he knew that he didn't mean to kill Kali, if he didn't tell his side of the story, he would be looked upon as a child-killing monster. I led Mark to believe that Kali's death wasn't his fault. Nothing could be further from the truth; it was simply a technique to make him feel more comfortable talking about his despicable deed. Minimizing a criminal's culpability is a common interrogation tool, but sometimes it can come across as patronizing and backfire.

Mark then asked me how much prison time he was looking at. There was no minimizing this aspect, and he knew it. I told him at least twenty-five years, adding that I would be surprised if he was ever released from prison. Mark protested that it was unfair that he would have to do a life sentence away from his wife and son. He had been living his own nightmare over the past few years, and he felt that it should count for something.

I countered that the general public wasn't going to care about him or his suffering, but ultimately, he had to come to terms with himself, his family and God. He offered to tell me how he killed Kali if I would arrange for him to see his wife and son. I promised to arrange it. He had finished his lunch by this time, but I was still eating.

Mark started out by saying that Kali did not suffer. I asked him how he killed her.

"I strangled her," he answered, "but I didn't do anything to her."

"You mean, you didn't have sex with her?" I asked.

"Yeah," he answered.

I knew that he was lying. All I could think about was how afraid that poor little girl must have been during her last moments on this earth. I found it absolutely astonishing that her killer was upset that he wasn't going to be given special consideration for his perceived "suffering" over the past few years. I just kept picking away at my lunch and asking what happened that night, making certain that I didn't appear too eager for his answer. Mark said that Kali rode over to his apartment on her Big Wheel and asked if she could play with his son Alex. Mark knew that her mother would not approve of

Kali going into his apartment, so he let her in and placed her Big Wheel in the kitchen so that no one would see it next to his apartment door. Mark said that Kali went upstairs with Alex to Alex's room and started playing with his toys while he went into his bedroom across the hall.

About ten minutes after Kali's arrival, Mark heard Judy calling out her name. He got nervous, fearing that he would get into trouble for having Kali in his apartment. Mark said that Kali walked across the hall into his bedroom at that time. Seeing the little girl in his bedroom, he panicked and strangled her to death. He concluded that he felt like he was dreaming during the whole event.

I personally believe that Mark was actually molesting little Kali but got spooked by her mother calling out to her. The sound of Judy's frantic voice calling out must have cut him like a knife through the open windows of his apartment. I don't believe that he panicked at all. I think that he made a cold, calculated decision to keep Kali from telling her mother what he had done to her. But I knew that I wasn't in a position to push him about the rape while we were in the restaurant. The only way that Mark would keep talking to me was if I let him stay in control of the conversation. Many child predators never admit to raping a child because it reveals just how sick and evil they really are. This murderer was attempting to rationalize his despicable actions as a panic response to what Kali's mother might do if she found her daughter in his apartment. I felt like saying, "Mark, that is an absolute lie and you know it!" Honestly, I would have said it in much more vulgar language. But I didn't. In these types of cases it is important to keep one's emotions locked away in order to achieve the real goal – legal justice.

Mark said that he carried Kali's body downstairs and placed her on the dining room floor. He then went outside with his son to collect his thoughts. While outside, he saw Judy in the playground area as she was searching for her daughter. When the panic-stricken mother asked him if he had seen Kali, he coolly replied, "No." Knowing that he now possessed an airtight alibi from the victim's own mother, Mark returned to his apartment and realized that it wasn't a dream when he observed Kali's body lying on the floor. He placed her body in a laundry basket, covered it up with a blanket, carried the basket to his vehicle, and placed it in the trunk. With his young son accompanying him, Mark drove to the Nor-Tel Company on Humboldt Street in Rochester, where he was employed as a security guard. He drove around to the back of the building and placed the laundry basket outside of the rear door to the utility room. He then drove with his son around to the front and went inside the main entrance. Mark told the two security guards on duty that he had left something at work and came back to pick it up.

While carrying his own child, Mark walked to the back of the building and retrieved Kali's body through the rear exterior door of the utility room. He then climbed to the top of an enclosed 30,000 gallon tank filled with liquid coolant, opened the hatch door and dumped Kali's body inside the tank. I asked Mark if he had cut Kali's stomach open to prevent her body from floating to the top of the tank.

"No," he replied. He explained that he had found a piece of heavy metal equipment in the utility room and tied it to Kali's body to weigh her down. I asked Mark if he had kept Kali's clothing or the blanket she had been wrapped in.

He replied that he got rid of everything, including the clothes basket. Mark added that he left Kali's earrings in her ears.

"It should have never happened. It was a waste," he offered.

"You're right, Mark." I responded. "It should never have happened."

Mark's eyes had become glassy. We sat in silence at our table for what seemed like a long time as the other patrons sat around us, oblivious to what had just occurred.

I paid the bill and Mark left a two-dollar tip. Afterwards, I drove him to my office. Mark sat in the front seat where he remained un-handcuffed. I had to maintain that he was neither in my custody, nor under my physical control until we reached my office at headquarters; otherwise, his verbal confession could be ruled inadmissible. Once we arrived in my office, I gave him the phone and he called his attorney. He was arrested that night and charged with the murder of Kali Ann Poulton. A year later, Mark Christie pled guilty to the murder and was given a sentence of twenty-five years to life in prison. He is serving out that life sentence in the custody of the New York State Department of Corrections.

If it had not been for Judy Gifford's intuition, her daughter's killer might have never been identified and brought to justice. Mark had an airtight alibi so he was not considered a viable suspect by the majority of the thirty-member investigative task force of local, state, and federal investigators. In fact, most of the other investigative teams went so far as to eliminate him as a suspect on the grounds that he did not have the means or the time to commit this crime. Had it not been for her mother's intuition, most likely Investigator Passmore and I would not have placed him in our sights.

When we hear of a disturbing crime such as this, we are shocked and fearful. We may keep a more watchful eye for a while, even though we don't really know exactly what we are looking for. Intuition is a powerful force, but when we sense a red flag or "get the creeps" about someone, it is easy for our minds to rationalize it away as paranoia, prejudice, or the illogical product of a bad day. After all, who wants to believe that a neighbor, trusted friend, talented coach, gifted teacher, loving family member or caregiver is not what they appear to be? We quickly become ashamed of ourselves and choose to ignore our suspicions. Every parent subconsciously weighs the potential risk to their children against the benefit of a particular outing, experience, or relationship. We know that living in a constant state of paranoia and locking our children away is not the right answer.

In response to the obvious need to better equip parents and communities to protect their children from sexual and physical abuse, in February 2005, the Faith Community Alliance of African American Ministers in Rochester held a meeting with representatives from local and state law enforcement, child protective services, and school officials. Among the attendees were Monroe County Sheriff Patrick O'Flynn, Rochester Police Chief Robert Duffy, Monroe County District Attorney Michael Green, and the Superintendent of the Rochester City School District, Manuel Rivera. The twenty-five member clergy group expressed a desire to commence a dialogue and formulate a community-based plan for their mission. They made it clear that they wanted to be active participants in this program, and challenged law enforcement to assist them in designing a proactive model for the rest of the nation to follow. According to Dr. John Walker, who chaired the meeting, nowhere else in the country have African-American ministers and local law enforcement come together for this purpose. At the request of Sheriff Patrick O'Flynn, I attended the meeting with him. Since I have spent the better part of twenty years investigating countless crimes against children, many of which are too despicable to describe outside of a courtroom, Sheriff O'Flynn assigned me the task of assisting the Men of Faith with their publicly-declared war against child abuse.

At Dr. Walker's urging, a team of people from the respective agencies was formed to speak to church and community groups. We offered basic information on how to identify, report, and prevent child abuse, and described how each of the respective agencies worked together both to investigate and prosecute offenders, and also to provide medical and emotional support to victims and their families. I spoke on the topic of seduction and sexual abuse in most of the presentations. My participation in this program has provided me with an opportunity to discover a silver lining inside the dark cloud in which most of my career has existed. God has given me an avenue to share my knowledge and experience, with the hope of preventing a new generation of children from being seduced and victimized. Another unexpected blessing has been hearing from many former victims who had always lived under a burden of guilt and confusion but were set free after studying the ways that a predator seduces a child and then uses guilt as a control mechanism. After having the common seduction tactics explained to them in an objective forum, these former victims finally realized that the abuse that they had suffered was not their fault as the perpetrator had led them to believe. There is no doubt in my mind that God inspired and designed these meetings. He brought together His representatives from both the church and law enforcement to help free many people of these demonic spiritual chains.

When Dr. Walker first suggested that I memorialize the content of my lecture in writing to serve as a resource for the many families who were unable to attend a presentation, I never really gave it a second thought. I just didn't feel up to the task. The daily grind of major crimes investigations didn't allow much time, or motivation, for anything else. Just ask my lovely and patient wife. She would tell you that working in the Major Crimes Unit isn't a career, it's a lifestyle. Then, out of nowhere, I felt like God spoke to my heart and inspired me to put pen to paper for the purpose of educating as many parents as possible.

The purpose of this publication is to teach all parents and caregivers how to hone their God-given instincts into an effective, knowledge-based tool to protect their children from the child predators who live among us. The source of the material presented here is approximately twenty years of experience in investigating and arresting child predators. This includes hundreds of interviews of child victims and their non-offending parents as well as interrogations of the perpetrators who offended them. This resource is not based on objective research and statistical analysis. Therefore, it should not be considered a scholarly, academic view of child sexual abuse, nor should it be compared with such publications. This book's content represents my personal perspective and is intended to offer a practical, simple presentation of how child predators operate in today's society. It will educate any concerned parent or guardian about how to recognize when a child predator is in their midst; how to protect their child from that predator; how to recognize if their child has already been offended by a predator; and what to do if their child discloses that they have been offended by a predator. For the adult reader who was sexually molested as a child, it is my hope that this resource may assist you in making some sense out of what happened to you, and help you understand that it wasn't your fault.

This book first lays a framework to help parents understand the common tactics that predators use to gain access to seduce and maintain control of a child. We will discuss specific defensive countermeasures against these tactics. We will study a dozen specific cases that will allow you to apply the principles that you are learning to real-life scenarios that unfold every day all around you. Along the way you will hear my opinion on matters that many parents wrestle with, such as a child's right to privacy versus a parent's right to know, children's cell phone and Internet usage, whether victims should fight back against violent attackers, and how to get your teenagers to open up to you. While you may not agree with every opinion I present here, one thing is certain: when you have finished reading this book, you will be far better equipped to protect your children. If you choose to fully educate yourself on this dark and difficult topic, you will be able to have more peace of mind as your children grow and navigate through many potential dangers.

CHAPTER 2

—∿∿—

RECOGNIZING A SERPENT

"*Now the serpent was more subtil than any beast of the field which the LORD God had made.*"

GENESIS 3:1

"**SUBTLE:** difficult to detect, elusive, not immediately obvious; characterized by skill or ingenuity; clever, crafty or sly; devious; operating in a hidden and injurious way; insidious."[1]

The people who sexually offend children come in all shapes and sizes. They are not limited to any one cultural, racial, economic or social group. They exist in all strata of our society. Ninety-nine percent of the pedophiles that I have

---

1. *American Heritage College Dictionary* (Boston/New York) Houghton Mifflin Company 1993 3rd edition; page 1355)

dealt with are males. Although female offenders do exist, my encounters with females have typically been as enablers to a male offender.

For the purpose of this publication, I have divided sex offenders into three basic groups. My descriptions of the three groups are based upon my personal contact with the many offenders I have interviewed and arrested during my nearly twenty years as a Major Crimes Investigator. These are not medically-certified psychological breakdowns of the different types of sexual offenders, for I am not an academic expert on sexual deviates. However, these simplified profiles will provide practical knowledge of how such criminals operate and seek out their next victim.

PEDOPHILES

Simply put, a pedophile is a person who fantasizes about having sex with children. On the surface, most of them appear to be very normal socially. Many of them are married and have raised families of their own, and have enjoyed a certain amount of success both personally and professionally. Generally, they are people who work very well with children, and children respond to them in a positive manner. But they harbor a very dark secret that they wrestle with daily, striving to keep it suppressed from the outside world.

Pedophiles seek to be among children for the purpose of sexual stimulation and gratification, yet many will never offend a child directly. While they typically subscribe to various forms of child pornography, they may never actually touch a child in a sexual manner. They satisfy their sexual fantasies vicariously by watching other adults molest children via different forms of media. I consider the latent pedophile to be just as guilty as the person who sexually offends a child. They are the sick voyeurs who feed their lustful desires by watching videos and photographs of children being molested or raped.

Pedophiles are known to save magazine and newspaper ads that depict children of all shapes and sizes modeling clothing and other merchandise in a secret stash, usually hidden in a safe place for private viewing. While this material is not considered child pornography, it is labeled "child erotica" because it serves the same purpose of stimulating sexual desire.

Over the past two decades I have investigated countless unattended deaths, suicides, and homicides. Some of these are referred to as "D.O.A" (Dead on Arrival) investigations, for the individual was discovered to be dead upon the arrival of the police and emergency medical personnel. Usually, there doesn't appear to be any obvious sign of foul play, so it is just a matter of taking a close look at the scene of the death, the body, the person's home and their background to substantiate that they did not die at the hand of another. During several of these investigations, the police or a member of the decedent's family stumbled upon their loved one's secret stash of child erotica or pornography. The deceased possessed an incredible amount of such material, safely tucked away in rarely-opened drawers or a secret locked room. Remarkably, most family members never knew about this sick characteristic or, if they did, they chose not to acknowledge it. One man had a secret shrine set up for a young female in the community who was raped and murdered over thirty-five years prior to his death. Fortunately, the girl's murderer had confessed and was still serving out a life sentence in prison. Otherwise, we could have spent an entire career trying to connect this deceased pedophile to the murder.

SEX OFFENDER/CHILD MOLESTER

A single occurrence of sexually offending a child puts a perpetrator into this category forever. Some child molesters are not pedophiles, but are simply opportunists who will sexually assault anyone who is vulnerable and accessible. Unprotected children often fit this criteria. Elderly women are also common victims of this type of sex offender, especially if they are estranged from their families or lack a consistent support system. The entire female gender is potential prey for this animal. A classic example of this type of offender will be shared in the case analysis section of this book.

CHILD PREDATOR

Some pedophiles' deep-seated desire to have sex with a child will eventually override their inner mechanism to suppress and control such action. When they choose to step out of their dark closet, they begin to reveal their true intentions as they maneuver to gain access to the child that they are targeting. The child predator's method of pursuing a potential victim is very similar to that of an animal hunting in the wild. Like the wolf or cougar who studies the flock to select an easy mark, the child predator seeks the one that is most vulnerable and accessible to him. He will use his profession or participation in a community program such as a church youth ministry, sports leagues, school activities, or recreational programs to become more familiar with specific children and their parents.

After the predator is smitten with a particular child, he will assess the child's circumstances. Are the parents over-burdened with their responsibilities? Is the child from a broken home? Is the child a social outcast? Is the child involved in some activity that the child predator is proficient at? Can he pose as a highly sought-after coach or tutor, appealing to the parents' desire to nurture their children to their fullest potential and thus the greatest scholarships? These are all criteria that the child predator ponders when selecting a potential victim. The predator will go to great lengths, expending both time and money, to place himself in what he would perceive to be the best position possible to grant him unlimited access to children and their parents. Once the predator attains an advantageous position, he puts his diabolical plan into action. The next chapter will discuss just how they do that.

From a parental standpoint, the child predator is the most insidious of the three profiles because he targets children. While most parents and children have been educated about "stranger danger," the child predator they should be most concerned with is the one that lives undetected among them and is usually someone they know and trust. Based upon what I know of these three types of offenders, if a parent protects their child from the child predator, they will automatically be protecting them from both the pedophile and the opportunistic sex offender.

WHAT CAUSES SOME MEN TO SEXUALLY OFFEND A CHILD?

Some experts believe that sexually abusing children is the result of learned behavior from the perpetrators own victimization as a child. Based upon my experience, I would agree with this theory only when children abuse other children. Children will act out what they have been exposed to when they are too immature to foresee the consequences of their actions. However, an adult clearly knows right from wrong and understands the potential consequences of their actions. While being abused as a child has caused many to suffer from depression, anger, and mistrust, I strongly believe that it doesn't cause the person to become an offender when they are an adult. I know too many victims of child abuse who would never consider abusing a child. In fact, many survivors would seriously consider killing a predator if they discovered one abusing a child close to them. It is true that I have interviewed and arrested predators who have claimed to be former victims, but I have arrested even more predators who said that they were never abused as a child. I consider the childhood abuse claim as an excuse and nothing more. My response to them in the interrogation room is that if they were a victim they should have known better than anyone how evil this crime is. In the end, they chose to victimize another child, knowing full well the harm that they would cause that child. God gave all of us a free will; how we use it is entirely up to us and no one else.

As a homicide detective, I can both understand and rationalize most acts of violence and what motivates them, including the crime of murder. Generally, it is motivated by love, hate, money, pride, revenge, or a combination of these. During the interview of a murder suspect, the experienced detective will determine what potential motives or hostilities a person may have had against the victim. Once that determination is made, it is easy for the detective to plug that motive in to the interview process and begin to convey empathy toward the suspect as to why they were "driven" to kill the victim. In other words, make the victim the bad guy, blaming them for making the suspect lash out at them. This process causes the suspect to feel less culpable, and thus more comfortable telling the detective what he did, as the detective has already revealed why it happened. Another way of empathizing with the suspect is to offer that he or she may have panicked after they confronted the victim and the victim reacted unexpectedly, which then "caused" them to kill the other person. Not that the detective agrees with or believes any of these rationalizations, but he must convey that he understands the suspect's perception of the situation so that the suspect will tell some semblance of the truth about what happened.

The crime of sexually molesting a child is different. It is a situation that one cannot easily rationalize or show empathy toward. Even the most violent and hardened criminals in our nation's prisons have a deep animosity toward child molesters. The child molester usually has to serve his prison sentence in protective custody or solitary confinement to protect them from being raped or killed by other inmates. I believe that God has put something in every man's heart to make them realize that all children are off limits. For this reason, unlike other crimes, the detective who tries to rationalize this act in the interrogation room will rarely be successful, for most suspects will sense that they are being patronized and lied to. The distrust that this creates inhibits the suspect from opening up. Some of the most evil predators that I have interviewed and arrested have confided that deep down, they knew that what they were doing to the child was wicked. Although these men still went forward with their crime, they knew that their actions would have ramifications that would continue beyond this lifetime. Even Jesus, the most forgiving and compassionate person to walk the face of the earth, gave a stern warning to those who "offend" a child and prevent them from seeking Him:

"But whoso shall offend one of these little ones which believe in me, it were better for him that a millstone were hanged around his neck, and that he were drowned in the depth of the sea."

MATTHEW 18:6 (KJV)

I interpret this Scripture to say that God has "a little something special" in the form of horrible punishment for those who offend children in any way and distract them from seeking Christ. Those who sexually offend a child would obviously fit into this category of sinners, and should thus be very concerned. I often refer to this passage while interrogating a suspected child predator. I get their attention by asking them if they have ever heard the term, "Millstone Justice." I know full well that they haven't, because I made up the term. Frankly, I always enjoy their facial expressions when I share the Scripture with them.

After accepting the Gospel of Jesus as the truth, I started the habit of praying before I interrogate a suspected predator. I ask God's Holy Spirit to guide me through the conversation, to give me the words this person needs to hear to tell me the truth, to give me the discernment to find the truth, and to use me as His tool to accomplish His will in this process. Because I investigate and seek the truth in everything I do as a professional, I have learned to always pray for God's wisdom, for things may not always be as they initially appear. I never want to wrongly accuse someone of committing such a despicable act if they did not. We read in the Book of Romans:

"The authorities are God's servants, sent for your good. But if you are doing wrong, of course you should be afraid, for they have the power to punish you. They are God's servants, sent for the very purpose of punishing those who do wrong. So you must submit to them, not only to avoid punishment, but also to keep a clear conscience."

ROMANS 13: 4, 5 (NLT)

This makes it clear that God has ordained law enforcement and given us His power to seek out and punish those individuals who break the laws, especially those who prey on the weak and the young. Therefore, it is paramount that those of us who are privileged to serve as police officers recognize that on our own day of judgment, God will hold us accountable as to whether we fulfilled our appointed assignment in a fair and righteous manner, according to His will. So it is important that I pray and seek His guidance in revealing the truth.

During the interview process, I sometimes feel led to direct my conversation to God, asking the suspect questions about their spiritual beliefs. Once we are in this portion of the interview, I just turn it over to God's Spirit and let Him direct the conversation. Many times I just sit back and witness the person literally crumble emotionally before my eyes as the Holy Spirit pierces their soul, exposing their filthy secret. Amazingly, some of these criminals confess to decades of undiscovered sexual abuse against a child within minutes of starting the interview. It was from these types of experiences in the interrogation room that I began to realize that God had His hand on these situations in a special way. God demonstrated to me during these interviews that this crime is very much committed on a spiritual plane. Man's selfish drive to feed his perverted sexual appetite regardless of the consequences opens a door to God's evil adversary. Satan is then able to enter into the situation and brilliantly manipulate men into pursuing these evil desires by any and every means possible. Ensnared by their own lust, they become slaves to it, reducing them to animal-like behavior that they themselves are deeply ashamed of.

While the secular academic community rarely recognizes the spiritual element of this evil crime, other professions are more willing to recognize and embrace the spiritual side of life. My wife, who has been a member of the medical profession for fifteen years, sees her field taking spiritual issues more seriously than it has since the dawn of the Industrial Age. Over the past decade, many of her colleagues have embraced the concept of treating the patient as a three-part being—body, mind/soul, and spirit—with remarkable results.

Medical professionals and social workers who specialize in the end-of-life stage, such as hospice and comfort care, utilize terms such as "crossing over" and "final journey" when a patient's death is imminent.

My own research while seeking the truth in regard to eternal matters, coupled with what I have been exposed to professionally, have led me to embrace the concept that human beings are in the middle of a spiritual war between God and the Devil. Our Creator desires us to know and experience Him through a loving relationship that can only exist in an environment where there is freedom to choose. The jealous Satan wishes to mar God's creation and tear us away from God so that we become unable to fulfill our God-ordained purpose of bringing Him the love and worship that He deserves. God has a specific purpose for each one of us and has blessed each of us with the abilities to enable us to fulfill it. However, Satan does not want anyone to realize their purpose, so he strives to corrupt our minds and hearts to distract us from achieving that realization. During this campaign of corruption he encourages us to use those God-given talents for our own selfish reasons to benefit only ourselves.

The Apostle Paul said: *"For we wrestle not against flesh and blood, but against principalities, against powers, against the rulers of the darkness of this world, against spiritual wickedness in high places."* Ephesians 6:12 (KJV)

I believe that men all around the world are inviting one of Satan's demonic minions into their hearts through their own lustful desires, soon finding themselves in spiritual bondage to this perversion. This is why I believe that we must fight this crime not only with traditional police investigative techniques, but also in the spiritual realm with prayer. Whether a person chooses to believe that spiritual beings play a role in this colossal conflict is entirely up to them. However, a lack of belief does not always equate to a lack of existence. When I look at the incredible weight and size of a 747 jumbo jet I have a hard time believing that it manages to get off the ground, but it always does.

We must prevent this crime from happening by being the most dedicated parents we can be, praying for our children daily and doing everything reasonably possible to keep them safe from the Evil One and his serpents. While we will never be rid of the child predator on this side of eternity, we can do our part by keeping our children out of vulnerable positions. We must be the dedicated shepherds of our flocks that God has appointed us to be. Nurturing and protecting our children should be the most important purpose of our lives. If every parent and guardian acted accordingly, sexual abuse toward children would not be able to exist. Without a population of potential victims to feed from, child predators would literally starve to death from the lack of unprotected children. The starvation of a predatory species can eventually lead to its extinction.

CHAPTER 3

—⟡—

WAYS OF THE SERPENT:
THE PREDATORY PHASES

*W*hereas some sex offenders prepare in secret to kidnap a child, most child predators lurk more openly within our midst, using methods that a trained eye can spot. He must be very cunning when preparing a child victim to become a willing or passive participant in fulfilling his sick desires without raising the parents' suspicions. The phases marking the progression of his pursuit usually consist of the trust phase, the courtship phase, the seduction phase, the offending phase, and the control phase.

THE TRUST PHASE

The first phase of the child predator's hunt is what we will refer to as the "trust phase." Once the predator chooses potential victims, he seeks to gain unsupervised access. The best way to gain access to a young child or adolescent is to first befriend their parents or guardian. The child predator's sole purpose in this phase is to gain the parent's or guardian's trust. He will invest a vast amount of time, energy, and resources into cultivating the relationship for the sole purpose of gaining their trust and access to their children. He is not concerned with how much time it may take—he is consumed with the hunt and eventual reward it will bring him. He may make several families his projects simultaneously.

In spite of the cynicism of our culture, gaining parental trust is all too easy in some environments, especially within a church community. As members of the Body of Christ, we are encouraged to open our hearts to one another and help where help is needed. This creates an optimum environment for the predator to disguise himself as a kind soul who offers stressed, overburdened parents the assistance that they have been praying for. The child predator will come up alongside an unsuspecting parent or family within the church body who is in dire need and provide selfless assistance and fellowship. This is how it starts.

This situation can occur in any community environment. Our society is inundated with these types of opportunities, creating a plethora of potential victims for the child predator to choose from: sports leagues, community recreation programs, after-school activities, apartment complex or neighborhood groups, etc. The child predator knows that most parents are over-extended emotionally, physically and financially, and in great need of some free time for themselves. The child predator is all too ready to relieve them of such stress, appearing to the unsuspecting parent as a "savior" willing to take the kids for a few hours so that the parents can take a break.

Single mothers are common targets of the child predator. Our communities are filled with single moms trying to manage a job and a family, usually with little assistance from the father. This situation makes her extremely vulnerable. Remember, a child predator is very sly and patient; he will not rush a mother into prematurely trusting him. He will assist Mom in many different aspects of her life, aligning himself as a trusted, reliable friend. Single women are very partial to having male friends in their lives just for companionship and to assist them with "manly duties" around the house. It may or may not include a romantic relationship. He will gladly fix leaky faucets, cut the grass, rearrange furniture, give advice on how to keep rodents out of the house, or amuse the baby for twenty minutes in the living room so that Mom can take a sorely-needed catnap. Often the single mother will refer to the child predator as "a Godsend."

Is every helpful soul who makes themselves available to parents and works well with children a child predator? Or, should a suspicious parent openly accuse a person of being a child predator simply because they are particularly selfless? No, obviously not. Without facts, no one should ever be publicly labeled a child predator. But parents should be aware of how these deviates build their inroads to a child. It is critical to understand that time spent together without offense builds trust by default, but that trust is not always deserved.

Often a parent will have concern, but they dismiss it as paranoia. It is here that many fail to act: once a suspicion has arisen, reduce both parent and child contact with this person, and then sit back and observe the person's actions within that community from a distance. The suspicious parent should do as a good shepherd does—quietly place themselves between the suspected predator and all children, making themselves an obstacle. If that person is truly a predator, he will eventually react in one of two ways. He may "telegraph" his ulterior motive, becoming more aggressive with his requests to have contact with the children; the emotional and often bizarre behavior stemming from an inordinate desire reveals the predator's true motivation. Or, the predator will simply move on to another "territory" or community because he senses that he is under scrutiny. The risk of exposure is disconcerting for predators, for they have their reputation and investments at stake. I believe that the more time and money the predator has invested, the more aggressive his response will be when you make yourself an obstacle. He may even try to turn the tables on the suspicious parent, accusing them of being overly protective and smothering their children. Or he may undertake a slander campaign, believing that his best defense is going on the offensive against the suspicious parent. Based upon my experience, if the suspected predator's reaction is consistent with one of the aforementioned responses, then the parent read the situation correctly and has prevented another child from becoming a victim.

If the parent is not satisfied in confirming or denying their suspicions, and still feels that this person is someone that the community should be concerned about, then the police should be advised of the situation. The police will document the concern and check the person out. The parent, acting as the complainant, does not have to be identified. The police can look into the individual's behavior merely as a precaution, even if there isn't enough evidence to arrest them. You never know what exists in someone's background until you take a peek. Even if the person checks out to be okay and doesn't possess a criminal history or past complaints for suspected criminal behavior, police keep intelligence files on suspicious persons. If they begin to see a pattern of the same types of complaints made against a certain person, then local law enforcement is aware that they have a potential child predator on their radar screen who has yet to offend but appears to be revealing his true intentions when around children for a sustained period. It is also possible that this person has already assaulted a child, but the victim has yet to disclose the crime. If this person is arrested for committing a crime against a child, the police and the local prosecutor's office will consider this type of intelligence invaluable. It can be used as corroborating evidence during a trial to demonstrate the suspect's pattern of behavior toward children, especially when the suspect's defense team attacks the credibility of the young victim or the person who alerted the police, and also when the suspect claims that his behavior was misinterpreted.

THE COURTSHIP PHASE

The trust phase eventually gives way to the courtship phase in the child predator's scheme. The predator's whole purpose in this courtship phase is similar to that of a young male suitor courting a young woman who has captured his interest. He wants to "romance" and impress the unsuspecting child into liking him and trusting him more than anyone else, including the child's own parents. He ultimately becomes the child's best buddy and confidant. Once the unwitting child starts to look upon the predator as his or her closest ally, he or she begins to confide in him about private matters, and the seduction begins. This process can take weeks, months, or even years.

Remember the fall of Adam and Eve in chapter three of the Book of Genesis? Satan appeared before Eve as a cunning serpent. At the time, he was not in an ugly reptilian form, for God did not curse him to an existence of crawling on his belly and eating dust until after he seduced Eve into committing the first sin. The serpent was thought to be attractive (Ezekiel 28:14-18); at least, we can say from the text that his physical appearance did not scare Eve. Otherwise, she would not have entered into a dialogue with him. Likewise, most child predators' physical appearance is not offensive. If anything, children are drawn to them. Their survival and success depends on their ability to conceal their true motives beneath an attractive, appealing exterior.

The child predator will shower the targeted child with praise, gifts, and special privileges in relation to the circumstances of their relationship. For instance, it is during this phase that the child predator/coach will show obvious favor upon the young athlete that he is targeting by offering them more playing time, even though it may not be deserved. The child predator/friend or child predator/extended family member will take the targeted child out to eat or to the movies to cheer them up and allow their parents some alone time. The friendly and outgoing child predator/neighbor who is a motocross bike enthusiast will take the targeted child to motorcycle races and eventually sets the child up with a motocross bike to use only when they are together. In all instances, the child predator will determine what the targeted child desires most and do everything in their power to make it come true for them. At first, this creates a bond between the predator and the child. However, the bond eventually transforms into bondage once the predator's true intentions are revealed to the unsuspecting child, as we will discuss further in the latter phases.

It is during the process of developing a bond with the targeted child that the predator will establish and utilize a common denominator to separate the child from their family or the group of other children under his supervision. The common denominator will often be identified early in the relationship and will help the predator to curry favor with both the child and their parents. The common denominator can be a sport, hobby, religiously-affiliated activity, or form of entertainment. Not many parents are really up on the hottest bands, video games, movies or amusement park attractions, but often predators will master these. They are tools in his arsenal, used to weave enchanting melodies for this sinister Pied Piper to play, deluding children with false promises. In some cases, a person rather than an activity is the common denominator. If the predator is a parent, then he can easily target one of his child's own friends. Tragically, in many of these situations the predator will have the targeted child accompany him and his child during sleepovers and trips out of town, providing him with ample opportunity to isolate the targeted child while his own child is sleeping or occupied elsewhere.

Because the child predator has already gained the trust of the child's parents, he is able to separate the targeted child from the rest of the family or group in subtle ways that wouldn't cause alarm. Examples of this behavior would include the predator offering to take the child out for an activity, thus allowing the parent an opportunity to have some much-needed time alone, or simply to ease the stress of dragging several children along on their errands. Or, the predator will convince the parents that the targeted child would benefit from receiving some "quality individual time" from someone, similar to what the Big Brother program would legitimately offer a child.

Consider the following three illustrations which demonstrate how the child predator can gain parental trust and access over time, enabling them to isolate and court the child.

1. A hired tutor *spends hours at the library with the targeted child, enabling them to ace a math test for the first time. The glow of success, coupled with the safety of those first library encounters with no harm done to the child, deflect the nagging questions of character and intent that might otherwise arise. The tutor and the student, who is now making considerable strides in his studies as a result of his tutor's much appreciated assistance, start meeting weekly over milkshakes at the ice cream parlor for their lessons. The child is getting A's instead of F's and seems to be blossoming under a "big brother"- type friendship. Later, the tutor begins driving the child home to relieve the parents of that burden. With the parent's safety concerns supposedly answered long ago, they stop asking the child where they were or why they weren't home exactly when expected.*

2. A music teacher *praises untapped talent and offers to conduct private lessons after school. The child's parents see the school as a safe place because it is bustling with activity after hours. The child's skills improve and nothing suspicious occurs. The music teacher begins holding music appreciation nights in his home with a group of promising* *students. The kids watch musicals and concerts, listen to re-cordings, or have jam sessions. No offense occurs. After some time has passed, the targeted child is encouraged to au-dition for the All-State band. The parents would have a hard time bringing the child to the audition, so the teacher offers to take them. After so many opportunities to build trust, the parents won't think twice when that teacher chaperones an overnight trip to a special event out of town.*

3. A youth pastor, *praised for his ability to connect with troubled teens, is able to coax a lonely child to open up. The parents are thrilled to see the change in their child and encourage them to attend youth events and "lock-ins" (overnight stays) at the church. The parents consider it safe because a number of adults are present. The courtship phase begins as the pastor begins to draw the child away for "one-on-one counseling" at said events. Or he offers to transport the child to and from church-related events such as revivals and Christian youth concerts.*

The point that I cannot stress enough by these ex-amples is this: **time without offense builds trust by default.** The child predator depends on this very important principle so that he can eventually isolate the child and evolve into the next phase of his diabolical scheme. Remember, during the courtship phase, both the child and parents are unaware of the predator's true intentions and motives. The child loves the attention and is enjoying all of the special perks that his or her relationship with the predator has provided them, and the parents genuinely appreciate that someone has taken an interest in their child. More often than not, the child becomes emotionally dependent on the predator during this phase of their relationship, due to periodic unsupervised contact. It is at this point that the targeted child becomes most vulnerable. Outwardly, nothing may appear amiss during the trust and courtship phases. This is why it is often difficult for everyone to accept and believe when a child victim discloses any level of inappropriate behavior during these phases.

It is not unusual for the child predator to be involved with several children at the same time, depending on his ability to have access to multiple prospects. His relationship with each child could be in different phases. For instance, he may be in the courtship phase with two children and actually began seducing and offending a third. A fourth child might have already disclosed sexual abuse to someone and rumors have begun to circulate in the community. Those close to him only know the predator to be the "nice guy" who loves and helps children and their families, or the "great coach," or the "gifted teacher" that he has portrayed himself to be. During these initial phases, the child predator has worked hard to manufacture and promote his deceitful mask and gain everyone's trust. He knows that once you have gained someone's trust, it is hard for them to revoke it without convincing proof. Therefore, it is common for a child's initial disclosure of sexual abuse to not be taken seriously. Tragically, the child will sometimes be ostracized because of it. This type of reaction is common when the child accuses someone who is highly regarded in the community, such as popular coach, teacher, youth pastor, or counselor.

If no one blows the whistle, then the serpent has mastered his disguise as an angel of light, and can continue preparing another child for the next phase of their impending victimization.

THE SEDUCTION PHASE

The courtship phase will eventually evolve into what we will refer to as the seduction phase. The child predator has successfully courted the victim into a psychological state where they have become so enamored with the predator that he or she is literally eating out of the predator's hand. Realizing this, the predator will begin to introduce the targeted child to inappropriate behavior.

At first, a predator's inappropriate behavior would be considered merely bad judgment if the child unintentionally discloses this behavior to another adult. For example, the predator will allow the targeted child to watch an R-rated movie with sexual content and nudity. The child predator will make a pact with the child that he will allow him or her to view such movies as long as they don't tell anyone. The predator is testing the child on two fronts. First, the predator needs to see if the child can keep a secret. Second, the predator needs to see how the child will respond to the movie's content. Most children are capable of keeping a secret because they are thrilled by the fact that some adult is allowing them to do something that their parents would never allow. If you have raised a child, you know that we parents never had to teach our children how to lie. That came naturally, because we are all born with a sin nature. But we have to remind our children continually to tell the truth. So in most situations, keeping a secret about something that Mom and Dad would never approve of would be fairly easy. The child predator knows this and will capitalize on it. If by chance the child discloses that they had viewed an R-rated movie while under the predator's supervision, the predator can easily apologize for the lapse of judgment or lack of knowledge about the movie's content. It can be easily portrayed as a simple mistake, permitting the predator the opportunity to assure the parents that it won't happen again. At this point, the child predator may move on to another child if he believes that the targeted child is incapable of keeping a secret, or he may try a different strategy, or he may wait for the child to become a little older.

If the child keeps the secret, the encouraged predator redoubles his efforts. He desires to accelerate the sexual desire of the targeted child, so he will place sexual imagery in front of them to accomplish this. He is confident that most children will be curious and motivated to watch the nudity scenes, especially if they are somewhere between eight and fifteen years old. The predator knows that children in this age group are maturing and their hormones are becoming active. He will be very subtle with the introduction of sexual imagery and monitor the child's reaction carefully. Based on the child's reaction, the child predator will then engage them in casual conversation about the images and acts that have been depicted. Again, the predator is acting as a trusted confidant with the target, reminding the child that this is their "little secret."

Flattery becomes one of the child predator's most useful tools during the seduction phase. He will pervert a young girl's desire to play dress-up. My daughters always enjoyed making themselves look pretty "like their mommy" when they were very young. They weren't acting sexual, but they wore dresses, high heels, sunglasses, and pretend make-up. They would prance around the house and say things like, "Look, Daddy, look! I'm pretty like Mommy!" or "Don't I look like a movie star?" Any parent can relate to these types of experiences with their children, especially little girls, whom I have found to be such precocious imitators of the most influential women in their life.

As he stimulates the child's sexuality, he begins to flatter them about their physical looks and body, and he will buy them clothes that make them look more sexually appealing. Eventually, the child becomes captivated by the interaction, especially when the child predator begins to take photos of the child modeling the clothes. During the execution of a search warrant at a child predator's home, it is common to find photos of five- and six-year-old female victims in their underwear or wearing sleazy clothing, posing in very provocative positions. I have seen very young girls exhibit this behavior after they have been victims of sexual abuse. They have learned how to use their bodies flirtatiously in order to manipulate men long before it occurs to other girls. Sadly, this scar often remains long after the offense has ended.

This type of activity is not limited to female victims. Young male victims are often manipulated by their offenders to pose naked or in their underwear for the purpose of being photographed. Young males, especially adolescents, are beginning to look upon themselves as sexual beings and feel the need to magnify their persona of sensuality to females around them. The predator will appeal to the male victim through this channel. For instance, the male victim may be led to believe that he could have a future as a male model, modeling underwear and unzipped blue jeans in the same provocative ways that he has seen others model these clothes. During a supposed "photo shoot" the predator will say something like, "You look so hot, even I'm getting turned on!" These types of comments can eventually lead to the predator making a sexual advance toward the young male, leading him to believe that these types of things normally occur in the world of modeling.

Provided that the targeted child can keep a secret and has responded to the child predator's flattery and casual, seductive conversation, the predator may then introduce the child to pornography and more graphic images of genitalia. At this point, the child's sexual knowledge and experience has been grotesquely advanced for their age, and they are fascinated by what they are viewing. The predator will then begin to seduce the child's mind with discussions about how gratifying sexual experimentation can be. He will introduce them to private masturbation, and engage them in conversations about how it had made them feel. The discussion will eventually gravitate toward the child predator offering to show them how to masturbate and suggest that they do it together, continuing to reinforce that "this will be our secret."

The child predator's presentation of sex to a young child is eerily similar to the way that the Devil seduced Eve into eating the forbidden fruit in the Garden of Eden. The Devil misled Eve into believing that if she ate the forbidden fruit from the Tree of Knowledge of Good and Evil, she would be like God. He pointed out how inviting, attractive, and delicious the forbidden fruit was. Satan suggested to the innocent Eve that God didn't want her to enjoy the forbidden fruit because God did not want her and Adam to be like Him, possessing the knowledge of good and evil. In essence, this is what the child predator does to our children. He introduces them to sex, which is meant to be a beautiful act between two married adults. He misleads the child into believing that he will be a better teacher about sex than the child's parents, either because the child's parents are incapable of showing them, or because the parents just don't want the child to enjoy a sexual experience. Adam and Eve knew that they weren't supposed to eat the forbidden fruit, just as most children have been taught not to allow anyone to touch their private parts. But just as Eve was seduced into believing a lie, the young child is seduced into believing that a sexual experience with this pervert will bring them pleasure or benefit them in some way.

THE OFFENDING STAGE

Once the predator has proposed his sexual agenda to the child as something very special and exciting that will gratify them like nothing else, with the child's permission, he commits the offense. In some instances, the child victim will not give their express consent, but they will be passive and feel confused but helpless to prevent it. They feel a deep sense of guilt for allowing it to occur. Some seduced children will enjoy the sexual abuse for a short season before they come to realize just what has occurred to them. As the offending stage progresses, the child's eyes begin to open to the horrific reality that the predator's motive was to molest them in despicable, unspeakable ways all along. After Adam and Eve consumed the forbidden fruit, Genesis 3:7 says that "their eyes were opened and they realized they were naked." God's light of innocence that covered their nakedness had been extinguished forever. Just as Adam and Eve found out after eating the forbidden fruit that the serpent had lied to them, the victim will eventually realize that they have been lied to. The child's joy-ride of seduction and sexual experience eventually dumps them into a living hell of severe depression and anger that haunts them for the rest of their life. They feel naked, forever stripped of their innocence by the predator. Their eyes have been opened to darkness and filth. The light of hope, love, and trust has been extinguished in an instant selfish act on the part of a person who was supposed to be their friend, nurturing, loving and protecting them.

Just as Adam and Eve wanted to hide from their Heavenly Father and cover their newfound nakedness, the child victim will begin to hide themselves emotionally in an attempt to cover their "nakedness" from their parents and those around them. Once a child has been sexually molested, they will begin to separate themselves from those most close to them. I have found the victim's overt avoidance of communicating with their parents and other authority figures to be the most obvious and consistent attempt to hide their nakedness. This can manifest itself in many different ways, depending on the child's personality and age. In a later chapter we will discuss the kinds of behavior that may indicate that a child has been molested.

THE CONTROL PHASE

Eventually, most children will desire to end sexual contact with the predator. They will attempt to disengage from him, but the predator will not allow the child to break free so easily. He has invested too much time, energy and resources to walk away from an investment that has just begun to pay off. He will begin to control the victim in any way possible, forcing them to comply with his sexual demands. He will have a plan in place to control the child to maintain their cooperation with him even though they have now become reluctant participants. How he controls the child will depend on the circumstances of their relationship.

For example, in the common scenario where the predator is the coach of the victim's athletic team, he will control the child by the amount of participation that he permits in games or competitions. If the victim cooperates with the predator's sexual demands, he or she will continue to "start" or receive more playing time, even when the child's skill level would normally not support such a move. Likewise, if the victim rebuffs the predator's sexual demands, then he or she will be punished by being removed from the first string line-up, even if it is detrimental to the team's success. The predator/coach is usually highly regarded for their ability and success, and they will utilize that position to their benefit to refute the child's first cry for help. The predator/coach will maintain their pious appearance, and politely share with the other parents that these types of false accusations will be made against him every so often when he has to "painstakingly" drop one of the players from the starting line-up. This phony act often works toward rallying the support of the other parents, as they don't want to believe that such a horrible thing could have occurred, let alone by someone whom they have come to trust and hold in high regard. The victim is then ostracized by their teammates and teammate's parents, wrongly identified as a disgruntled athlete and liar. Incredibly, some team parents will look upon this situation as an opportunity for their own child to advance in the line-up. I am sorry to say that I have seen this scenario play out too many times. Sometimes even the victim's parents will be openly unsupportive of their own child because of the skillful manipulation of the predator during the courtship phase. Child predators will seek to "hook" the victim on some sort of activity, material reward, or privilege prior to the offending phase in order to utilize it as a control mechanism later. In essence, the predator transforms the child into a prostitute. The child will continue to provide sex in order to maintain privileges or material rewards. We will review some real examples of this tactic in the case analysis section of this book.

Often the predator will resort to intimidation tactics to keep the victim quiet and cooperative. They may threaten to harm them or someone in their family. Some child predators have even threatened to harm the victim's pet if they didn't keep quiet about the sexual abuse. Yet another diabolical control mechanism is to prey upon the child's sense of guilt. The predator will brainwash his victim into believing that he or she is partly responsible. They may even threaten to expose the child as a sexual deviate or homosexual. This tactic is especially effective with adolescent males, who fear the social stigma that they would bear if their participation was revealed to their peers. The child predator knows how to use these fears to coerce the victim. If the victim still refuses to cooperate, it is not uncommon for the predator to threaten exposing them via the provocative photographs that he took during their sexual encounters. With today's advanced technology, the victim may even have been photographed without their knowledge. While the photographs primarily are taken to memorialize the sexual encounter for the predator's own future stimulation, when needed he will use them as a tool to force cooperation.

The control phase can last a lifetime. Long after a child has broken free, they may still feel the heavy chainlinks of despair, resentment, hopelessness and hatred that connect them to their abuser. Even though the predator no longer has physical or psychological control of their victim, they will always possess a part of every child that they have ever sexually abused. This is because he stole something from them that they can never retrieve – their precious, innocent childhood.

SECTION II

—∭—

CASE EXAMPLES

TRUTH

—⌇⌇⌇—

"What is truth?"

PONTIUS PILATE

*"The truth is what God knows and speaks;
and when He looks into men's hearts
He sees the truth (about them)
most of which is ugly."*

PATRICK CROUGH

SECTION II

—ᴧᴧ—

INTRODUCTION

*D*uring my career as a police officer, I have participated in numerous on-the-job training sessions. Many of these sessions were dedicated to analyzing and critiquing the actions of police officers during critical incidents, some of which included officer or civilian casualties. The purpose was not to point blame at the officers involved, but to fully understand the scenario and then implement specific training in the hopes of preventing it from reoccurring. It is in this spirit that I offer some real case histories that were investigated either by me or by one of my colleagues in the Major Crimes Unit. I have not embellished any facts. The cases are presented here in the same manner that they would be presented in a court of law. A citizen who has performed their civic duty by sitting on a jury for a similar case would hear and see the same types of facts and evidence. The only thing that a jury would not be able to hear are the personal convictions that I share while discussing each case. I have chosen not to name names. While each documented case is a matter of public record, it is not my intention to bring further attention or embarrassment to the victim, their families, or the suspects' families.

In an attempt to cover a wide spectrum of potential scenarios, each case includes a different set of circumstances that you may encounter as a parent. At the end of each case, we will review the facts of the threat and possible counter-measures. At issue is not only the predator's behavior, but also the actions of the victim's parents. This is not to point blame at them, but to apply the principles that I have shared with you thus far. Certainly, there is no fool-proof system for determining if a child is in danger of becoming a victim of sexual abuse. But each of the following scenarios will portray certain characteristics that an enlightened parent should be able to identify and take appropriate protective measures before their child becomes a victim.

Some readers will find the content offensive. Frankly, it is. If someone reads a book about war and the experiences of soldiers on the battle field, they will encounter disturbing, graphic detail about the hellish nature of war that will resonate in their minds for a long time to come. But the reader would receive a helpful education from the material, and it might even change their opinion on certain matters. From my vantage point, we are in a battle for our children on both spiritual and physical fronts, and every parent should obtain as much "intelligence" on the enemy as they can in preparation. So I encourage every parent to press forward through the material, if at all possible. The wisdom I have gained in life came not from success and smooth sailing, but rather from unwanted controversy, failures, and painful experiences. This book is intended to provide a future benefit to the reader with the hope of preventing loved ones from becoming victims of a child predator.

CHAPTER 4

—៳៳—

CASE EXAMPLE 1
THE HELPFUL NEIGHBOR

A four-year-old boy was molested by a middle-aged man who was a close friend and neighbor of the victim's parents. The suspect and his physically handicapped wife befriended the boy's parents, who were considerably younger than them, shortly after they moved into the large suburban apartment complex. The suspect was a popular figure in the complex. He was friendly with the management and the uniformed police that patrolled the neighborhood; he was seen as an honorable man. The suspect displayed an immediate affection toward the young couple's son, which developed further as he and his wife spent more time with them. He would constantly hold the two-year-old boy, frequently having him on his lap. Eventually, a close bond of trust and friendship was formed between the two families. The unsuspecting young couple allowed the man to take their son on frequent walks around the apartment complex so that they could have some time alone. Later on, the suspect was permitted to bring the child to his apartment for lunch. The little boy's parents eventually experienced some trouble in their marriage, and they separated temporarily. Although the suspect's wife was frequently confined to bed because of her condition, the suspect offered that he and his wife would baby-sit the boy for free to allow the mother time to seek employment. She must have been so relieved to receive this generous offer during such emotional upheaval and financial stress. The suspect, who was not otherwise employed because he was collecting benefits for a disability, watched the young boy for approximately one year.

The boy's mother became concerned with her son's behavior when he kept "humping" her while sitting on her lap. When she asked her son why he kept humping her, the boy disclosed that "Jim" humps him and plays with his "binkie." The boy was referring to the suspect by name and his own penis when he used the term "binkie."

After the boy's mother called the police, I was assigned the investigation. The boy was described to have below-average verbal skills, which is always a benefit to the child predator because the handicap makes it more difficult for the child to articulate what occurred. For this reason, I interviewed the young boy in a therapist's office, where he was given anatomically correct dolls along with other toys. The boy was encouraged to play, but was not directed on which toys to use. As we suspected, without hesitation the boy undressed the adult male doll and the young male doll and then demonstrated the different types of sex acts that the suspect had performed on him.

The victim was deemed incapable of testifying in a court of law due to his lack of verbal skills and his inability to withstand a rigorous cross-examination, so the case was not prosecutable. Child sex abuse cases that make it into the courtroom usually lack physical evidence. This factor alone makes these types of cases very difficult to prosecute. Without physical evidence of the abuse to corroborate the defendant's confession, the child's testimony is absolutely necessary. When a child is unable to testify under oath and articulate what the accused did to them, the criminal charges are immediately dismissed. Unfortunately, this is not uncommon. I have obtained a confession from a child molester, and yet been unable to arrest and charge him with the crime because the victim was incapable of testifying in court because of their age or a mental or emotional handicap.

I still executed a search warrant at the suspect's residence, and we found "child erotica," which corroborated the suspect's lust for little boys. The suspect had a hidden stash of magazine and newspaper ads and candid photos showing half-dressed little boys neatly stacked together. We know the erotic value of these types of photos is enough to stimulate the child predator as intensely as child porn would, but because possessing these photos is not against the law, we were not able to arrest him. We also found numerous photos taped to the suspect's bedroom dresser that depicted the young victim engaged in various activities. Some of the photos depicted the victim lying on the suspect's bed or sitting in the bathtub naked. While this corroborated our suspicion, it is not illegal to possess these kinds of photos either. But it was very clear to everyone who viewed this collage that this man had a sick affection for this child. We also found pairs of clean underwear belonging to the victim in one of the suspect's dresser drawers. While having the little boy's clean underwear in his own drawer may not be a crime, it clearly indicates to me that his relationship with the child was out of balance and typical of what a child predator would do.

We discovered that the suspect also had a prior history. He had been convicted of committing an identical crime against a young boy fifteen years prior to this incident. He had confessed to the crime and served jail time. Because it occurred so long ago, he was not required to register as a sex offender in New York State. This allowed him to fly under the radar and have unlimited access to other children. I wonder how many other little boys this man came into contact with during those fifteen years.

Because the suspect refused to be interviewed and contacted a lawyer, I was not able to speak with him. The only way I was able to salvage the case was to contact his lawyer and explain that we were willing to wait for the child to mature and attain the verbal skills required to testify against his client in the future. I offered that he could allow his client to plead guilty to a much lesser offense now with the promise of no jail time, but he would be placed on the sex offender registry and have an extended probation. The suspect's public defender believed that I was going to pursue the case when the victim was a year older, so he advised his client to take the plea deal and not risk going to prison. Truthfully, I wasn't as confident as I had led them to believe regarding the victim's ability to testify in a year. The reality is that young victims are unpredictable whether they have a disability or not, and child predators capitalize on the fact that many are unable to testify in court. Due to the circumstances, I felt that it was essential that we use what we had to get this degenerate registered as a predator, which would make it illegal for him to be alone with a child and raise a warning to other parents. It was a bitter pill for us to swallow, but it was the best that we could do under the circumstances.

Applying what you have learned about the trust and courtship phases, let's identify some of the signs of potential danger. First, this man had an immediate open attraction to the young boy. He constantly held him on his lap, and he frequently asked the parents for permission to take the young lad out of the house. The suspect courted the parents and the victim by taking the child on walks alone and into his apartment to serve him lunch. Perhaps the parents had heard glowing reports of the suspect from other residents. Or perhaps since the suspect and his wife were older, the relationship had a parental flavor, prompting the couple to see the suspect's behavior in a grandfatherly light. Whatever the reason, this is where the parents could have exercised better judgment. I consider it unwise to allow a man whom you have known for less than a year to take your young child out of your home for unsupervised visits. The suspect's eagerness to be alone with the child, and his affectionate behavior toward the child while in the presence of the child's parents, were red flags. Many of us love being with children. But if the motive is simply to enjoy the child's company, that can be done under the parent's watchful eye. If you encounter an over-eager adult, you can test your suspicion by allowing limited supervised contact only. If the person is a predator, they will be disturbed by this, and they will either begin "telegraphing" or they will move on to more promising targets; if they have sincere motives, then they will take it in stride.

This predator, like others, patiently invested a vast amount of time and resources to gain access to his target and the trust of his parents. Once the suspect had won the family's hearts through the trust and courtship phases, he knew that the time for the kill had come. The mother needed inexpensive childcare, and the predator was able to exploit this vulnerability, stepping up immediately under the guise of a trusted friend. Because the suspect had seemed trustworthy up until that point, and the mother's need was undoubtedly desperate, any suspicions that she still might have had were overruled. While there are many who are worthy of our trust, as parents we should never stop checking up on our children's activities when they are in the care of others. Set specific ground rules for caregivers (for example, "do not bathe the child") and test for compliance to those rules. Ask your children questions about what they did that day, and listen very carefully.

Since molestation usually occurs when there are no witnesses, the fact that another person is nearby can seem to negate the possibility of an occurrence. In this case, the parents may have been disarmed by the fact that the wife was home, even though they understood that she was frequently confined to her bed. This situation allowed the suspect to have the young boy all to himself frequently in the privacy of his own home. The abuse occurred in the suspect's bedroom while his wife was downstairs watching television or sleeping. As parents we must understand that predators are skilled at isolating a child, even in their own home when others are present. They will see moments of opportunity that we cannot see.

CHAPTER 5

—m—

CASE EXAMPLE 2
THE STEPFATHER WHO LIKED
TO WATCH PORN

$\mathcal{T}$he victim was a ten-year-old female and the suspect was her thirty-year-old stepfather. The victim's mother was employed outside the home during normal business hours. The suspect was employed as a short-order cook at a diner and worked mostly late evenings. Consequently, the victim was alone with her stepfather for a large portion of the day while her mother was at work. The man did not possess a criminal record, nor had any sexually-related allegations ever been made against him. In fact, he had become friendly with a few of the Northeast district uniformed patrol officers who patronized the restaurant.

One day, the victim walked into her elementary school and disclosed to one of her friends that her stepfather had been having sex with her. The victim's friend went home and told her mother, who notified the school. The school called the New York State Child Abuse Hotline, who contacted Monroe County Child Protective Services (CPS). I was assigned to assist the CPS worker and investigate the child's allegations.

I contacted the victim's mother at her place of employment and set up an interview with her and her daughter. Unbeknownst to me, the victim's mother had learned of her daughter's allegations just prior to my contact and had already confronted her husband of six years, kicking him out of the house. While her reaction was very appropriate, this development put me at a disadvantage in the investigation because it eliminated my opportunity to surprise the suspect with an unplanned visit and interview. My concern was that he would consult an attorney, who would always advise against an interview. Child sex abuse cases are difficult to prosecute without a confession from the perpetrator. Most jurors and even judges do not like to convict someone for sexual abuse when the case rests solely on the voice of a child. In fact, some jurors have even said afterward that they believed the victim's testimony, but chose not to convict the defendant because they felt that the police and prosecutors "did not have enough proof." I will never understand that rationalization, but that is the hard reality of these types of cases.

During my interview with the victim and her mother, I learned that the suspect frequently watched videotapes of graphic heterosexual activity. The victim disclosed that when she was seven years old, her stepfather began showing her his porn tapes while her mother was at work. He then began to masturbate in front of the victim, buying her secrecy with money and gifts. Over the last year he had begun to coax his stepdaughter into being his sexual partner, imitating the acts that they viewed on his porn videos. He continued to maintain the victim's silence with money and gifts, adding the threat that she would get into trouble for being a willing participant if anyone found out what "they" were doing with each other. But her tender conscience could no longer bear the burden of keeping such an evil secret. Like so many other young victims, this young girl was too ashamed and afraid to tell her mother, so she disclosed the abuse to a friend.

After taking the victim's sworn statement, I commenced my search for her stepfather, who had shacked up with some friends since being asked to leave by his wife. After making my presence known at his favorite hangout (a bar and pool hall near the diner), I met up with him at the restaurant the following day. Surprisingly, he voluntarily accompanied me to one of our substations. I allowed the suspect to sit in the front seat next to me, un-handcuffed. Luckily, he had not contacted a lawyer yet. Amid our small talk during the ride to the substation, I prayed silently to God that He would give me the words to pierce this man's heart to tell the truth.

As we were driving, the stepfather couldn't contain himself and addressed the allegation. Typical of these types of interviews, he denied touching his stepdaughter in a sexual way. He acknowledged watching porn movies while she was alone in the house with him, but claimed that he never forced the girl to view them with him. In fact, he asserted that his stepdaughter watched some of the porn movies on her own without his permission. The suspect repeatedly insisted that he would never touch any child sexually because he had been molested when he was a young boy. He offered up all of this information without me asking him one question. I just listened quietly, conveyed empathy to his situation and kept driving.

This man made a tactical mistake by using his alleged victimization as testimony of his innocence. If he had just denied the allegations, he would have left me little to work with during the interview. As a person who frequently interviews these types of criminals, I viewed his statement and rationalization as a weakness to exploit to uncover the truth. The suspect was trying to gain my respect and shift my sympathy from the real victim to himself. Whether or not he was truly a victim of child abuse did not make a difference to me because, in my mind, it would never justify anyone molesting a child. The suspect continued to declare his innocence. His continued denials did not come as a result of me repeatedly accusing him; it stemmed from his own guilty conscience dealing with the knowledge that his stepdaughter had brought his dirty deeds into the light.

Once we arrived at the substation and got settled in one of the interview rooms, I advised the suspect of his Miranda Warnings by reading them verbatim from the rights waiver card that I carry in my wallet. Like so many others, he voluntarily waived his rights and agreed to speak with me about the allegations against him. At this point I felt led to read him his stepdaughter's sworn statement, which was three pages long and spelled out in graphic detail many of the disgusting acts that he had performed on her. When I finished reading the statement I looked across the table and observed the suspect sobbing openly with tears streaming down his face. Quietly I told the suspect that it was a very profound statement for a ten-year-old girl. The suspect agreed with my assessment, but then he raised his voice and exclaimed that he did not do any of those things to her, slamming his beefy hand down against the table to emphasize the denial.

Ignoring the outburst, I quietly reminded him of the extensive sexual and physical abuse that he claimed he had been subjected to as a young child. I suggested that anything that had occurred between him and his stepdaughter may have been the result of the abuse that he had suffered. Maintaining my soft tone of voice, I then told the suspect that I believed that he did do "some" of those things that his stepdaughter was accusing him of, but deep in his heart he did not mean to hurt her. The suspect knew that what he had been doing to this little girl was evil and despicable. My role as the interrogator was to tap into that guilt and then exploit it by displacing the blame onto something or someone else, which gave him an easier avenue to admit to his wrong-doing. In this case, I blamed the person who the suspect claimed abused him. I encouraged the suspect to take responsibility for his actions against his stepdaughter, emphasizing that not doing so would make it very difficult for her to deal with the emotional damage that goes along with being a victim of such crimes. I then reminded him that he should know this from his own personal experience. He agreed.

I challenged him that either he was going to be viewed as a tragic product of his own sexual abuse, or as an evil man who has no compassion for a little girl who calls him "Daddy." The suspect began to sob openly, with his heavy body heaving up and down, his face buried in his arms. It was time to extract the confession. I asked the suspect in a sympathetic whisper if he wanted to tell his stepdaughter that he was sorry for what he did to her. Keeping his head buried in his arms, he shook it up and down, signifying "Yes." The suspect then lifted his head up, looked at me with his bloodshot eyes and stated, "I did some of it, but not all of it." He then placed his head back down and began sobbing even more uncontrollably than before. It was obvious that the suspect needed some time to gain his composure, so I left him alone for several minutes. His open lamenting could be heard in the investigator's office, located at the opposite end of the hall from the interview room.

Upon my return to the interview room, it was apparent that it was going to be difficult for the suspect to talk about the things that he did to his stepdaughter. This man was so ashamed that he couldn't look at me or respond to my questions. He couldn't even bear for me to ask him questions out loud. In an attempt to help the suspect get started and feel more comfortable, I offered to write down some specific questions on my notepad and he could simply answer yes or no. I suggested that he write his answer after each of my questions and place his initials next to each of his answers. He agreed. I asked the suspect to show courage and be truthful with his answers, and to focus on relieving his stepdaughter's emotional burden. When we are fortunate enough to have a child predator expressing guilt, as an interrogator, I must exploit that moment to the fullest in my attempt to obtain the truth.

Please be warned, the following paragraph is graphic, for it depicts what this predator did to the young victim. Unlike Hollywood's depiction of a police detective's job, there is no glamour in this kind of work. It is both filthy and emotionally difficult. While this part of my job is nauseating, it is essential, for it transfers the burden of proof from the young victim. No longer does everything rest on their tiny shoulders for a guilty verdict. When a lawful confession is obtained, the little voice of a child victim becomes as loud and powerful as the roar of Niagara Falls.

The questions that I wrote out and the suspect's written responses included the following:

"Did you kiss her?"
Response: "Yes."
"Did you touch her?"
Response: "Yes."
"Did you touch her vagina?"
Response: "Yes."
"Did she touch your penis?"
Response: "Yes."
"Did you touch her vagina with your mouth?"
Response: "No." Later in the interview the suspect admitted to committing this act.
"Did you touch her vagina with your penis?"
Response: "Yes."
"Did you put your penis in her mouth?"
Response: "No." Later in the interview the suspect changed his response to "I don't remember," but he said that it could have happened, if his stepdaughter said that it did.
"Did you ever ejaculate on her?"
Response: "No." Later in the interview the suspect said he leaked what he described as "pre-cum" from his penis on his stepdaughter during some of the sexual encounters with her.
"Did you ever touch your stepdaughter's anus?"
Response: "No." Later in the interview the suspect said his penis might have rubbed up against his stepdaughter's anus.

Once we had completed this exercise, the suspect appeared more comfortable with talking openly. As a result, I memorialized the results of our discussion in a four-page written statement, which described what he had done in more detail. The suspect was subsequently arrested and remanded to the Monroe County Jail in lieu of $25,000 bail or $50,000 bond. Several weeks later, minutes before the suppression hearing was to start, he voluntarily pled guilty to the charges in exchange for a reduced sentence of twelve to fifteen years in state prison. The plea bargain saved the young victim from having to face the man who repeatedly raped her, and from the rigorous cross-examination of a defense attorney. The lawfully obtained confession is the equalizer in these cases. It forces the captured predator to walk into a public courtroom and take responsibility for their actions before the world.

Based on my experience, stepfathers and foster fathers are common perpetrators. Obviously, this factor alone is not a red flag, but when the stepfather, or any father for that matter, is known to view pornographic media and assorted material on a frequent basis, it is unwise to leave a child in that man's sole care. Unfortunately, the mother in this case, like so many others, was unaware of the potential risk of leaving her daughter with a man that she knew had a penchant for sexual fantasy. Not every man who views adult porn with their mates will molest the children around them, but it indicates a potential risk. Additionally, based on the background work completed in this case, it appears that the mother had not consistently questioned her daughter about her interaction with her stepfather or her other daily activities while she was at work. Had she done this daily, she might have picked up on something from her daughter's responses. Her daughter might have disclosed early on that her stepfather was watching porn while in her presence. Knowing this particular mother, I am certain that she would have rebuked her husband for such behavior and prevented the situation from escalating into sexual abuse. I would counsel any mother in this predicament to urge her husband to get rid of all porn and to seek counseling, especially if he is addicted to viewing porn. For obvious reasons, guns and pornography of any kind should not exist in a home where children reside. I would further counsel the mother who discovers that her husband is addicted to pornography to find alternative care for her child until she is confident that her husband is free of such bondage for an extended period of time and is no longer a risk to her child. Frankly, knowing what I know and seeing what I have seen, I personally would never allow such a man to be alone with my child for any amount of time.

Understandably, most people have a hard time believing that a loved one could commit such a despicable act against their own child or one that they are close to. No one expects these types of things to occur in a family setting or a similar environment where our children are considered secure. This is what makes these crimes so devastating. Too many times, the people whom we have come to love and trust are the ones that victimize our children. The purpose of this book is not to scare parents or make them paranoid of everyone around them, but to make them aware of how potential tragedies can be avoided. When it comes to our children's safety, we need to think as a shepherd does of his flock, anticipating danger when certain factors indicate a possible threat. If you as a parent choose to ignore these potential risks, the results could be tragic.

CHAPTER 6

—ɱ—

CASE EXAMPLE 3
THE HIGHLY-ESTEEMED COACH

"The human heart is the most deceitful of all things, and desperately wicked. Who really knows how bad it is? But I, the Lord, search all hearts and examine secret motives. I give all people their due rewards, according to what their actions deserve."

JEREMIAH 17:9-10 (NLT)

The following case is in no way a representation of the many great people who serve as athletic coaches and mentors to our youth. It serves as an example of how child predators will place themselves in this position to gain access to children for their own selfish purposes. The predator in this case was a thirty-nine-year old former Olympic champion gymnast from an Eastern European nation. His wife and business partner was also a world-champion gymnast, and they had three children of their own. They had established themselves as a highly respected, successful coaching tandem, both nationally and internationally. Their large state-of-the-art gymnastics facility was second to none, and served as a training center for nearly five hundred gymnasts from preschool to college age, beginners to Olympic competitors.

If you are familiar with the Olympic champions from the former Soviet Union and Eastern European countries over the past forty years, you know that much of their success was due to the Spartan, warrior-like existence in which they were forced to live and train. Children who appeared to be gifted with certain athletic abilities were plucked from their homes and families at a young age. They became the property of the state; their lives were not their own, but that of the oppressive and authoritative government. The life of the child athlete was controlled in every aspect, and their trainer had supreme authority over them. These Eastern-bloc nations enjoyed unprecedented success, building dynasties across the board in the respective sports.

After years of defeat and humiliation, amateur athletic sports programs in the United States began to buy into the Communists' method for success, recruiting coaches and athletes to venture across the Atlantic and set up shop stateside. Soon thereafter, many parents in America were doing everything in their capacity to place their children under the tutelage of these Eastern European trainers and coaches, or American coaches who adopted their maniacal training style. What American athletes and their parents experienced was nothing short of culture shock. The Eastern European style of coaching demands loyalty and unchallenged authority. Typically, parents are not allowed to interfere or even politely question the coach in regard to their training methods or their degree of control of the athlete's life. And their services do not come cheap. Some parents have even taken out a second mortgage on their house to pay the coach an exorbitant fee in the hope that their child would develop into an Olympic champion.

The thirteen-year-old victim in this case was a member of an elite junior female team of approximately ten gymnasts that competed internationally. All of them were gifted athletes, candidates for a Division I college athletic scholarship or Olympic hopefuls. Like most of her teammates, the victim had been coached by the suspect and his wife since she was in preschool. The bond between the coaches and gymnasts and their families was strong and long-standing.

At the request of Doug Randall, Bureau Chief of the Monroe County District Attorney's Office Domestic Violence and Child Abuse Bureau, I became involved in this investigation, which had been opened a few days earlier by a local village police department. The suspect had already been confronted by the victim's family and was aware that a police investigation was ongoing. This was a major setback from an investigative standpoint, because the suspect had retained a lawyer immediately and refused to be interviewed.

The victim's parents had become suspicious of their daughter's away message on their home computer, fearing that their daughter was having inappropriate contact with an older boyfriend over the Internet. Additionally, the parent of another gymnast had informed them that the coach had been having inappropriate discussions with his adolescent female students at the gymnastics school. The concerned parent further advised the victim's parents that their daughter had observed the coach brushing his hand up against the victim's body as they would walk by each other during training and practice sessions. Based on these developments, the victim's parents decided to install spy software on their home computer to secretly monitor her online conversations.

When I met with the victim and her parents, they showed me printouts of twenty intercepted instant messages (IMs) between their daughter and her coach. By their substance, the IMs appeared to be communications between girlfriend and boyfriend in a coded format in an effort to conceal the sexual nature of the conversation. They made reference to specific sexual acts that the two parties had committed with each other in the past. Most of the conversations centered on the topics of oral sex, vaginal penetration with the coach's finger and penis, orgasms, and masturbation.

When I interviewed the victim, she stated that her coach started to have explicit conversations with her about her sexual development, including the size of her breasts, several months prior to physical contact. The coach later began rubbing the victim's legs and abdomen area, touching her in a sensual way when he stretched her out after training sessions. The victim, who had idolized her coach since she was five years old, said that she began to enjoy the way that her coach was touching her and the way that he was flirting with her. She admitted that she enjoyed it when her coach would brush his hand against her buttocks when he didn't think that any of the other gymnasts were watching. The coach also began communicating with her over the Internet daily. He was appealing to her budding sexuality and grooming her to become his willing partner by sharing his sexual fantasies about her. At this point, the victim knew that she was engaged in behavior that her parents would never approve of, but the attention was exciting to her. She shared that part of her "felt weird" about what was going on, but she really didn't know how to disengage from it. The newfound relationship confused her young, immature mind.

The victim explained that her coach had been spending more time with her than the other gymnasts, keeping her after practices for extra one-on-one training time. Some of the victim's teammates observed the coach's actions toward her and began to ask questions. The victim downplayed what was happening and told them that she didn't know why the coach was acting that way toward her and no one else. One-on-one training time with the coach was reserved for only the top one or two competitors on the team. Some of the victim's teammates began to view her as the "coach's pet," but felt the favoritism was not warranted, as they did not consider her to be one of the top competitors. Some of her teammates became jealous, which eventually caused dissension on the team and among some of the parents. Many of these parents were paying big money for the coach to teach their daughters, and if one girl was receiving extra attention, it would only be a matter of time before they were going to make an issue of it.

The victim admitted that she was afraid that her coach would become angry with her if she told him what her teammates had been saying about her. The victim thought that her coach would stop spending extra training time with her if she broke away from him. The victim had seen her coach become angry with other gymnasts in the past and then ignore them. As a result, their individual performance in competitive events would drop. The victim viewed this potential outcome as catastrophic to her future as a gymnast. Clearly, she was in over her head, and that's just where he wanted her.

The coach and the victim communicated over the computer about their sexual activity for close to a year. As the touching grew in frequency, it became more invasive and intimate. The emboldened coach would instruct the victim's parents not to return for their daughter until later in the evening because he was spending more individual time with her. On at least one of those nights, the victim's father showed up and found his daughter and the coach still in the gymnasium with all of the lights off. On another occasion, a teammate's parent was supposed to give the victim a ride home after practice, but the coach refused to allow her to leave. He insisted that she remain with him alone. Much to the coach's chagrin, the parent refused to leave without the girl; he remained there until he contacted her parents and obtained their permission to leave her behind. I admire this particular parent for his actions. He did not bow down to this arrogant coach when it came to the safety and welfare of a child that he had been entrusted with temporarily.

One night, the coach showed up at practice and handed his cell phone to the victim, instructing her to play a video that he had prepared for her. The victim stated that the video depicted the coach naked and masturbating, which included a close-up of his penis while climaxing. When she returned the phone to her coach, he asked her if she had enjoyed watching it. The victim said "yes," but she really thought that the video was disgusting. The victim was afraid to tell him the truth.

Eventually, his fantasy became reality. The touching and caressing evolved into sexual intercourse in the "pit." The pit was a very large boxed-out area filled with thousands of foam cubes that ensured soft landings for vaulting and tumbling exercises. It was the size of a large above-ground swimming pool, and approximately six feet deep. The victim reported that she engaged in both oral and vaginal sex with her coach in the foam pit after practice sessions. Incredibly, sometimes other teammates were still in the facility at the time. But because the sides of the foam pit stood six feet above the floor surface, it was difficult for anyone to see what was going on inside of it, even while standing on the practice floor mats below. No one would ever question what they were doing, because it was common practice for the gymnasts to "fluff the pit" after practice when the coach told them to. Fluffing the pit meant getting in it and moving the foam cubes on the bottom to the top so that they would not stay compressed. It served as a form of physical conditioning because it was a very strenuous activity. The victim was assigned this duty of fluffing the pit more often than other gymnasts as the sexual encounters increased in frequency.

The victim stated that her coach would ejaculate his semen either on her or into her mouth or vagina during these incidents. The victim said that she would spit it out of her mouth into the foam pit. I viewed this as a potential positive for my investigation, because if we were able to locate the coach's semen in the foam pit, we would have a very strong case against him. Hearing these gruesome details is not for everyone, including most cops. For the successful investigation and prosecution of the case, it is vital that the police detective becomes skilled in placing the child victim at ease, gently extracting all of the dirty details. The investigator must be able to at least give the appearance of being comfortable talking to the victims about this horrible stuff. Many of these children become willing participants, but they have been brainwashed by the child predator into thinking that they will get into trouble or that someone will get hurt if they tell. If we are incapable of masking our own disgust, how can we expect the young victims to be comfortable talking to us about what had been done to them? As you can imagine, the police investigator who is not properly trained and skilled in interviewing victims would be a detriment to every case that they worked.

Corroborating a young victim's testimony with physical evidence can change the landscape of an investigation, especially when your suspect is a person of prominence. Since the coach had already retained a lawyer and would not make himself available for an interview, our next priority was to draft search warrants for his home and the gymnasium. The probable cause for the search warrants was the victim's sworn statement and the IM messages between the coach and the victim that her parents had intercepted. The writing of the warrants took us into the late hours of the night, but it was paramount that we execute both search warrants immediately, before the coach was able to destroy potential evidence. While seated at his kitchen table in his pajamas, a county court judge studied both search warrants and signed them.

We later found out that the coach and his family were in Lake Placid for the New Year's holiday. This development made it a little easier. I hate going into someone's home to execute a search warrant late at night when children are present. It can be terrifying to the children to have several police officers come into their home and take it over from their mom and dad. This is the place that they are supposed to feel safe. Too many times I have seen the fright in their young faces as they are corralled into the living room with their parents while we turn their house upside down. I resent their father for putting them through such an exercise. The perpetrator's children always end up being secondary victims in any criminal cases I work, and it always breaks my heart.

Search warrant teams executed both warrants without any interference. The coach's home and business computers were seized and secured as evidence. Our crime scene technicians turned off all of the lights in the training facility and scanned the corner of the foam pit where the encounters had allegedly occurred with what we call an "alternate light source" lamp. This special light causes trace evidence such as body fluids and semen to turn a florescent greenish-yellow.

At first, things didn't look too promising. Most of us were going on fumes as it progressed into late morning. I politely asked the technicians to hang in there and move a mat that was covering an area of the pit that we were scanning. The mat was large and heavy, requiring several of us to slide it out of the way. The effort was well worth it. When the evidence technicians shined their lamps over the area, it was like we were looking at a cluster of diamonds in the darkness of a large cave. Four foam blocks had what appeared to be semen on them. By the pattern of the dried fluid, it appeared that this might have been from one of the times that the victim had spit her coach's semen out of her mouth.

My hope was that the county Public Safety Lab would be able to match both the victim's DNA from her saliva and the coach's DNA from his sperm. That would be an absolute lock. As an investigator, I always keep looking ahead at possible defenses that the suspect might offer up to discount the physical evidence. Because this facility was owned and operated by the coach and his wife, I could already foresee the suspect claiming that he and his wife had sex with each other in the pit when the facility was closed. If we were able to recover a sample of semen with traces of the victim's DNA mixed in it however, there would be no possibility of formulating a defense against such damning evidence. The fact that the semen was right where the victim said it should be was great corroborating evidence, but the cruel reality is that a jury is always going to look for a legitimate excuse not to convict someone of this stature. If the suspect's wife chose to get on the witness stand and explain the evidence away, it would sway at least one or two of the jurors against a guilty verdict. And sure enough, as soon as it became public that we had recovered potential semen in the foam pit, someone started broadcasting that the coach and his wife made love in the pit all the time.

Later that following day, the coach voluntarily surrendered with his attorney at our Eastside substation. After escorting them into a conference room, I handcuffed the coach and searched him for weapons. I found his cell phone in his pants pocket and seized that as potential evidence, which was a lucky break for us since he had used it for the video recording of him masturbating. As expected, the coach's attorney would not allow us to interview his client, so we booked him on two counts of rape in the second degree, three counts of criminal sexual act in the second degree, and one count of sexual abuse in the second degree. We transported him to his arraignment in the respective town court, where the judge set the bail at $50,000 cash or $100,000 bond. The coach was then transported to jail.

It is important to think several steps ahead to determine the best course of action while working a case such as this. I decided not to charge the coach with any of the sexually enticing discussions he had with the victim over the Internet in state court, for I felt that we would get more bang for our buck in federal court. At first, I took some heat for making this decision without consulting with those ranked above me, but eventually everyone agreed that it was the best alternative. The reason is that the defendant would face more potential prison time in federal court for the Internet crimes than he would for the actual physical crimes in state court. As bizarre as that may sound, it is the harsh reality in some of these cases. As planned, I contacted FBI Special Agent Jason S. Fickett, who was working out of the Rochester office at the time. He was instrumental in assisting us with getting the computers and cell phone analyzed by a forensics team. Our department's computer forensic examiner specialist had retired shortly before this case came in, so we had to solicit assistance from the FBI or Secret Service. I felt that it was only appropriate to allow the Feds to lodge their own charges against the coach for the electronic crimes. And Special Agent Fickett wasted no time.

The coach had been bailed out of jail by some of his supporters. However, he was arrested approximately two weeks later in his driveway by Special Agent Fickett. He was charged with violating Title 18 of United States Code 2422(b), a federal statute that prohibits people from utilizing or attempting to utilize a facility or means of interstate commerce to persuade, induce, or entice a minor to engage in any sexual activity for which any person could be charged criminally. Because computer messages travel across state lines to a mainframe and are then routed back to their destination, even if the messages are only traveling next door it becomes a federal crime due to the interstate travel of the signal. After he was booked and processed, the coach was transported to the local United States Magistrate for his arraignment and taken back to jail with no bail.

The second arrest came on the heels of a public smearing campaign against the victim by the coach and his supporters. They were already attempting to publicly humiliate this young girl and turn people against her. Unfortunately this type of reaction is not uncommon when we arrest a person of prominence in the community, where everyone comes out and supports the accused rather than the victim. It is tragic that many people did not consider that the victim did not bring this behavior upon herself. She didn't go to the gym one day and decide that she was going to seduce her thirty-nine-year-old coach. She wasn't even in high school yet. Those connected to either the victim or the suspect should just remain silent and allow due process to take its course. Fortunately, the second arrest on federal charges and subsequent incarceration showed that we meant business and possessed a strong case against the coach, which quieted some of his more vocal supporters.

Approximately eleven days after the coach was placed back in jail, the victim's mother called me to advise that her daughter had disclosed additional information about what had occurred in the foam pit. After a few sessions with a counselor, the victim felt more comfortable and less afraid to share more details. Once the offender is placed in jail, the victim will feel less threatened. Especially after they have met with a victim advocate or counselor to talk about their concerns, they will often feel safe enough to speak more openly about past events. The victim came to my office the following evening with her mother to share the additional information. The victim indicated that the sexual encounters had occurred more frequently than previously acknowledged. While they did occur in the aforementioned corner, the victim stated that her coach would use the foam blocks to wipe his sperm off their genitals and then cast them around the entire foam pit. The victim also disclosed that her coach had instructed her to shave her vaginal area, and he shaved his genital area. At his request, she gave her coach a pair of her thong panties to wear. On at least one occasion he wore her panties under his sweat pants to practice and showed them to her when no one was looking. Welcome to my world, where there is nothing too bizarre to satisfy the insatiable lust of a child predator. This man, who at one time had the honor of representing his home country and even winning an Olympic medal, had now reduced himself to wearing a pair of his young student's panties.

We had limited our initial search to a small area of the pit based upon the victim's earlier testimony. This new information prompted me to apply for another warrant to conduct a second search of the entire foam pit in the gymnasium. A person's constitutional right against unreasonable searches in this country is considered sacred; a second bite at the apple to search someone's personal property or business is rarely granted by a judge unless you can provide a compelling reason. In the second warrant application, I carefully articulated that we had limited our first search of the foam pit to a very small area based upon the victim's initial testimony, but we desired to expand our search based on recent additional information from the victim. Thankfully, the judge granted our second request. It was well worth the effort.

This time, we conducted the search during regular business hours and went in with an army of technicians and equipment. All of us assisted with the physical search, which was conducted in the dark with the alternate light source lamps. We recovered approximately one hundred foam blocks that appeared to have dried sperm on them. The people who were assigned to assist me in the execution of the search warrant worked extremely hard. They processed the entire scene like an organized assembly factory as I blasted rock and blues music over my boom box. I even allowed the coach's defense lawyers in to observe our operation, simply to impress them. My supervisor, Doug Comanzo, was very helpful and supportive, pitching in for the steak dinners and pizzas I brought in for the crew as a sign of my gratitude during the ten-hours-long search. This was just another example of how good managers empower their people to get the job done. While he had not been our supervisor for long, Sargeant Comanzo has great people skills and a sincere heart to do what was right. To an old dog like me, that goes a long way.

Because DNA analysis is very expensive, there was no way that the county was going to pay for all one hundred foam blocks to be analyzed. That may happen on television, but in the real world, money is always a concern. So I examined all of the blocks and picked twenty that I thought would offer us our best shot at locating both the victim's and coach's DNA mixed together. All we really needed was one foam block that had DNA from both the coach and the victim. This case was receiving national and international media coverage, so it was very important that we build a solid case to support the victim, who was under incredible scrutiny.

Praise God, we hit the jackpot. We felt as if we had found the elusive Holy Grail. Our Public Safety Lab located both the victim's DNA and the coach's DNA from his sperm on one of the first five blocks that I had submitted for analysis. Now the world would know that this man had violated a young girl that he was being paid an exorbitant amount of money to mentor and coach. He had violated her trust and the trust of her loyal parents. He was finally exposed to be the slippery serpent that he truly was. Everyone would now know that the victim was telling the truth, and that she was not the disgruntled athlete that she had been labeled. The powerful voice of public support that he had been receiving all but disappeared when we shared the news with his "dream team" of defense attorneys. The coach pled guilty in state court to the sexual crimes, and in federal court to the computer crimes for enticing her. He agreed to waive his right to appeal for a lesser sentence, and was given sixteen years in prison.

The best conclusion we can hope for in these criminal cases is when the defendant walks into court and admits to what he did. It eliminates public scrutiny against the victim by removing all doubt that this person did in fact commit such despicable acts against a child that told the truth. It relieves the child from further embarrassment that goes along with having to relive their victimization in a courtroom while testifying at a trial and being subjected to a rigorous cross-examination by their offender's defense attorney. There is no doubt in my mind that when a child is forced to testify in a public courtroom against their offender, they are re-victimized both mentally and emotionally by the experience.

I find my greatest sense of purpose when investigating crimes against children. After I discover where the truth lies in my investigations, I do everything in my official capacity to put forth the best prosecutable case that I can so that the defendant will be motivated to make a plea agreement and confess in a public courtroom. I find more satisfaction when the defendant pleads guilty in child sexual abuse cases than any other cases because by doing so, we have lifted a huge emotional and psychological burden off the child victim and given them their life back. If that child has any chance of recovering from such a devastating experience, they need to know that their offender acknowledged that the sexual abuse was their fault, not the child's. A secret apology with no consequences has proven, too many times, to not be enough.

Showing tremendous courage, the victim went to a new gymnastics facility to continue training and attempted to compete amid unbearable pressure and gossip during the subsequent prosecution process of the suspect. It was as if she and her parents were being blamed for the disruption of some of her former teammates' training and causing a distraction in the American gymnastics community. There is no doubt that her overall performance suffered as a result. Even though the criminal case is now closed and the coach is serving his prison sentence, the victim and her parents have been left to pick up the pieces of their lives and continue on. I can only hope and pray that this young girl's future will take a turn for the better, for she is gifted and had great aspirations before her trusted coach betrayed her. I know that the journey will be difficult, but she has two great parents who love her unconditionally and will support her.

While I believe that athletic programs are a great activity and have an important place in our children's development, we Americans have placed way too much emphasis on success. I view this as a recipe for disaster on several fronts. First, the children can be under unbearable pressure from competing at a level beyond their maturity to handle. This prevents them from simply enjoying the sport as a way to recreate and learn. Second, parents who place their children under the unchallenged authority of any sports coach are jeopardizing their own relationship and parental authority. Once a parent surrenders their child to another adult in such a manner, they have lost a part of that child's respect, if not entirely. When the child athlete realizes that their coach possesses authority over their parents, it will create a rift between them which could last a lifetime. Third, the child predator longs for parents to hand over their children to their absolute control, so if possible he will place himself in the position of coach to gain unlimited access to potential child victims; once he has successfully established himself, he will gleefully exercise that control.

This predator used his authority, as well as his cultural influence and personal success, to gain the control of this young girl's entire life with her unsuspecting parents' consent. As a result, the relationship between the coach and the athlete, and the coach and the parents, became way out of balance. I don't blame the parents of this young girl; I blame this child predator for his diabolical manipulation of them. But I must warn every parent: do not allow your judgment to become so clouded by your hopes for your child that you fail to recognize the danger. The coach was able to manipulate this young girl while he drew her sexuality to the surface by flirting, teasing, and touching her in very sensual ways. There was a part of this victim that obviously enjoyed this type of interaction, but there was another part of her that felt confused by this man's actions toward her—a man that had become the most authoritative male influence in her life over the past eight years. When he found out that she was showing a normal interest in boys her own age, he immediately intervened and mandated that her parents not allow their daughter to date or even socialize with boys. He told them that boys would become a distraction to her training and ultimate success as a competitive gymnast, and he simply would not allow it. The parents conceded to his demands, thinking that they were doing the right thing by their daughter. In addition to being cut off from socializing with boys her own age, the victim was also alienated by some of her teammates because of the amount of special attention she had been receiving from the coach. Little did her parents know that the coach that they had invited into their home countless times for dinner and family get-togethers was targeting their child, drawing her away from the rest of the "flock" of her peers, just as a predator corners their prey.

When it comes to sports and the coach factor, I understand the delicate balancing act on the part of the athlete's parents, especially fathers. My youngest daughter began riding horses at a young age and soon began entering competitions. As her skill improved, her need for a more advanced riding coach and trainer increased. As a result, she ended up with one of the best trainers in this area of the country. I can tell you that he was paid a good chunk of change to coach my daughter. This accomplished coach was a single man in his early thirties and, according to every woman in the riding facility including my wife and daughter, very handsome. When he spoke it was like those old E.F. Hutton commercials—everyone stopped what they were doing and listened. His status at the riding facility was that of a demigod. So you can imagine the reaction of my wife and daughter when I questioned his character and judgment now and then. Frankly, they were under the man's spell for the three years that my daughter was under his discipleship. In a sense, I was powerless.

I never suspected the trainer of any wrongdoing, nor did I ever observe him act in an inappropriate way with my daughter or any other child. Lord knows, I was watching him, just waiting for an opportunity to knock him off his pedestal. But other than raking us for a lot of money, this charismatic coach never overstepped his bounds. I will tell you, the recipe for disaster was there. He owned my daughter's heart and my wife thought he was above reproach. That is, until she eventually came to realize he was a mere mortal just like the rest of us. I share this personal experience with you to demonstrate that it could have happened to my family if beneath all of his charisma, success, and good looks, the coach had actually been a child predator. My beautiful but iron-willed blonde daughter would have followed him into Hell if he had asked her to. And there were plenty of opportunities for that to happen when we dropped her off at the barn for hours-long training sessions.

I understand and appreciate the pressure that a parent can be under in this type of situation. If I had severed the relationship between my daughter and her trainer based on mere suspicion, I'd still be residing in the dog house today. But if this man had overstepped his boundaries as an instructor in any way, I would have confronted him and discontinued my daughter's riding lessons to protect her. Then I would have gladly driven to the local lumber yard and purchased the necessary building materials to build a spacious addition onto our dog's house in the backyard.

When it comes to dealing with our children's influential and demanding instructors, we must rely upon godly wisdom, good judgment, and common sense. While many successful coaches will, for good reasons, insist that there be no parental interference with respect to the team line-up, game plan, and overall management of the team, most coaches will never challenge the parent's authority over the athlete. When the coach begins to make or push for decisions that only a parent should make, regardless of what their motive may be, their actions should be questioned and challenged. When it comes to your children's safety and welfare, take no prisoners: never allow another adult, no matter who they are, to operate outside of the boundaries of their relationship with your child.

CHAPTER 7

—ɯɯ—

CASE EXAMPLE 4
"TIME TO BE NICE"

"*Bend down, O Lord, and hear my prayer; answer me, for I need your help…Send me a sign of your favor. Then those who hate me will be put to shame, for you, O Lord, help and comfort me.*"

PSALM 86:1, 17 (NLT)

"*And through covetousness shall they with feigned words make merchandise of you: whose judgment now of a long time lingereth not, and their damnation slumbereth not.* "

PETER 2:3 (KJV)

This case involves the molestation of an adolescent female by her own father. The suspect was a successful home builder and businessman, living in an upper middle-class community with his family. The young woman had broken down and disclosed to her boyfriend, and later a school counselor, that her father had been sexually abusing her for the past nine years. The school year was just one week old and our reported victim was starting her senior year in high school.

After being assigned the case via the New York State Child Abuse Hotline, a child protective worker and I drove out to the large high school, located in one of the more affluent Eastside suburbs of Monroe County. It was a warm September afternoon when we walked into the school building. The stale hot air reeked of adolescent body odor and overactive hormones. We met with the seventeen-year-old student in her counselor's office. I was immediately taken back by both her physical appearance and mannerism, which belied her young age. She wore no makeup and had her long, curly hair pulled back away from her face, a look more customary for a woman in her twenties or thirties. She possessed a social maturity well beyond her years. This girl shed no tears during our conversation with her; she held a steely composure while I asked the difficult questions typical of these types of interviews. I asked the victim how long the sexual abuse had been occurring and she responded matter-of-factly, "As long as I can remember."

I was astonished by this young woman's story. The victim's father had been molesting her since she was in the fourth grade. As she physically matured, the molestation gradually evolved into sexual intercourse, oral sex and countless acts of sodomy. Since she had reached puberty at a relatively young age, this poor girl had been forced into performing the role of her father's sexual partner in her mother's place for nearly her entire childhood. The abuse always occurred when the victim's mother was either at work or out of the house running errands. "Time to be nice," was the father's pet phrase to the victim when he wanted her to report to his bedroom for a sexual encounter. The victim stated that she would stare at the bedroom ceiling and make pictures in her mind out of the plaster formations while her father raped her. In other words, the victim would allow her mind to drift away from the brutal reality of what was occurring to her. This is how this remarkable young woman survived the countless sexual assaults.

The young woman's allegations were difficult to digest, even for me. As a father of two daughters, I will never understand how a man could violate his God-ordained role to nurture and protect his children, forcing his own flesh and blood to commit these deviate, despicable sexual acts. But as shocking as this brave young woman's allegations were, I believed that she was telling the truth. What sealed my belief was her disclosure of her father's favorite phrase, "Time to be nice." Many of the child predators that I have arrested had little pet phrases for their victims when they wanted the child to acquiesce to sex. Sexual offenders are creatures of habit, just like the rest of us. The victim's description of her escape mechanism also rang true. No child is capable of making this up, nor do they know the significance of this information to the experienced police investigator.

The victim's father rationalized the molestation to his daughter by telling her that it was her "duty to be nice" to him. As a little girl she didn't like doing these horrible things with her dad, but she didn't know any better; she was told that this is what all daughters had to do. By the time she reached puberty, the victim was forced to have sex with her father two to three times per week. As the victim matured, she learned that the behavior was in fact wrong. When the victim's protests became more frequent, the father increased his control. He prevented her from having a boyfriend her own age. He became insanely jealous, even visibly hostile, when a young man came to the house to call upon his lovely, blossoming daughter. To the average person, this reaction appeared to be that of an overly protective father. Yet it was due to a far more sinister reason that most people would never have imagined.

What led this young woman to finally expose a dark family secret and disclose the years of sexual abuse was her father's jealousy, and his arrogant belief that he would never be held accountable. When the victim's father made her give him sex to use the car and then reneged on the deal because she refused to stop seeing a young man, she broke. She disclosed the abuse to her boyfriend, who promptly broke up with her because he was afraid of her father. This was too much for the victim to bear, so she reached out to a school counselor for help. I thank God this child didn't consider following through with her thoughts of suicide, like so many do.

I eventually met with the victim at the sheriff's Eastside substation to take her sworn statement, which detailed a compelling, heart-wrenching account of an entire decade of molestation and rape. I had already conducted a background investigation of the victim to determine whether she could have an ulterior motive for these allegations, but I found no evidence that would support any kind of sinister plotting on her part. My investigation revealed a solid, above-average student who had no history of lying or behavioral problems in school. To the outside world, this young woman was a mature, happy girl.

On the following day, during the lunch recess, my partner Investigator Passmore and I met with the victim for the purpose of making a control phone call to her father. This is when the police investigator facilitates the recording of a phone conversation between two people with only one of the participants' permission. In New York State, it is legal to secretly record your conversations with another person without their knowledge. This can be a very effective tactic to build corroborating evidence of an allegation. As if she hadn't been through enough already, we were asking this young lady to make a phone call to her father to engage him in a conversation about the years of sexual abuse that he had subjected her to. It was certain to be an excruciatingly painful moment for her, but we needed a recorded conversation between them that would demonstrate culpability to a jury. For just a moment, put yourself in this child's position to grasp the enormity of such a task. If she was unable to make the call, and her father didn't confess to the crime, a conviction was highly unlikely. If the victim's father invoked his right to decline an interview and requested a lawyer, the only corroborating evidence we could count on was him acknowledging the sexual abuse during a recorded conversation. Too many juries have told prosecutors after they handed down a "not guilty" verdict that they believed the child victim's testimony, but felt that there wasn't enough evidence to convict the defendant. This makes no sense to me, but when you put twelve people together in a jury room, this often happens in these types of cases.

It was sunny and warm as Officer Passmore and I set up the recording device while the victim sat in our unmarked police car in the high school parking lot. I thought she would be more comfortable sitting in our vehicle rather than in a school administrator's office. After I instructed the victim on what I needed her to say to her father, I had her call his cell phone. She did an excellent job at saying the things that she was told to say. We could not hear her father's responses while she was talking to him, but by her comments we could tell that he was making admissions and attempting to convince her not to speak with the police. While the control call was necessary, it saddened me deeply to require it of this young woman. She began to cry as the phone conversation continued, but she was courageous and hit the mark. After she hung up, Investigator Passmore and I listened to the micro-cassette recording. While the phone call proved to be fruitful for the case, it turned my stomach. The suspect repeatedly begged his daughter not to have him arrested, saying that he was sorry for what he had done to her all of those years. At one point, the victim asked her father why he didn't just go out and pay a prostitute instead of forcing her. All he could say was that she was right and he would get the victim counseling. What really disgusted me was the guilt trip: "think about your mother and your grandparents and what it would do to them" if she were to tell the police and send him to prison. He tried to blame her for his actions and their pending consequences. Understandably, the victim was an emotional wreck after making this call, so I accompanied her back into the school counselor's office. Upon my return to the Major Crimes Unit I requested a copy of the micro-cassette, and I secured the original tape as evidence.

After completing the necessary arrest paperwork, I called the suspect and invited him in for an interview. I told him that his daughter had filed a report against him and I just wanted to hear his side of the situation. He was quick to deny the allegations, offering that perhaps she had filed the police report as revenge for his recent stand against her behavioral problems. His tone and mannerism exuded confidence, a stark contrast to the whining and sniveling that we had heard a few days before. He agreed to meet with me that evening at the Eastside substation. The suspect said that he planned to bring his oldest son, with whom he had been staying since his eviction by the child protective workers, to share with me what a "vindictive person" his daughter could be. I didn't share that I planned to take him to jail that very night. Honestly, I sincerely hoped that this man would come in and continue denying his daughter's allegations. I wanted to bring in the tape and embarrass him with the playback of him admitting to the crimes, whimpering and begging his daughter for mercy. But much to my chagrin, God had another plan that would not allow me to play the role of a vengeful tormentor.

When the suspect arrived at the substation, I sized him up. He was a man of short stature with a wiry, strong build and gray hair. His hands were that of a working man. His ruddy complexion and crooked nose gave him the appearance of an old-time boxer who had weathered one too many bouts. The suspect's son apparently assumed that he was going to accompany his father to the interview room, for he automatically arose from his chair to follow along. I could sense their consternation when I directed him to remain behind in the lobby on the other side of the locked door.

After we sat down in one of the interview rooms, I advised the suspect of his rights. He voluntarily waived them. I didn't feel the need to build a rapport with this man, so I directed our conversation straight to the issue at hand. I didn't attempt to downplay the magnitude of the charges; I simply remarked that these were serious allegations. The suspect stated that he understood the seriousness of the matter, but he didn't know why his daughter would be saying such things about him. I then asked the suspect what he thought should happen to a person who molests their own children. With stern conviction in his voice he replied, "They should go to jail!"

I nodded in agreement. I then informed him that I had met with his daughter on a couple of occasions and I was impressed by her. I had looked into his daughter's background and I had learned that she had never been in any kind of serious trouble throughout her entire school career. She had achieved high grades, and the teaching staff considered her an excellent student of exemplary character. The suspect agreed with their assessment. I noted that his daughter's allegations were difficult to comprehend with respect to the time frame of nearly ten years. I told him that she appeared to be telling the truth and I believed that something had occurred between them sexually. The suspect again denied any sexual contact with his daughter. I ignored the denial, reasserting that I felt that something did happen with his daughter, and I understood that it was difficult for any man to talk about. I offered that either he was a "good" man who may have used some very bad judgment, yet willing to make things right by taking responsibility for what he did; or, he was a bad man who not only sexually molested his own daughter over many years, but was now going to make her carry around the emotional burden of his selfishness for the rest of her life. I told the suspect that his unwillingness to take responsibility for his actions against his daughter, forcing her to live with such a burden, would be reprehensible conduct for a father. I could see by the expression on his face that he was starting to crumble, so I prayed that the Lord would give me the right words and guide me wherever He wanted this interview to go. And I just kept talking. I told the suspect again that I truly believed that his daughter was telling the truth, but that he was a "good" man who had struggled with at least one major character flaw in his life, as many of us men do in today's world. I noted that it was not uncommon for us to victimize our family and children, the very people we love and care about most. I suggested that the stress of making a living, providing for your family and making your marriage work, can lead a man to act out in ways he wouldn't normally act.

The suspect responded, "I have been under a lot of stress lately...but I didn't do this."

"Do you believe in God?" I asked.

"Yes." He answered.

I asked him to consider that God would hold him very much accountable if he did in fact do these things to his daughter but refused to own up to it in a public forum. I advised that admitting his fault to his daughter in private was not good enough. If she was telling the truth and he didn't take responsibility, everyone would assume that she was a liar. I could see the suspect's posture dropping. It was as if God's Spirit was convicting this man's heart, transferring the weight of his daughter's enormous emotional burden back onto him. I didn't let up on him because I wanted the weight of what he had subjected his daughter to over so many years to become unbearable and break his spirit. At that very moment, I felt like God was speaking to this man through me, guiding the direction of the interview. I know of other experienced police interrogators who have had this feeling while trying to convince the suspect of a horrible crime to admit the ugly truth, a truth that he had never intended to confess. It is during these moments that many of us feel that we are truly working for God, doing exactly what He created us to do.

"Would you give up your life for your children?" I asked the suspect.

"Of course I would," he answered soberly.

I had asked him this question for a very specific reason. I know that every man likes to be a hero, especially when he knows that he is in dire need of redemption. I told the suspect that this moment was a true test of such a statement. Now his daughter was crying for help. I continued softly, "She can't carry it around anymore…She doesn't want to destroy the family…She doesn't want to put her daddy in jail…She doesn't want to upset her mom and grandparents, but she just can't go on living this way any longer."

I was transforming the issue from confessing to saving his daughter from her pain. Most suspects never want to admit to such a despicable deed of molesting any child, let alone their own child. But if I can get the suspect to focus on the child's pain rather than their own guilt and the potential consequences they are facing, many of them will experience a moment of emotional vulnerability and take responsibility for their actions. It is a small, short-lived window of opportunity, so when it opens, the police investigator must seize the moment and close it. The police community commonly refers to the detectives who successfully obtain admissible confessions on a frequent basis as "closers." Like door-to-door salesmen, we usually have only one shot to sell the truth to the suspect. Certainly, it is a difficult sale to make to a child predator. He has everything to lose and nothing to gain by telling the truth about his actions against a child. However, it is possible if the police investigator can identify the suspect's emotional vulnerabilities and methodically work on those weaknesses during the interrogation. Unless someone is a complete sociopath, most everyone is emotionally vulnerable in some capacity.

The words just kept coming out of my mouth, but it felt as if they weren't coming from me. I told the suspect that this was his opportunity to sacrifice his own life and reputation to save his child's life. I asked him to release his daughter from her shame and lay down on his own sword for her. I like to offer the suspect a visualization of the perceived heroic deed of rescuing the child that he victimized. At this point in the interview it was no longer a matter of whether he had done this; now it was a matter of taking responsibility. I told the suspect that if he did not own up to what he had done, then he would be telling the world that his daughter is nothing more than a liar. I advised him that his lack of courage to tell the truth would most likely destroy his daughter, never allowing her the chance to recover emotionally and live a normal life. By this time, the suspect was looking down at the tile floor with tear-filled eyes.

"She's not a liar... She didn't lie," he muttered.

"Is she telling the truth about everything?" I asked.

"Yes," he responded.

I was amazed. Within twenty-five minutes of waiving his rights under the guise of innocence, the suspect admitted to nearly ten years of raping his own daughter. This does not normally happen in these types of interrogations. I give all the credit to God. The Lord used me, a sinner, as His vessel, providing me with the words needed to convict this man's heart to confess his sin at a pivotal moment in the investigation. I truly believe that it was a loving God's intention to relieve this poor child of her colossal lifelong burden. There is no doubt in my mind that God constantly uses police officers and investigators as tools to accomplish His will, and He will do it despite our own prideful intentions and wickedness.

The suspect subsequently signed a written confession. He was then arrested, formally charged at his arraignment and taken to the Monroe County Jail. Unfortunately, he later decided to take his case to trial, forcing his daughter to testify against him. At the time of the trial, this poor girl was a college freshman, attending her first semester of classes. She had to painfully describe in detail the despicable acts that her own father forced upon her to complete strangers in a public forum. Her father's gamble did not pay off. He was found guilty by the jury and sentenced to fifteen years in prison.

Tragically, according to the victim's counselor, the victim's mother still was not entirely in her daughter's corner. This proved to be too much to bear, and the young woman had a meltdown after she testified in court. She eventually failed all of her classes that semester and was expelled from school for poor academic performance. Kristina Karle, the Assistant District Attorney who prosecuted the case, went above and beyond the call of duty, as she usually does with all of her child abuse cases. She wrote a long letter to the university, explaining the unique circumstances that this student had endured during her first semester. The school was gracious and allowed the victim to repeat her classes.

Remember the taped control phone call that we had the victim make to her father? The judge overseeing the trial ruled that we could not use it. Ms. Karle and I did not understand the judge's reasoning for the decision, which was the first and last time we have ever had a taped call thrown out. The District Attorney's Office Appeals Bureau also felt that the judge's ruling was incorrect. I thank God that I did not need to use the tape during the interrogation of the suspect. The defense attorney thought that I had, and he tried to get the confession thrown out under the "Fruit of the Poisonous Tree Rule." If I had used the tape during the interrogation, then the judge would have ruled the confession similarly poisoned, and the confession would have been declared inadmissible. The God who knows the beginning, middle, and end of all things had put His plan in place, helping me obtain the confession without using the tape. Otherwise, I am certain that we would never have convicted this predator at trial.

This case exemplifies how this type of crime can go undetected for years, even decades, if the child never discloses the abuse or if they have no champion to defend them when they are too young to know how to defend themselves. In this case the victim reportedly had disclosed the abuse to her mother on several occasions when she was younger, but her cries for help went unanswered. Children must not be ignored when they indicate that something is not right. Some of the most horrible depictions of man's evil behavior have been expressed only by the small voice of a little child.

Even after the trial, the victim's mother was not as supportive of her daughter as we would have liked. With the family's main source of income now behind bars, the victim's family suffered serious financial losses. This hardship strained the relationship between the victim and her mother. This is part of the collateral damage that goes along with these types of crimes when they occur within the family unit. While one weight is lifted, another is placed back upon the shoulders of the victim. They cannot help but feel responsible for the hardship brought upon their family. Many victims will even regret disclosing the abuse. And when the other parent and family members are not entirely supportive of the victim, the pain is unimaginable. It is vital to a victim's recovery that the parents be the unequivocal champions and defenders of their child, regardless of the personal consequences. But sadly, this type of situation is not uncommon. Some mothers have chosen to turn a blind eye or deaf ear when they suspect that their lover or bread-winner is abusing a child. Some have even told their child that it was the child's responsibility to say no to the abuse to make it stop. In some cases, the mother places too much emphasis on her own emotional and/or financial needs, allowing her fear of an uncertain future to overshadow her understanding of the immediate emotional and physical danger to her child. In other cases, the mother was herself a victim of protracted domestic violence and thus too ill-equipped to take the appropriate action on behalf of her child.

Only God knows what is in store for this young woman. I hope and pray that she is no longer alienated from her mother while her dad serves his well-deserved prison sentence for what he did to her. I simply pray that her mother comes to this point of view before it is too late.

CHAPTER 8

—⁄⁄⁄—

CASE EXAMPLE 5
CHILD PREDATORS AND
DAY-CARE FACILITIES

*O*ne of the teachers at a day-care facility observed a four-year-old female and the father of another female student exit an empty classroom. After the man left the facility a short time later, the teacher pulled the little girl aside and asked her what had happened with her classmate's father. She disclosed that the man performed a "special check" of her vagina. The teacher immediately told her supervisor, and they dialed 911. The young victim was transported to Strong Memorial Hospital, and Investigators Tom Vanthof and Patrick Ponticello from the Eastside substation responded to the hospital to assist with the preliminary investigation. The young victim told the investigators that her classmate's dad took her into the bathroom and told her that it was a "special check day." He then removed her pants and licked her vagina. The investigators notified the Major Crimes Unit, and the case was turned over to Sergeant Doug Comanzo and Investigator Steven Peglow, who responded to Strong.

With the assistance of the day-care staff, the suspect was identified. Investigator Peglow subsequently put together a photo array of six mug shots that included a police photograph of the suspect, since the man had been arrested before, and showed it to the teacher who had observed him with the victim in the classroom earlier that morning. She positively identified the man in the police photograph to be the same man she observed in the classroom that morning.

Interviews of the day-care staff revealed how this clever suspect gained access to someone else's child. The charismatic middle-aged man had claimed that his daughter suffered from separation anxiety, and he requested permission to remain at the facility in the morning to allow her time to transition into her new environment. Unaware of his ulterior motive, the day-care staff became comfortable with the suspect's presence over time. They unwisely allowed him to hang around the children's classrooms instead of limiting him to the lobby and waiting area. Now that he had obtained their trust and access to the other children, he simply waited for the staff to be distracted. While they were greeting other children and parent arrivals, he quickly lured a little girl into the bathroom to sexually assault her.

Investigators Peglow and Ponticello then went to the home of the suspect's daughter. She lived with her mother, since her parents were divorced. Investigator Peglow interviewed the young girl while her mother was in another room. She confirmed that her daddy took her classmate into the bathroom at school to "give her a check." The mother advised the detectives that her ex-husband had already been investigated for abusing their own child. Investigator Peglow had conducted that investigation. He attempted to interview the suspect, but he refused to be interviewed and retained a lawyer. The suspect was never arrested because it was determined that his daughter was unable to understand the concept of being sworn under oath to testify in a court of law. As a result, the case had to be closed because the allegation could not be substantiated.

A background check of the suspect revealed that he had been convicted for aggravated harassment and endangering the welfare of a child approximately two years prior. According to police reports, the suspect called a phone number that he had randomly picked out of the local telephone book. The call was answered by a ten-year-old boy. The suspect, being the sick puppy that he is, ended up talking the young lad into masturbating during the phone call and describing the experience to the suspect. It takes little imagination to guess what the suspect was doing during the call.

The most violent moment of the suspect's known criminal history occurred fifteen years prior to the day-care offense. He broke into a residence and abducted a twenty-year-old female, forcing her into the trunk of his vehicle. The suspect later admitted that he had randomly picked the victim out of the phone book. He drove her to his residence with the intention of raping her, and God only knows what else. Shortly after they arrived at his apartment the suspect's neighbors called the police, for they heard the young woman screaming as the suspect wrestled with her. The victim could not withstand the trauma of facing and testifying against her assailant in court. As a result, the suspect was allowed to plead guilty to a non-felony. Tragically, this man never served the appropriate prison sentence for this violent, pre-meditated act, remaining free to offend again.

The day after speaking with the suspect's ex-wife and daughter, Investigator Peglow interviewed the victim at the Bivona Child Advocacy Center. The center offers interview rooms specifically designed for young victims, providing a less intimidating, child-friendly atmosphere. The little girl related the same story to Investigator Peglow, who has a knack for interviewing young children. The victim further told him that the suspect "wiggled his own pee-pee" as he touched her. When Investigator Peglow asked the victim what she meant by "wiggle," she dropped her little hand to her waist and simulated male masturbation. The child went on to say that "white stuff" came out of the suspect's penis and fell on to the bathroom floor. The suspect had explained it as "special cleaning fluid." The time frame that the suspect had to work with was literally no more than five minutes, if that. For the suspect to have achieved ejaculation in just a few minutes, he must have had himself sexually stimulated in anticipation of the attack before he even walked in the facility. His own daughter was aware of his filthy act, but this was not enough to deter him from behaving like a predatory animal.

Deputy Russ Reynolds, a crime scene technician, was dispatched to the day-care facility to process the bathroom. Utilizing an alternative light source designed to highlight body fluids and other trace evidence, Deputy Reynolds and Investigator Peglow observed several spots of suspected seminal fluid on the bathroom floor. What made this particular discovery more remarkable than usual was that the bathroom floor had already been cleaned with bleach. Deputy Reynolds swabbed the spots and sent the samples to the Monroe County Public Safety lab for analysis. A few days later, the lab advised us that the swabs did indeed contain semen.

At that point a decision was made to pick up the suspect for an interview. Additionally, Investigator Peglow drew up a search warrant for the suspect's vehicle and also the studio apartment that he rented in the northeastern part of the county. Most predators will have child porn in their possession, and it can dramatically impact the case and add years of incarceration to their sentence. Sergeant Comanzo assigned me to assist Investigator Peglow with the interview. Since the suspect had already refused to be interviewed for the alleged incident with his own daughter, we decided to video record and wear a body wire to audio record a non-custodial interview with him outside of his place of employment. We figured that the suspect would not talk to us very long, if at all, so we decided to capture whatever dialogue we could. Based upon his past police contact, we were anticipating that the suspect would not admit to the crime. However, if we could catch him in a lie, it would be nearly as good as a confession. Having his lies on video would serve as undeniable proof. No matter how proficiently a police investigator can testify to a defendant's untruthful statements, a video of him lying is much more damning in court.

Because the suspect would not be in our custody, we did not have to advise him of his rights. As long as he is willing to speak with us voluntarily, we can ask him anything that we want. But he has the right to stop the interview and walk away whenever he wishes, and we must assure him of that at least once during our interview to demonstrate to the court that the suspect knew that he was not in custody. This strategy defeats a defense lawyer's argument that the suspect thought he was under arrest. In that scenario, a judge would have to rule any incriminating statements made during the interview inadmissible in court because in New York State, police can not talk to a suspect without a lawyer if the police have already filed for an arrest warrant. Also, if the police possess an arrest warrant for a suspect, the suspect cannot voluntarily waive his right to a lawyer without his lawyer actually being present. Needless to say, police investigators in New York State have been forced to operate with at least one hand tied behind our backs, so we have to be creative at times. This can put the detective's safety at risk, since he is exposing himself to potentially dangerous suspects in their own element with no immediate physical control. At times, such risks are required in order to keep an investigation active and fruitful. In this particular case, we felt that the calculated risk was in our favor, for this suspect did not have a history of violence toward police. But there is always a first time for everyone, especially when they are desperate, and this suspect was certain to know that the crimes that we were interviewing him about would demand serious jail time. Video recording suspect interviews is not a technique that police departments normally utilize in our jurisdiction, so we were stepping outside the norm. I had video recorded a murder suspect's confession sixteen years before this, but that was done at the direction of the District Attorney's office because it was a cold case that lacked physical evidence. I believe that was the only video-recorded confession taken in this county. I knew that we were going to upset the *status quo*, but I didn't care. Our young victims needed us to corroborate their testimony in the best way possible.

I was quite comfortable with the recording equipment, since I had some experience with wearing a body wire when I was a young undercover officer investigating illegal narcotics and gun trafficking. Investigator Peglow demonstrated that he was a fast learner as we prepared for the interview. Investigator Patrick Ponticello would operate the mobile surveillance platform to videotape and audio record our interview.

The suspect was managing an Italian restaurant that was located in a large mall in the Greater Rochester area. It was about 5:30 PM when Investigator Peglow and I approached the suspect at the front counter of the restaurant. The restaurant was located in the large eatery area of the mall, and it was bustling with mall patrons ordering food and eating at café tables. The suspect directed us to meet him around the back of the restaurant. Investigator Peglow politely asked the suspect to step outside so that we could talk with him for a few minutes, and he agreed. We casually escorted the suspect to a spot on the sidewalk in front of the eatery and carousel area to ensure that Investigator Ponticello had a clear shot of us with the video camera from the surveillance platform.

The suspect leaned up against the glass of the large windows of the dining area as Investigator Peglow explained our purpose for being there. He did a nice job of laying out the circumstances of the investigation, and I made sure that the suspect understood that he could stop the interview and leave anytime he wanted to. I was pleasantly surprised that the suspect didn't request his lawyer, given his history with Peglow nearly a year ago. The suspect denied any knowledge of the incident. We even offered the scenario that he simply helped her use the toilet, but he denied any contact with her. He made the serious mistake of denying that he went into the bathroom with the little girl or even by himself. This was huge, because if the semen recovered on the bathroom floor turned out to match his DNA, we had him telling a substantial lie on video. Even if we gained nothing else from the interview, we had already made our case. We eventually ended the interview and the suspect returned to work.

Investigator Peglow and I met up with Investigator Ponticello, who we affectionately refer to as "Ponch," at a local barbecue joint near the mall. Our dinner was delicious and the conversation upbeat as we discussed our next move. Both Peglow and Ponch ooze motivation and enthusiasm when it comes to working an investigation, and possess a real willingness to learn. Working with these young lions made the job fun again for me, especially with this suspect in our crosshairs. There is no better prey to hunt than a child predator, and my two comrades were like a pair of pit bull terriers wanting to bite something.

We were satisfied that we had made our case, and confident that the suspect's DNA would match the semen that had been collected from the daycare facility's bathroom floor. We decided that we would return to the mall, arrest the suspect, and continue to videotape our interaction with him. We planned to execute the search warrant on his vehicle in the mall parking lot and then transport the suspect back to his apartment to execute the search warrant for his residence. I put crime scene technicians Dan Luffman and Scott Shear on notice. Investigator Peglow drove back to our office to finish the arrest complaint, while Ponch and I opted to keep the suspect's vehicle under surveillance until he left work later that night. The plan was to arrest the suspect at his vehicle. But of course, hardly anything ever goes as planned.

Just as Ponch and I were setting up our surveillance on the suspect's vehicle, he got into it, drove out of the mall parking lot, and headed eastbound. Ponch and I kept a loose tail on him and eventually lost him in traffic. We drove to the suspect's apartment, located in a rundown motel, and observed him driving out of the parking lot. By this time it was dark, so we stayed close to him and followed his vehicle to a nearby gas station. Ponch and I thought that our target might be gassing up to leave town. He was supposed to be working until 10:00 PM, and it wasn't even 8:00. We figured that the suspect knew that the jig was up and was going to make a break for it. I instructed Ponch to turn the video recorder back on and contact Investigator Peglow to advise him of the situation. Wearing the body wire, I stepped out of the surveillance vehicle and walked toward the suspect as he was exiting the gas station's store. I asked him where he was going. The suspect said that he was on his break and heading back to the restaurant. This was hard to believe, since the mall and the suspect's apartment were on opposite sides of a heavily populated county.

I directed the suspect to the back of his vehicle and I arrested him. After placing him in handcuffs, I advised the suspect of his rights. Ponch moved the suspect's vehicle away from the gas pumps and I walked him back to his car. I then began questioning the suspect, explaining that I thought he had been less than honest with us earlier in the evening at the mall. Eventually, the crime scene technicians arrived and executed the search warrant on the suspect's vehicle as I continued to interview him. Ponch returned to the surveillance vehicle and kept the video recording going. The suspect was still unaware that we were being taped. Now that he was in custody and he had waived his rights, I spoke to the suspect in a more accusatory tone. I told the suspect that I didn't believe him and I advised him to start taking responsibility for what he did to the little girl at the day-care facility. I also revealed that his own daughter witnessed him going into the bathroom with her classmate, so his continued denials were making her out to be a liar. He didn't like that, but he still wouldn't budge from his story. The suspect then suggested that his daughter was confused. I replied that I would not have any respect for him as a man or a father if he stuck to his lies, which would force both his own daughter and the young victim to testify against him in a public courtroom. While he continued his denial, this thought seemed to strike a chord inside him. The concept of his own daughter testifying against him appeared to be the Achilles' heel that I was searching for.

Investigator Peglow showed up at the gas station and fell right into step with the ongoing interview. When the crime scene technicians were finished executing the search warrant on his vehicle, we transported the suspect to his apartment to execute that search warrant and continue our interview with him. Prior to entering, I had the technicians set up a video recorder on a tripod in the corner of the room. After waiting a few minutes, Investigator Peglow and I escorted him into his apartment as the crime scene technicians were searching the cramped residence. We had the suspect sit down in a stuffed chair directly across the room from the video recorder. I advised the suspect that the technicians record all search warrants. We never told him that it was recording everything we were all saying and doing. Investigator Peglow continued to methodically interview the suspect, conveying empathy and repeating the choice he had to make: either admit the truth about what occurred with the little girl, or we would subpoena his own daughter to testify against him. The suspect eventually admitted to masturbating in the bathroom while the little girl was with him, but he would not admit that he had touched her. I challenged his confession, stating that he was slick for not admitting to the more serious crime of touching the child in a sexual way. Like sharks in bloody water, Peglow and I were moving in on the suspect, biting away at his half-hearted denials as he sat hunched up in the chair, looking down at the floor.

I pointed out the numerous porn flicks that he had in his room featuring teenage girls. "You've got a problem here," I said, leafing through the DVDs that the technicians had laid out on the bed. I read off many of the disgusting titles aloud for the video recording. I wanted the judge and jury to hear what the suspect had been using to slake his lust. "I bet you don't get a whole lot out of watching this stuff. Do ya? It is a sickness isn't it...it's like an addiction isn't it? I mean, how do you feel after you watch it? Like crap?"

"Well, that's why I go to the group," he responded,

referring to his sex offender group therapy sessions.

I continued, "I mean, you're a slave to that. You don't have just one or two of these. You've got some heavy stuff. You're a slave to that. You're in bondage. You ever hear that term before?"

"Uh-huh," he responded.

"You're in self-made bondage. You're in a bad place, my brother...a bad place."

"You must be a Christian," he responded as he looked up at me.

"Yes I am," I said, "but I am not any more righteous than you in the eyes of God. I've got my problems too. But that stuff there," I pointed to the DVDs, "indicates to me you're in some serious pain...You're forty-five years old, living in a motel room watching porn and masturbating. I'm not saying that to you in a judgmental way...my heart goes out to you."

Investigator Peglow and I talked to the suspect non-stop, continuing with the theme of keeping the little girls off the witness stand to save them from the trauma. After about three hours of prodding, probing, cajoling, challenging and comforting the suspect, he finally gave it up. It ended with this conversation:

"Please let the other little girl off the hook," I pleaded. He had already admitted to going into the bathroom with the little girl and masturbating, but refused to admit to touching her. His half-hearted admission got his daughter off the hook from having to testify, but we would still need the victim to testify that he licked and touched her vaginal area if he didn't corroborate her account of what happened.

If we got the suspect just to admit to touching the little girl while they were in the bathroom, we would have a rock-solid case against him, and we would not have to rely solely on the testimony of a four-year-old girl for the most serious part of the of the crime.

"Reach down in your soul and pull it outta ya," I continued. "Do it for the child. I am gonna ask you again, and all you need to say is yes or no. Is the little girl telling us the truth about what happened in the bathroom?"

"She didn't say anything about...I didn't make her touch me..." He started giving it to us but we had to remain patient and not get overly pushy.

"No," Investigator Peglow responded. "Michael... Look at me for a minute...Did you touch that little girl while you were masturbating?"

"Um...Just prior to," the suspect answered.

Jackpot!

It was obvious that the suspect was still not telling us the entire truth, but he told us enough to corroborate the little girl's account. The suspect never admitted licking her vagina, but there was no reason for a four-year-old girl to lie about such a fact. The suspect knew that touching the child's vaginal area with his mouth or penis is a more serious crime under New York State law, which would equate to much more time in prison. Therefore, he consciously limited himself to admitting only to touching the child's vagina with his hand. But at this point it didn't matter; we charged him with both touching and licking the little girl's vagina. We had plenty of evidence, including his sperm and a video-taped confession, to convict him on every charge. Praise God, our strategy had worked and this mope was going away for a long time.

The suspect's arrest received a substantial amount of media coverage because it occurred in a preschool day care. As a result, another four-year-old girl disclosed that the suspect had molested her in a similar way, on a different day, at the same facility. Investigator Peglow testified at the grand jury hearing. The suspect was indicted on numerous counts of criminal offenses for molesting both girls. He was looking at a total of about sixty years in prison if convicted on all charges. The suspect's defense lawyer requested a suppression hearing on the interview in an attempt to get the suspect's confession thrown out. I testified at the hearing. It was a fruitless battle for the defense attorney, since the suspect was seen and heard on videotape being treated with respect and dignity yet later confessing to a good portion of the allegations. The suspect eventually negotiated a plea bargain and was sentenced to twenty-one years in prison. He waived his right to appeal. Assistant District Attorney Kristina Karle agreed to the deal due to the victims' ages, and Investigator Peglow and I agreed with it as well. These little girls would have had a difficult time testifying in a court room packed with curious citizens and the media.

If the case had gone to trial and the suspect had been convicted, he would have had the right to appeal the conviction. If the suspect wins an appeal then we have to do it all over again, usually many years later. And that is never easy. Child victims and witnesses grow up and forget things, or move away to an unknown place. Police officers become unavailable to testify after retiring, moving away or even dying. Evidence can be accidentally destroyed or lost over time. And lastly, there is never a guarantee that the presiding judge is going to give the convicted criminal a stiff sentence. We never know what to expect from our appellate courts in New York State, especially the highest court, the New York State Court of Appeal. Therefore, it is a huge success whenever we can get a child predator to walk into court, admit to the crime, and be incarcerated for over twenty years without having to require the little victims to be re-traumatized in a public courtroom.

Let us do a quick recap of this case. This child predator misused his God-ordained position of father, using his own four-year-old daughter as the "common denominator" to gain access to other children. He charmed the day-care staff with his charisma, and bided his time to gain their trust. They became comfortable with his presence in areas of the facility that he should not have been in without proper supervision. Child predators are masters of manipulation, and they can quickly seize a moment of an exposed vulnerability. Inside what was supposed to be a safe refuge for our little ones, a venomous serpent was quietly slithering around in search of its next victim. The day-care staff let their guard down, never thinking that a parent of one of their students could be so evil, and two young children paid the price.

This case screams that we can never be over-protective when it comes to the safety of our babies or those that we have the responsibility to protect. If you send your children to a day-care facility, don't be afraid to ask hard questions about their security protocol. Make sure that they do not allow male parents inside the facility without proper supervision, no matter who they are or how long they have been affiliated with the day care. Frankly, I would be suspicious of any male staff as well. It is my sincere opinion that men have no place supervising little children in such facilities. Do not allow yourself to rest in the assurance that a clear background check is required before staff is hired. Similarly, the absence of the name on a sex offender registry is not a sufficient safeguard of your child's safety. It helps, but it is no guarantee; besides, these checks are not done on the parents, delivery people, repairmen, or anyone else that may have a *bona fide* reason to enter the facility. A strong security protocol with staff dedication to constant vigilance is paramount. Parents can also contact the state agency that issues operating licenses and regulates these facilities. The agency is responsible for ensuring that they stay in compliance with the state's policies and procedures. They would serve as a great resource to determine if the facility that you are considering is safe and consistently operating within the state's guidelines.

Parents should monitor a facility as much as possible before choosing it. Now that you know more about how a predator thinks, ask yourself: could I easily pierce these defenses if I wanted to? And do not forget these rules wherever you are: do not assume that someone is "safe" because they are a father, and do not assume that your child is safe even for a moment without careful supervision. As we saw in this case, a false sense of security is all that it takes for a predator to see his opportunity and pounce.

CHAPTER 9

—〰—

CASE EXAMPLE 6
"MY BEST FRIEND'S DAD."

"*Wash me clean from my guilt. Purify me from my sin. For I recognize my rebellion; it haunts me day and night. Against You, and You alone, have I sinned.*"

PSALM 51:2-4A (KJV)

Investigator Sergeant Gary Caiola summoned me into his office and instructed me to close the door. A Monroe County Child Protective Service supervisor had called to notify him that an adolescent girl had just disclosed to her mother that her best friend's father had molested her for three years. Sergeant Caiola advised me that the suspect was a successful OB/GYN doctor. The suspect was well known by the doctors and staff of the REACH Program at Strong Memorial Hospital, which is dedicated to diagnosing and treating children who have been either sexually or physically abused. Furthermore, the victim's mother worked as a nurse practitioner in the REACH Hospital. This case was bound to cause shock waves and collateral damage in the community.

As instructed, I made contact with the victim's mother and set up an appointment to meet her at a bagel shop near to the hospital. We sat at a table outside, since the late spring weather was cooperating and we would be afforded more privacy. She said that the suspect was unaware of her daughter's disclosure, and her colleagues at the REACH Clinic were keeping it under wraps. The middle-aged single mother shared that her fourteen-year-old daughter had separated herself from her best friend over the past several weeks. The girls had previously been inseparable, practically living together since they had been in elementary school. When the mother suggested that the victim have her friend over to celebrate her daughter's birthday, she refused. The victim's mother asked her what was going on between them. Her daughter then disclosed that her best friend's dad had been molesting her since she was ten years old. I also learned that the suspect was the victim's mother's personal OB/GYN doctor. Needless to say, at first glance this woman had absolutely no reason not to trust this man and his integrity.

The following evening I met with the victim and her mother at the Eastside substation to take her statement. She reminded me of my daughters when they were her age. Her slight build and young face were slowly developing into womanhood. I could tell by her facial expressions and body language that she was reluctant to talk to me, so I spent a little extra time developing a rapport with her. After talking about school, her friends and what she was planning for her upcoming birthday, she appeared to relax. Before I started the questioning, I explained that I just needed her to be truthful, and I assured her that I wasn't going to do anything in this investigation that she did not approve of. This seemed to gain her confidence and trust. I believe that it is important to tell victims, especially children, that they have some control of what is going to happen in an investigation. When a person becomes the victim of a physical crime, their life is taken over for a period of time by the person who offends them. Empowering the victim by making them part of the solution helps them transform from victim to survivor.

The victim confirmed what her mother had shared with me the day before: her best friend's father had been touching her in sexual way over the past three years when she slept over at their house on weekends and during the summers. His routine was to give them both back rubs at bedtime as they lay in their beds. Eventually, he would reach around to her front and rub her breasts. The victim admitted that it felt good to her, but it also confused her. The victim knew that what he was doing to her was wrong, but she was afraid to tell anyone because she didn't want to cause any trouble with the suspect's family. She had become an integral part of that family, and she loved them all very much.

The suspect constantly spoke with the victim over the computer. He insisted that she call him by his first name. The suspect became very openly affectionate toward the victim as her sleepovers increased in frequency, many as the result of his personal invite. At times they were alone and he would grope her with his entire body, humping her, and touching her more intimately. On at least three separate occasions, the suspect reached into the victim's underwear and rubbed and fingered her vagina after promising her how good it would make her feel. Obviously, he was grooming her for sexual intercourse.

The victim eventually told a younger female cousin what the suspect had been doing. In response, the cousin instant messaged the suspect on the computer and told him to stop touching the victim. But incredibly, the suspect did not stop. This man was on a mission to have full-blown sexual intercourse with this young girl, no matter what the consequences; and he was arrogant enough to think that he was going to get away with it even after someone warned him to stop. He ended up ruining two families, a successful medical practice, and his reputation because of it.

The victim and her best friend started growing apart when they reached the seventh grade, and they eventually stopped spending time together regularly. This absence gave the victim space to realize that the suspect should never have done this to her. A year later, the emotional burden had become too heavy, and when the opportunity presented itself during their conversation about her lack of contact with her best friend, she finally confided in her mother.

I called the suspect at his medical practice and left him a message to call me back at my office. When a police investigator shows up at someone's residence or workplace it draws more attention than I care for, especially when my goal is to get the person alone to speak with them. Family and co-workers ask too many questions and can cause the suspect to feel embarrassed. A humble, soft approach is usually successful in drawing them out for a meeting. Under the guise of discretion, I explained that I wanted to avoid bringing attention to something that could prove to be very embarrassing for the accused. I don't do this with all my suspects, just the ones who hold a prestigious position in our community and have a lot to lose. Generally, they will keep a lid on things and attempt to talk their way out of everything.

As I had hoped, the esteemed doctor returned my call a short time later that afternoon. In a very friendly, non-judgmental voice, I advised him that a young female had alleged that he had touched her inappropriately. I kept it vague over the phone and I asked him to meet me in person so that I could explain further. I could sense both his apprehension and his desire to find out exactly what I knew. At first, the doctor offered two lame excuses for not meeting with me. He said that he was waiting for his wife to return home from a week-long church retreat, and he was on his way to his son's lacrosse game. Put yourself in his position for a moment. Can you imagine having a police detective calling you and accusing you of sexually molesting a child? If you were innocent, you would be out of your mind to know the details, and who was telling such a heinous lie. On the other hand, if you knew that you were guilty, you would need time to think things through, offering excuses that pale in comparison to the detective's reason for wanting to talk to you. One doesn't have to be an experienced police investigator to see through this feeble attempt to buy more time to concoct a false story. Even educated and professional people are not above making this mistake. I have learned over the years that people don't need any extra time to remember the truth. It is imprinted in their memory. However, they do need the additional time to fabricate lies and then keep them straight.

My concern was that if too much time elapsed he would have time to consult with a lawyer, who would obviously instruct him not to speak with me. Since there were no witnesses or physical evidence, it was important that I engage him in a conversation. So I advised the doctor that the allegations against him were very serious, and I suggested that he reconsider attending the high-school lacrosse game in order to meet with me as soon as possible. He said that he understood and agreed to the meeting.

We decided to meet near the doctor's residence at a Starbucks in Brighton near the border of Pittsford, two of the more affluent towns on the east side of Monroe County. Approximately twenty minutes later we were greeting each other and shaking hands after I observed him step out of a white mini-van. The vehicle fit the persona that the victim's mother described—a family man who loved being around his children and their friends. He was a man of medium height with a slightly thin build, and he was casually dressed in a button-down shirt and khaki pants. His close-cropped gray hair and glasses supported his professional position. This guy looked about as straight as anyone could look. I reassured the doctor that he was not under arrest or in my custody, and that I just wanted to meet with him to give him the details of the allegation and ask some questions.

At his request, we walked alongside a short red brick wall adjacent to the coffee shop and sat down in front of the small boutique-style jewelry store that was next to Starbucks. The late-afternoon sun was shining brightly on our faces, making the mid-sixties temperature feel much warmer. We must have looked like two old friends having a private conversation to the constant stream of customers that walked past us to and from the coffee shop. It was the perfect setting for this interview. As far as he was concerned, we were on his turf. He appeared relaxed and confident that he could explain this whole misunderstanding and make me go away. And that is right where I wanted him to be, for people will speak more freely when they feel relaxed. Everyone has a story to tell; I just allow them to tell it and then work from there. When people are willing to talk openly, even when they are lying, it provides me the opportunity to get into their head to discover how I can convince them to tell the truth.

I advised the doctor that I was conducting an investigation into the allegations of inappropriate touching that were made against him by a fourteen-year-old female. At first, I identified the female as a friend of his daughter's, but later identified her by name. The doctor referred to the girl by her nickname, saying that he knew the young girl very well and looked upon her as one of his own children. I explained that the victim had stated that he fondled her breasts on numerous occasions while she slept over with his daughter at his house over a two- to three-year period, and that on at least one occasion he had touched her vaginal area. The doctor quickly denied that he ever touched the victim in a sexual manner. He offered that the touching was inadvertent and occurred during physical horseplay with the victim and his daughter. I replied that the victim didn't describe it that way; she said that he would fondle her breasts when he gave her back rubs at bedtime. He acknowledged that he gave both girls back rubs at bedtime since they were very young. Again attempting to rationalize the young girl's complaint, the doctor offered that these back rubs also included the rubbing of their stomachs and chests before they developed breasts.

"Wow, thanks for putting yourself in the ballpark so quickly, doc," I thought. He was trying to be slick by offering such a bizarre explanation to deflect the victim's allegations. However, the strategy backfired. He unintentionally provided me something to work with in the interview because he voluntarily placed his hands on the victim's chest. This intelligent man probably figured that he could bamboozle the friendly but simple-minded investigator. I viewed this attempt as a sign that he had something to hide. Now it was just a matter of finding out exactly what it was.

I politely countered that the victim alleged that the inappropriate touching started when she was ten years old and continued until she was thirteen, even after she had developed breasts. I then provided the doctor with the victim's description of how the touching would occur: he would move both his hands under her shirt and reach around to her front and then fondle her breasts for a little while. He would then ask her if it felt good and if she enjoyed it. I told the doctor that the victim said that it did feel good when he touched her breasts, but it left her confused.

He denied touching the victim, claiming that she misinterpreted what was going on. Consider how incredible his response was. Imagine: a parent finds out that a friend's father has been regularly giving their daughter back, tummy and chest rubs on her bare skin. I'm very confident that any parent in their right mind, including the good doctor, would take issue with that behavior. For the next ninety minutes the doctor continually denied touching the victim's breasts in a sexual manner. The doctor's attempts to explain away the touching as non-sexual backfired on him. He did not realize that he had already admitted to the crime. The law states that the touching of the sexual or other intimate parts of the body is considered to be sexual contact if it is done for the purpose of sexual gratification of either person. The victim had already told me that she became sexually aroused as a result of him touching her, and that he would make it a point to ask her how it made her feel.

Since the doctor was voluntarily talking to me and not requesting an attorney, I continued to pursue the truth. He had not admitted to touching the victim's vaginal area yet, nor had he taken responsibility for his actions, so we had a long way to go. Each incriminating truthful statement that I can extract from a suspect strengthens our criminal case and lessens the child's burden, especially in the arena of public opinion. A portion of that burden was removed by the doctor's inadvertent admission to the reported crime.

The doctor stated he was sincerely concerned for the victim and how she was dealing with the situation. He said that he was not angry with her for making such allegations against him, for he would never hurt her in any way, and he felt bad that he had caused her such pain. Gee, what a humble and caring man—I wanted to puke right there. Does this sound like an innocent man to you? If you were being falsely accused of touching a young girl on numerous occasions spanning several years, wouldn't you be a little upset with her for concocting such a story about you, knowing full well that it would be the end of your professional and family life as you know it? When a suspect feigns such concern for the victim and suggests that they were confused, he has something to hide.

The doctor asked what was going to happen from this point on. I told him that I had to speak to the victim and her parents because they wanted to know what his explanation was and if he accepted responsibility for his actions. The victim was seeing a therapist to sort out her feelings and determine if she would be supportive of taking criminal action against him. I told him that she was undecided at the present moment. Since she was a minor the decision of prosecution wasn't really hers to make, but ultimately, we would need her cooperation in a criminal prosecution. Continuing to be completely honest with him, I advised the doctor that I was going to meet with the District Attorney's Office and a criminal complaint would most likely be filed against him sometime next week. He knew the severity of the situation, so there was no sense in trying to downplay his actions. Sometimes that would be an appropriate strategy, but I had too much respect for the man's social and intellectual ability. He would be able to see through that and we would lose whatever rapport we had developed up until that point.

The doctor then asked me what my role was in all of this. I told him that I was working on behalf of the victim to determine if her allegations were true. I told him that I currently was in the investigative stage and needed to meet with him to hear his side of the situation. Then I would assess whether he is a man who made a very bad mistake in an isolated incident with one girl or a man that this community needs to consider a threat to other young girls. I reinforced that his voluntary cooperation would assist me in making that determination. The doctor said that he understood. I continued my monologue: I believed that the victim was telling the truth. He needed to consider what his continued denials would represent to her. If her allegations were true then he needed to take responsibility for his actions. I warned that if he didn't admit to the truth then he would be calling the victim a liar, which would only add to this child's pain.

The doctor had already stated several times during our conversation that he wanted to do what was right for the victim and help her. I had agreed with him each time and re-inforced the fact that she would never heal emotionally until he took responsibility. I let him know that the victim was upset, but she cared for him and his family very much. She was devastated by the thought of what this public disclosure would do to his medical practice and his whole family. I re-minded him that it wasn't right for a young girl to bear such a burden, and he should consider releasing her from it. Appearing downcast, he answered, "I know that."

I suggested that he have the courage to do what was right for the victim and own up to the truth. I told him that his explanations were weak at best and would only cause her more harm in the end. He nodded and said, "I know that."

I looked at the doctor and asked, "Is she telling the truth about how you touched her breasts?"

There was a long pause as the doctor looked off into the distance. He then lowered his eyes toward the sidewalk and said, "Yes."

I then asked him if the touching occurred on multiple oc-casions over the two- or three-year period as the victim had said that it did. Again, he replied, "Yes." However, he qualified his an-swer by saying that he really didn't remember how many times it had happened and he didn't realize that the timespan was so long.

As many predators do, the doctor maintained that the sexual contact was not done for the purpose of his sexual gratification, but it was the result of his affection for the victim. I told him that I believed his explanation to a point, but I felt that he was not being honest with himself. I told the doctor that his affection for the victim turned into lust when he stepped over the line and started touching her breasts. It is typical of a suspect to rationalize his despicable actions against a child. It is their way of saying, "I'm really not the scumbag everyone is going to think I am when they hear about this."

I told the doctor that his way of justifying his bad behavior didn't make sense. A man of his profession should and does know better. To make my point, I went back in time and asked him about receiving an instant message from the victim's cousin to stop touching her. He acknowledged that he had received the message and confronted the victim about it. I countered that if the touching was out of sincere affection rather than lustful desires, why did he confront the victim in secrecy about the message instead of in front of a witness, such as his wife or daughter or both? I told the doctor that if he was really touching the victim in a non-sexual manner, then he would have wanted to vindicate himself. I concluded that his dealing with the message secretly demonstrated dishonorable intentions. I challenged that his actions spoke louder than his empty words. He nodded and said, "I see your point."

I answered that I believed that he had a sincere affection for the victim, but somewhere along the way it turned to lust. I asserted that I believed the victim completely, including the part about him touching her vagina. I told him that the victim felt partly responsible for what happened because she gave him permission to touch her there. I asked him to consider the victim's emotional welfare and accept the entire blame for this incident if it was in fact true.

The doctor said that he understood what I was saying and he fell silent for a moment. He then asked me if he could talk to me "off the record." I explained that everything we discussed would be documented in my police report. The doctor said that he understood and then remained silent for an additional minute. I asked the doctor what he would think if he were in my position. He responded that he would be thinking exactly the way I was thinking about him. He then asked me what I would do if I were in his position. I replied that I would take full responsibility for my actions and put myself in God's hands. I then asked if he had considered asking God to help him stop touching the victim. His answer surprised me: he had asked Christ to take the desire away from him but He never did. I then offered that God must know that he was incapable of stopping on his own, and God might be answering his prayers now by bringing this to the surface.

I informed the doctor that I was a follower of Jesus Christ. I suggested that the Lord was behind our meeting together to release him from this terrible secret. I pleaded that the Lord wanted to save him from destruction, and his eternity was hanging in the balance. The doctor said he agreed with that assessment. I advised that the victim needed him to validate her account of what occurred between them if it was true. If he really cared about her emotional well-being, he needed to do what was right and face the consequences for his actions. He responded, "You're right."

I could tell that God had His hand in this interview because our discussion then turned to some Biblical passages that deal with lust. We talked about the sins of adultery and murder committed by King David and the lasting effect that it had on his family even though God forgave him. We also talked about the ultimate price that Samson had to pay for his lust. As I like to do in so many of my interviews, I mentioned the passage in the Gospels where Jesus warned that it would be better for a man to be thrown into the sea with a millstone hung around his neck than to face God's wrath for leading children away from Him. I urged him again to release this child from her burden and admit to the truth about all of his actions, and to confess that it was the result of his own lustful heart and selfishness. The suspect responded, "You're right," and then exhaled deeply.

After two solid hours of talking in the afternoon spring sunshine like two old friends, I asked the doctor if the victim was telling the truth about him touching her vaginal area. The experienced interviewer knows when it is time to ask the pivotal question. We feel it. The interviewing of a subject, whether he is a reluctant witness or suspect, is an evolutionary process. We must patiently guide the subject off the treacherous path of prideful denial and onto the path of righteousness that ultimately leads him to the edge of truth. The process includes a certain amount of give and take, cajoling the subject, challenging the subject, stroking the subject's ego, probing his mind, and eventually "closing" him. I knew that the doctor had followed me to the edge of truth.

However, the edge was that of a very high cliff that he was afraid to cross over. It was my job to convince him that the edge of truth was merely a line that he needed to step over to set both himself and the victim free from the emotional and spiritual bondage that he had placed them under. I felt confident that I had convinced him to have the courage to tell the truth. Praise the Lord for His guidance, my timing had been right. The doctor hesitated for a brief moment and then replied, "Yes, but it happened only once." It is at moments like this when I know I work for God. And I know many of my colleagues feel the same way when they lawfully convince someone to step over the "edge" and tell the truth.

I thanked the doctor for his honesty. I told him that I admired his courage to set the record straight and free the victim both from her burden and from the social stigma of being labeled a liar and troublemaker. I knew that he and his family would be facing difficult times ahead. I offered my support and told him that we are all sinners in the eyes of God and none of us are more righteous than the next. Sadly, his wife was due to arrive home that evening from an out-of-state church retreat. I sincerely felt bad for her and their children. Through no fault of their own, their lives were about to change drastically.

We talked for an additional twenty minutes. I shared with him that the Lord breaks His people down when they are in rebellion against Him, but after they repent, He eventually builds them back up to serve Him in an entirely different way. I encouraged the doctor not to lose hope.

After I arrested the suspect, I had to testify in a suppression hearing. His lawyers attempted to get his confession thrown out, but the judge didn't agree with their argument and ruled the confession legal. Several months later, shortly before the trial began, the doctor pled guilty to a felony charge. As a result, he lost his license to practice medicine and was placed on probation for ten years. His attorneys were able to convince the judge not to give him any jail time. As you can imagine, the plea bargain created a lot of controversy and public outcry. However, the man who once proudly wore the title of "Medical Doctor" was stripped of that and he had to exchange it for the label, "Registered Sex Offender." Personally, I was not thrilled with a disposition that required not even weekends in the county jail. But I have learned to not get caught up in the prosecutorial part of any case. Rather than driving myself mad with things that are out of my control, I hand them over to the Lord. I have confidence that He will deal with the situation in His own time. Some of you may think that is a bit weird or even a cop-out. But that is the way I deal with it to maintain my focus on the job that I am meant to do — seek the truth.

In review, this predator used his own child as a "common denominator" to gain and maintain access to his victim. This situation was a tough one to fathom. In the mother's defense, she had sufficient reason to trust this man. He was a pillar of the community who loved children, and a good family man. He was her doctor. Even her coworkers admired him. These insidious criminals can be difficult to identify. However, if this mother had been aware of how a child predator courts and grooms a potential child victim, she might have seen some of his actions in a different light. For instance, she would have known that his communicating with her daughter over the Internet was a red flag and warranted her asking questions. He used the Internet as a tool to maintain his contact with the victim until her next visit. It enabled this predator to talk privately about inappropriate subjects with the victim, piquing her curiosity and enticing her to have sex with him. And personally, I would avoid allowing your child to sleep over any of their friends' houses too frequently. In this case, the predator used the constant contact to become close to her, and then to isolate and seduce her.

When the suspect became a physician, he agreed to honor the Hippocratic Oath. He ignored that promise when his actions injured the emotional and mental welfare of a young girl whom he selfishly used to fulfill his own sexual desires. He misused his professional position as the mother's personal doctor to manipulate her trust, and he subsequently violated his God-ordained charge to care for another parent's child. Shame on this man for putting such pressure on a young girl, who looked upon him as a second father, seeking only acceptance and love from those she had become close to and admired. A secondary consequence of this crime is that it undermines any foundation of trust that the victim has established up to that point in their life.

God's Word tells us, "To whom much is given, much is required." The suspect was blessed with a higher education, a successful medical practice and professional prestige that most men could only wish for, and a beautiful family who loved him. But he threw it all away, not in one foolish act of indiscretion, but in three years of scheming, plotting, lying and molesting his daughter's best friend. In the end God held him accountable, and He took away his privileged lifestyle, forcing him to wear the scathing label of "child molester." His wife and children have been forced to endure the punishment with him. Because of his selfish actions they have become the secondary— and often forgotten—victims. This type of crime is not restricted by social and economic boundaries, plaguing even the most educated and wealthy people in our community. No matter what the outward appearance of a man, we can never tell what evil lurks below the surface in his soul. God's Word sums this up in 1 Samuel 16:7: "The Lord does not see as man sees; for man looks at the outward appearance, but the Lord looks at the heart." NKJV.

After an offense has occurred, the parents of the victim often cry wistfully, "If I had only known..." or "If I had been made aware of this before..." This case shows that we can never be too careful when it comes to the welfare and safety of our children. We should never trust any adult who becomes too close with our children socially, no matter who they are or what position they hold in our community.

CHAPTER 10

—〰—

CASE EXAMPLE 7
"A FULL MONTY...OR...THE STANDARD TWENTY AND A TORTURE"

I never get used to working these types of crimes, but I have become somewhat desensitized over time. The weight of the tragedy does not diminish, but specific facts of a case lose their shock value when you hear similar details over and over. This case challenged even my calloused perspective.

A single mother of two prepubescent boys had become friends with the gentle giant of a man who lived in the apartment building next to hers. At 6'3" and 350 pounds, he was an imposing figure that filled any doorway, but possessed a gentle spirit and spoke with a soft tone of voice. The friendly, trusted neighbor was home during the daytime hours because he worked the night shift as a security guard at the world headquarters of an international corporation located in downtown Rochester. This made it convenient for the mother to rely on him in a pinch to look in on her eight- and ten-year-old boys while she was out making a living to support them. She had to make do with what she had and take advantage of every helping hand available to help supervise her sons.

The big man and the boys became buddies. He became their surrogate father, someone to look up to. As time went on, both boys were spending more time with the suspect at his apartment, playing his challenging computer games. But there was one stipulation to those visits: they could only visit the suspect one at a time, never together. After the suspect moved out of the apartment complex, the mother allowed her sons to visit the suspect separately and even stay overnight at his new residence, located in a rural town several miles away. What the boys' mother didn't know was that this trusted friend had been doing unspeakable things to them for three years.

It was a casual conversation with her younger son about spanking that revealed to the mother what this so-called friend was really about. In that context, the victim disclosed that the suspect allowed him to play video games on his computer during the first two visits to the suspect's apartment; however, on the third visit the suspect told the victim that he had to do a "Full Monty" before he was allowed to play video games. Since the boy did not know what the term meant, the suspect explained that it involved being tortured. The young boy's desire to play the video games outweighed his concern about the physical pain, so he consented to the man that he had come to trust and admire. I viewed this young lad's decision as a sad testament to just how much social acceptance and adult attention he was lacking.

The suspect helped the boy remove his clothes and then proceeded to whip him on his bare buttocks with a leather-braided belt. If that wasn't enough, the suspect then forced his finger up the child's small rectum and squeezed his testicles. After screaming and withering in pain for several excruciating minutes, the victim was allowed to play video games as his reward. This was just the first of countless torture sessions to which the victim subjected himself. The sessions expanded to include squeezing the boy's nipples, big toes and thumbs until he was crying and begging him to stop. After enduring torture, the victim was rewarded for his submission and silence.

After the victim's mother received this startling revelation from her younger son, she questioned her thirteen-year-old boy. He had withstood similar abuse for various gifts and rewards that included playing on the suspect's computer. The older boy was whipped more frequently than his younger brother. He was subjected to at least twenty lashes during each session, and his nipples would bleed from being squeezed so hard after being whipped.

The distraught mother called the police and the case was referred to the Major Crimes Unit. I was assigned to oversee the investigation, and I requested Investigator Thomas Passmore to assist me. We interviewed each of the boys and their mother. We learned that the suspect had been threatening to shoot both boys if they told their mother. The boys viewed these threats as very real, for they were familiar with the suspect's collection of long rifles and shotguns.

After Investigator Passmore and I finished taking the boys' sworn statements, I asked the older one to make a recorded control phone call to the suspect to engage him in a conversation that would corroborate their allegations. Capturing the suspect talking about one of these torture sessions or setting up a future session would seal this man's fate in a courtroom. The boy asserted that the suspect would never talk about his transgressions over the phone, but I convinced him to give it a try. I appealed to the gregarious boy's imagination by telling him to pretend that he was working as an undercover cop. After setting up the recording device in my office and reviewing what we needed him to say, the victim made the call. When the victim asked him what he'd have to be subjected to in order to come over that weekend to play video games, the suspect was guarded. He told the victim that he just woke up and was getting ready for work, and instructed him to call back in the morning.

On the following morning Investigator Passmore and I met with the victim at the Bivona Child Advocacy Center to place a second recorded control phone call. It was obvious that the suspect did not want to talk about their secret on the telephone. Thanks to the boy's diligent effort, the suspect did at least acknowledge the question of what the lad would have to do by answering, "We'll discuss it when you come over." While this fell short of an admission, it was far from a denial. I viewed the conversation as progress and decided to give it another shot in a few days.

We met with the victim at the Bivona Center a few days later to place a third call. The victim did an awesome job pleading with the suspect to tell him what he'd have to be subjected to before he would be allowed to play video games. He explained that he needed to mentally prepare for what was in store for him. In response we could hear the suspect answer, "the standard twenty and a torture." That incriminating statement translated to twenty lashes on the victim's bare buttocks with a leather belt and a session of twisting and squeezing his testicles, nipples, big toes and thumbs. Our persistence had now paid off. This corroborating evidence was, as they say in those credit card commercials, "priceless."

Early the next morning, Investigator Passmore and I picked up the suspect as he was concluding his shift as a night security guard. We met with him in the cavernous lobby of the corporate world headquarters building downtown. It was still empty; hundreds of employees were probably just beginning their morning commutes. After introducing ourselves as Monroe County Sheriff's Investigators, I asked the suspect to accompany us to our office so that we could ask him some questions. Without asking us what it was all about, he agreed and followed us to our unmarked police vehicle which was parked directly outside the lobby doors. The Kodiak-bear-sized man quietly took a seat in the back. He was not handcuffed. We took a calculated risk with our safety in the hopes of keeping the subject cooperative and willing to talk.

After escorting the suspect up to our office, I advised him of his Miranda Warnings, which he voluntarily waived. I chose not to attempt to establish a rapport with the man. I felt led to direct the conversation to the issue at hand, so I advised him of the allegations that were made against him by his friend's two sons. He offered no visible reaction to the statement so I kept talking. I then used a displacement of blame tactic. I told the suspect that I believed that he must have been physically and sexually abused as a child, because the behavior that these two young boys described was very sadistic.

Using this statement as a threshold, I began questioning the suspect about his childhood. I wanted him to feel as though I was looking at him as a victim. If a suspect acknowledges that he was sexually abused as a child, then he will feel more comfortable admitting to his own transgressions, since we have laid the groundwork in his mind that what he did wasn't really his fault. Of course, nothing could be further from the truth. I don't consider myself any more righteous than the suspects I confront, especially in the eyes of God. However, I know from my own sinful nature that we human beings will sometimes rationalize our bad behavior to lessen our sense of guilt. A skillful police interrogator knows how to tap into his own wicked thoughts and behavior to help analyze those of others. Being able to relate to another man's evil actions in order to motivate him to a confession is a dangerous, dirty consequence of this job. Since my goal is to obtain the truth, no matter how nauseated it makes me, I will do whatever I can to comfort the suspect with irrational justifications in order to accomplish that goal. The pharisaical detective who chooses to place himself on a higher plane than his suspects will always lack success in the interview room.

At first, the suspect denied that he was abused as a child. However, within a few minutes he acknowledged that his father had abused him both physically and sexually. His father had walked out on the family when he was in the fourth grade. I asked the suspect to tell me about the abuse that he had suffered at his father's hand, but he refused, saying that he did not want to relive that time in his life. I found this quite ironic, for he didn't seem to have a problem reliving those moments when he was torturing these two young boys. Without even asking the suspect if he committed the aforementioned crimes against the boys, I continued as if he had already admitted to his guilt. I gently pressed the suspect for the truth by asking him if he thought that God was going to hold him accountable for his actions. This tactic worked, for the suspect answered, "Yes," thereby making his first admission to the boys' inconceivable allegations. His admission resonated during the long silence that fell upon the room.

I then asked the suspect to describe what he did to the boys. He answered, "The same unspeakable things my father did to me." The suspect added that he was still very angry with his father and would kill him if he ever saw him again. The suspect gave us a written statement admitting to all of the boys' allegations of sadistic sexual abuse and torture. He confessed that he became sexually aroused when torturing the boys. Surprisingly, we never had to use the taped phone conversation between the suspect and the older victim during the interview. He admitted to the crimes within fifteen minutes of being advised of his Miranda Warnings. When we ask God for His guidance and allow Him to use us as His vessel—and not try to do it all ourselves—good things happen.

After the suspect was finished giving us his written confession he voluntarily provided us with written consent to search his residence, which was located on the west side of the county. He accompanied Investigator Kevin Garvey and me to his apartment. In our search, we seized his computers and various media, all of which contained child pornography. We also seized his long guns and the leather belts that had been used to whip both victims.

Shortly after his arrest, the suspect pled guilty and agreed to serve twenty years in prison to avoid a much longer sentence that could have resulted at a trial. I take great satisfaction in the fact that we were able to obtain this type of disposition without having to subject the child victims to the additional trauma of testifying in court. It re-establishes my sense of purpose in doing what I do.

I truly believe that we had stumbled upon a man who possessed all the ingredients of a potential serial killer of young boys, and it was just a matter of time before his sexual violence escalated into a perverted climax of murder. Judging by the victims' descriptions, the violence had been escalating over time. The only question that remained was whether he would have killed these boys, or whether he was just practicing on them for pleasure until he chose other victims to whom he was less connected.

Over the span of three years, the suspect brainwashed these two young boys into voluntarily subjecting themselves to excruciating pain and sexual abuse to play video games. In essence, these two young boys had become this degenerate's personal prostitutes. As much as I have seen and dealt with on this job, this fact was hard to digest. I have a horrible feeling that these two young boys are going to carry around tremendous emotional baggage when they are old enough to comprehend what they were seduced into. I hope and pray that they have a solid support system in place when this awful realization hits them.

My heart goes out to all single mothers, especially those who must work outside of the home in order to support their children. Many of them have limited resources that they can depend on to supervise their children while they are working. I understand that they are stuck between a rock and a hard place, and they must accept assistance from those individuals that they have come to trust over time. This single mother's sons were lacking adult male companionship and role models, which is a common curse of the many broken homes in our society. She believed that this soft-spoken, gentle friend was a good influence. She fell prey to a false sense of security. If she had been made aware of how child predators operate among us, she might have been more diligent to debrief her sons daily. There is no doubt in my mind that she would have discovered years earlier what this man had been doing, or she might even have been able to prevent it.

It is critical that we parents take the time to effectively communicate with our children every day. Find out the who, what, where, when, and how of the time that your child was out of your control. Your daily discussions must continue through their teen years, for you need to establish a baseline on their responses and mannerisms. Consider it a low-tech but effective polygraph tool: it will enable you to know when they are holding something back or even lying. Focus your discussions on the people most close to your child and the people that they appear to be drawn to.

Remember, one of the predator's most effective tools is manipulating a child into silence. This cloak of secrecy is easily kept when the parents are unable to consistently communicate with their children. Parents can eliminate this tool by drawing out their children every day to find out who is treating them special. The child predator knows that parents today are too exhausted, too distracted, too busy, too selfish, or too ambitious in other areas of their lives to take the time every day to find out what's going on in their child's life. We parents need to examine our hearts with a clear and honest vision, and then make the appropriate adjustments to be the best shepherds that we can be, listening to everything that our children are telling us.

CHAPTER 11

—ᴍᴍ—

CASE EXAMPLE 8
THE POPULAR SCHOOL TEACHER

A fourteen-year-old boy returned home one fall afternoon and informed his mother that a former male schoolteacher, whom he had been working for over the past six months, had been showing him photographs of boys and men having sex with each other. The boy's parents appropriately forbid their son to continue working for the man. However, as you probably know by now, that wasn't the extent of what this young teen had suffered during his association with this man. A week later, the boy shared the rest of the story with a female teacher. The school officials immediately notified the student's parents and the police.

Monroe County Sheriff's Investigators Steve Peglow and Larry Crawford were assigned to investigate the allegations of sexual contact between the youth and the fifty-five-year-old man. Their interviews uncovered the actions of a child predator that had been cloaked as a highly revered science teacher with more than thirty years of experience in his profession.

The victim told the investigators that the teacher, who was friendly with his parents, had recruited the victim to work part-time for him at his residence and car business. Over the late spring and summer months while he was working for him, the teacher had engaged him in nearly a dozen separate incidents of sexual activity that included masturbation, touching, oral sex and sodomy. First, he began to show the victim photos, videos, and computer images of men and boys having sex together. He would reward the victim for his silence by buying him gifts and taking him out to eat, all while he was getting paid. Being at a pivotal age of his sexual development, the victim became easily aroused by the images, and he was seduced into masturbating along with his teacher while they viewed them together. The activity eventually escalated into masturbating and performing oral sex on each other. The suspect took nude photographs of the victim and kept a "fantasy book" that chronicled both the acts that he had committed and the sexual fantasies that he desired to convert into reality. The youth told investigators that he was enjoying the activity sexually, but it troubled him greatly because he knew that it was wrong, and that he was going against what his parents had taught him. He expressed his concerns to the teacher on several occasions, but his protests were ignored. When he could no longer bear his sense of guilt, the boy told his parents about the dirty photographs. He knew that his parents would not allow him to continue working for the suspect, and this would stop the vicious cycle of the unwanted sexual contact. The victim said that he was too ashamed to tell his parents about the sexual contact. Obviously, the victim needed to get all of what occurred off his chest, so he made a full disclosure to a female teacher at his current school.

Investigators Steve Peglow and Larry Crawford drove to the suspect's house early the following morning. They met him as he was backing his vehicle out of the garage. The suspect exited the car and greeted the detectives in the driveway. After identifying themselves, the detectives asked the suspect to voluntarily accompany them to their office, which was located at the Monroe County Sheriff's Office headquarters building in downtown Rochester. Without hesitation the suspect agreed, but asked to cancel an appointment that he had that morning. He also wanted to return a potted plant that he was carrying to the house. The investigators accompanied the suspect into his garage and kept an eye on him from the door as the suspect went into the kitchen area with his briefcase and set down his plant. Both investigators noted that while the suspect was doing this, he hastily opened his briefcase, pulled out a file folder, and placed it in a cabinet underneath the sink. Neither of them asked the suspect what was in the file. The suspect was then transported un-handcuffed to headquarters. Based upon the investigation thus far, these detectives were certain that this man was getting arrested. In fact, they had the authority to place him under arrest when they observed him backing out of his garage. However, the probability of a genuinely fruitful interview is significantly lower after you have placed someone under arrest, especially in these types of investigations. Sex offenders are control freaks and tend to be more willing to talk when they feel in control.

Once at headquarters, Investigator Peglow commenced the interview with the assistance of his senior partner, Investigator Crawford. Upon waiving his rights, the suspect stated that he knew why the detectives wanted to talk to him, and he expressed a desire to get the matter resolved. It was obvious that the man had a plan to try to talk his way out of the situation. From an interviewer's standpoint, this type of attitude is a good thing. Incredulous lies and false explanations in the face of convincing evidence and credible testimony can sometimes be just as good as a confession.

At first the discussion centered on the suspect's passion for specialty cars and his thirty-four year career as a middle-school science teacher. The suspect told them that he operated a very successful business restoring and selling vintage vehicles. Many of his customers were from other parts of the country and around the world. The suspect reported that he had employed male students from his school over the years to work for him at his residence and his car shop, which was located on another property in the same town. The suspect also mentioned that he raised ducks for use in his science classes. The suspect, who never married, confirmed that he hired the boys to cut his grass and clean up his residence, the shop, and his vehicle inventory.

The suspect assumed that the detectives wanted to speak with him in regard to a recent complaint from the parents of a male student that he took home with him without first obtaining their permission. The suspect said that he was "just trying to help out" this student. The suspect portrayed himself as a child advocate, dedicated to helping boys mature into productive young men.

Investigators Peglow and Crawford asked the suspect if he knew the victim. The suspect confirmed that the victim had worked for him up until recently. He claimed that they had parted ways over "some disagreements" and added that the victim had become "demanding and domineering." The suspect said that the other boys who worked for him asked the suspect to get rid of the victim because they didn't like the way the he had been "bossing" them around. The suspect explained that he was just trying to help the victim because of some problems at home. He alleged that the victim was angry and upset because his mother slept with his younger brother.

The suspect admitted that he touched the victim at various times. He would pat him on the back as a reward for doing a good job, or he would give the victim a back rub. The suspect said that the victim gave him shoulder and back rubs when he was working on the computer. The suspect even admitted hugging the victim out of affection. The suspect said that his "strong" relationship with the victim made the other boys who worked for him jealous. The suspect claimed that he attempted to get rid of the victim to keep peace with the other boys, but the victim refused to leave him alone. According to the suspect, his attempt to fire the victim caused the victim to become more domineering, where the victim would continually call him, leave him messages and page him if he did not call him back. He said that the victim was calling him to tell him what to do.

When asked if there had been any inappropriate touching between them the suspect quickly answered, "No." The detectives could tell that he was ready for the question by the next part of his response. The suspect added that he had to let the victim go because "things were getting out of control." The suspect said that he had just talked to his neighbor about the situation the night before. He purportedly told his neighbor that he was making plans to change his lifestyle because he had to stop being around these kids. The suspect alleged that the victim had threatened revenge: if the suspect fired him, the victim would make his life difficult. The suspect told the detectives that he was worried about his job, his business, and his good standing in the community. He exclaimed, "I'm done if this gets out!"

The suspect asked the detectives to call the victim's school counselor to corroborate his story. He indicated that this school counselor was "upset" with the victim for the way that he was treating the suspect. It was very obvious to the investigators that this guy was trying to portray himself as the real victim in this situation, as many child predators do. They purposely place themselves in a role that grants them access to children. When a child exposes them for what they really are, they offer the same defense: they were selflessly extending themselves, trying to help a child with a need, but they were forced to stop because of the victim's behavior. Predators know that most adults don't want to believe that they are capable of such allegations, so they will prematurely judge the child to be untruthful based upon the suspect's claim that the child is upset or a troubled youth.

When the suspect realized that the detectives weren't buying what he was serving them, he changed tactics and asked, "would hugging…and both getting hard-ons, count?" He then told them that that might have occurred with the victim. He admitted that he possessed porn magazines and nude photos on his computer that the victim may have found on his own since he had a key to the suspect's shop. He also stated that there was a cot for napping at the shop—as the victim had described—and he went on to ask, "If this gets into the paper, even if I didn't do anything…is there any way to fix this?" Then he asked, "Can I talk with the parents?" The man knew that he was sailing through the tumultuous waters of a police interview on a ship of deceit, and it was sinking despite all of his efforts to save it.

After a short bathroom break everyone returned to the interview room. Offers of food and drink were politely refused. The interview continued with several minutes of small talk before the detectives directed the conversation back to the suspect's relationship with the victim. The suspect described his relationship with the twelve-year-old like that of a marriage without the sex. He again admitted to patting the boy on his buttocks, rubbing his back and shoulders, and hugging him while they both had erections, but the suspect said that this was all done out of his "affection" for the lad, not sexual gratification. The suspect said that he feared that people would think that he was a homosexual because he never married and had always wanted his own son.

Investigators Crawford and Peglow left the suspect in the interview room under the watchful eye of two uniformed deputies and returned to the suspect's residence to execute a search warrant. Remember the file folder that the suspect had quickly taken out of his brief case and stowed under his kitchen sink? It was the first place that they looked. Their good police work and patience were rewarded. Inside the folder they found photographs of naked boys, including one of them holding a duck. Similar damning evidence was located on the suspect's computer and at his shop. The investigators located two photos of the victim posing naked in a dresser drawer at the suspect's shop, just as the victim had described.

Armed with the two photos of the victim, Investigators Peglow and Crawford returned to their substation and asked the suspect to describe his relationship with the victim again. After he described the relationship as affectionate but non-sexual—for the third time—they placed the photographs on the table in front of him. He held both photographs for a moment as he looked at them. Then he said, "Better I don't say anything." When he was confronted with irrefutable evidence, the suspect finally realized that he could no longer talk his way out, and he cried uncle. The investigators remained steady and unemotional throughout their day-long interview with this suspect. While he didn't confess to the crimes, he certainly provided them with a truckload of incriminating statements and obvious lies that could be used against him at trial. This is an example of excellent police work.

The suspect was arrested that same night. He was arraigned before a town justice and remanded to the Monroe County Jail in lieu of $25,000 cash bail or $50,000 bond. Investigator Peglow met with the victim the following day and showed him the two aforementioned photographs. The victim asserted that the photos were taken by the suspect with his Polaroid camera during one of their sexual encounters.

The investigation was far from over. A few days later, Investigator Peglow and Deputy Robert Clar interviewed a second student who came forward to file a complaint. The fifteen-year-old male victim had not been a student in the suspect's seventh-grade science class, but he said that the suspect always used to stare at him in the school hallways as students passed between their classes. Understandably, this made the victim uncomfortable. This is eerily similar to how an animal must feel when it senses a predator lurking nearby, scoping out its next victim. Eventually, the suspect walked up to the victim and introduced himself. For the rest of his time in seventh grade, the victim did not have much contact with the suspect other than a casual greeting in the hall, but the unnerving long looks continued.

The suspect made his move the following school year. He dispatched another male student to approach him about working for the suspect. The victim told the other student, whom he did not know very well, that he would consider it. That same day, before the victim had even arrived home from school, the suspect called his parents to set up a meeting to discuss the terms of their son's employment. This clever predator went on the offensive to gain the parents' trust for access to this child. The victim started working for the suspect at the end of that school year. The victim had been led to believe that he would be working with other kids, but he realized shortly after he started that he was the only boy working for the suspect. The suspect would always make it a point to pick up the victim and drive him to and from work.

What started out as a few hours per week job quickly evolved into working twelve-hour days, several times a week. Most of that time was not devoted to working, but just hanging out and going places with the suspect. They would play Monopoly, go for ice cream, eat out at restaurants, attend car shows, and drive the suspect's vintage specialty cars around the county. Eventually, the suspect allowed the victim to drink beer while he was with him. The victim was paid for every minute that he spent with the suspect. The victim stated that he really did not want to spend so much time with the suspect, but the suspect would manipulate him into feeling guilty for not wanting to hang with him. Once the beer was introduced into the relationship, the suspect made a secret pact with the youth to keep his silence, thus seducing him into going against his parent's authority. The suspect's web of seduction and deceit was nearly completed.

Had these parents been aware of how child predators operate, they would have been more diligent in debriefing their son on a daily basis in regard to his daily activities with this man. They would have realized that what was supposed to be a small part-time job turned into an out-of-balance social relationship, with the victim spending way too much unaccountable time alone with this man. They might have uncovered that their son was being manipulated by him. Instead, the victim's parents extended their trust to a higher level when they agreed to allow their son to accompany him on a four-day trip to another state. It was during that trip that the suspect began hugging the victim. Shortly after their return home, the suspect began hugging the victim more frequently. The hugs eventually turned into groping sessions, where the suspect would run his hands down the victim's back and grab his buttocks while thrusting his hips forward into the victim. When the victim confronted him, the suspect would say that he was just joking around. Then he would put the victim on the defensive by telling him to not be so homophobic.

Approximately five weeks into the summer vacation, the victim said that the suspect called the victim into his bedroom and showed him pornographic magazines. After viewing the material, the suspect stood up and began masturbating and rubbing the victim's penis. Horrified, the victim left the bedroom. The suspect said, "You know, I've been good for five weeks…I couldn't help myself."

While driving the victim home that same day, the suspect stopped at his car shop. While inside the car shop, the suspect called the victim into his office where he was seated. He then molested the boy in a similar manner as before, except this time he tried to have anal sex with him. The victim refused and was eventually taken home.

The victim refused to return to the suspect's house for several weeks. During that time he received numerous telephone calls from the suspect asking him to come back to work for him. The suspect tried to bribe the victim with a trip to the Corvette Museum in Kentucky. He even encouraged the youth's parents to let him go. Despite much persistence, the victim refused. Incredulously, the suspect continued to pursue the victim via countless e-mails. The suspect blamed the victim for what happened between them. The suspect excused his behavior as an accident and said that he thought the victim wanted it to happen. The suspect even tried to bribe the victim with a car. I commend this young man for his courage and unwillingness to be seduced and manipulated any longer by this evil serpent. This insatiable animal was relentless in his pursuit of this child, ignoring his repeated protests to leave him alone. The victim's parents became suspicious of the suspect's numerous attempts to contact their son and their son's refusal to work for him any longer. The victim's father called the suspect's home and left him a message to stop calling their son and stopping by their house unannounced. Still, the victim had not told his parents the real reason that he did not want to return to his employer.

Over a year later, it was announced in his tenth-grade class that the suspect had been arrested for inappropriate behavior with a minor. It was known throughout the school system that a lot of boys had worked for him over the years. The victim said that his stomach did a flip and he got a sinking feeling upon hearing the news. The victim's teacher must have observed his reaction to her announcement, for she approached him after class to see if he was okay. The teacher did an excellent job of making the victim feel comfortable enough to tell her about his personal experiences two summers before. While he did not give her a full account, it unsealed his dark, secret burden. Had this teacher not observed the victim's reaction to the announcement and then taken the time to speak with him in a manner to gain his trust and unlock the recesses of his conscience, this young man might have carried an overwhelming heaviness in his heart for his entire life. Child victims are more likely to make their initial disclosure to another adult besides their parents because of their embarrassment. In these two cases, both victims decided to share their secrets with a female teacher that they felt they could trust. If you work closely with children, please be sensitive to the fact that God may call upon you to play this important role someday. The actions of these teachers serve as an inspiring example of what to do and how to behave if this occurs.

Due to the mandated reporting requirement in New York State, the school had to notify the Monroe County Sheriff's Office and the victim's parents about his disclosure to his teacher. Plainclothes Deputy Robert Clar was assigned to the investigation that commenced on this victim's behalf, and he worked in concert with Investigators Peglow and Crawford. Because he was ashamed, the victim initially shared only part of what occurred. It was only after Deputy Clar read through all of the e-mail conversations between the victim and the suspect that the victim acknowledged that more sexual touching had occurred. I believe that this young man was molested much more severely than he was willing to admit, and I completely understand his reluctance to do so.

Investigator Steve Peglow was contacted by the father of a third victim, who was currently away from home attending college as a freshman. The victim's father stated that the suspect recently contacted his son, who had been the suspect's student and employee when he was twelve years old. The suspect advised this victim that he had been arrested for molesting another male student and said, "We need to get our stories straight." When the victim refused to cooperate or communicate further with the suspect, the suspect began harassing him. This led the boy to contact his father and apprise him of the situation.

Investigator Peglow eventually met with the victim in person. While the victim denied ever having sexual contact with the suspect, he complained of being harassed. Investigator Peglow felt that the boy was hiding the truth because he was ashamed, so he advised the victim to call his college campus police to file a harassment complaint against him, and he invited him to call him anytime. Later that evening, the victim paged Investigator Peglow. When they spoke over the telephone, the victim divulged that he had been molested by the suspect over a five-year period, and some of the sexual encounters had occurred while they were alone in the suspect's classroom.

Investigator Peglow met with the victim at his office several days later and obtained a three-page sworn statement that was filled with filthy and despicable acts. Some of it is similar to the activity already described earlier in this case example. However, over the course of five years, the suspect forced this student into participating in numerous acts of sodomy while watching homosexual pornographic films. His lust for this adolescent was so out of control that he would issue him a pass excusing him from study hall for "one-on-one remedial education" in his classroom. Once the victim arrived, the suspect would cover his office windows and have sex with him. Incredibly, these evil encounters occurred several times per week while the victim was in the seventh and eighth grades — unnoticed for nearly two years.

The abuse continued as the victim progressed through high school. The suspect bribed him as he did the others, promising him a car and promising to bequeath him the car shop upon his demise. When that wasn't enough to keep the victim cooperative, the suspect threatened to expose the victim. When the victim tried to terminate the relationship on numerous occasions, the suspect would call and e-mail him relentlessly. He would even dispatch another youth to give him a message to "call him or else." This poor boy never had a chance. The predator had his claws and teeth deep into his psyche. The young victim was no match for this cunning and manipulative serpent, who had led him to believe that there was no way out. Feeling hopeless, the victim was unable to break free, and he subjected himself to five years of sexual abuse and sodomy at the hands of a man who was supposed to be his advocate and mentor. This is exactly what makes these types of crimes and the people who commit them so contemptible.

The suspect was charged with additional crimes for what he did to this victim. Eventually, Investigators Peglow and Crawford determined that the suspect had employed thirty young boys over many years. Many of them refused to cooperate with the investigation, insisting that nothing inappropriate had occurred with the suspect. However, there was good reason to doubt their denials. The detectives obtained a list of boy's names that the suspect had possessed. All of the boys had similar physical characteristics in terms of build, eye and hair color, and overall appearance. As many child predators do, this one pursued boys with a specific physical profile.

Further investigation revealed another of the suspect's diabolical strategies to gain access to the boys that he was interested in. Near the end of each school year, the suspect taught a unit on reproduction. As part of the curriculum, the class would incubate and hatch ducklings. When the school year ended, the suspect would hand-pick which students would be allowed to raise a duckling at home over the summer. The condition for this task, considered a privilege, was that the suspect be allowed to come to their home regularly to bring food and check on the duck's progress. It didn't go unnoticed by other teachers and former students that the students who were chosen for this task were always boys. This was a ploy to learn more about each boy's family situation and their vulnerability. Once he chose his targets, the suspect would befriend the boy's parents in order to obtain their trust, thereby laying the foundation to spend time alone with their son.

Unfortunately, most of the boys were reluctant to testify because they were ashamed and afraid of being exposed in a very high-profile public trial. One victim even threatened to kill himself if he was forced to testify. These circumstances placed the prosecutor in the difficult position of having to allow the suspect to plead guilty to only one count of Sodomy in the Third Degree. Adding to this tragic outcome, because this was the suspect's first conviction he was sentenced to only six months in jail, probation, and registration on the sex offender list. However, this child predator could not control his ravenous ways and soon violated a condition of his probation. He was immediately sentenced to four years in prison. While this punishment was not nearly extensive enough for the thirty-year-long wake of damage and emotional carnage he left behind, it was significantly better than the original sentence. Whenever a convicted child predator receives a lesser sentence than the crime would normally require, I take comfort in knowing that God will eventually deal with the unrepentant predator as he states in the Psalms:

"They are like worthless chaff, scattered by the wind. They will be condemned at the time of judgment. Sinners will have no place among the godly. For the Lord watches over the path of the godly, but the path of the wicked leads to destruction."   Psalm1:4b-6 (NLT)

This case exemplifies so many facets of how the child predator operates in our midst. He masked himself in the profession of a trusted educator, and was considered to be one of the most likeable and popular teachers among his peers. This allowed him unlimited access to potential victims of his choosing. He strategically utilized more than one common denominator—his specialty car business and the baby ducks—to maintain access to his chosen targets. This also provided him access to the victims outside the parameters of his job and allowed him to cultivate a personal relationship with each of them. He focused on boys, whose ages ranged from twelve to fifteen years old, where it is natural for them to seek attention and praise from the influential adult males in their lives. At this age they are also becoming curious about their own sexuality, so they are more open to experimentation.

A background investigation into the suspect's past revealed that complaints of sexually abusing male students were made against him as early as 1972, and as recently as 2000. Even public allegations (before the ones that prompted this investigation) did not deter him to cease his offensive behavior toward other children. Why he was still employed as a teacher in a public school district is beyond my understanding and an affront to the students, parents, and other teachers in that school district. It demonstrates how child predators can be elusive manipulators, twisting around the truthful statements of a child to avoid being detected, stopped and held accountable for their actions. Even while being interviewed by the detectives, the suspect did his best to manipulate the situation by attacking the credibility of the victim. He was quick to slander the victim and his parents, saying that he and the victim had "some disagreements" and that the other boys who worked with the victim supposedly didn't like him and wanted him fired. The suspect went so far as to describe the victim as demanding and domineering, and claimed that he was just trying to help the victim due to problems at home.

To anyone unfamiliar with how child predators court their targeted victims, the suspect at a glance would never appear to be any cause for concern. This was a highly-respected teacher who took the time out of his own personal life to help young boys develop into productive young men through his interaction with them separate and apart from school. At face value, who wouldn't admire this man? These are the people we write stories and movies about for what they do on behalf of our young people above and beyond the call of duty. That is the tragedy of this situation. There are wonderful people in each of our communities and schools who sacrifice their time and resources for the right reason—helping children to be all that they can be. We need more people like this. The child predators that use this tactic are ruining it for the rest of us. Every time one of them is exposed, it causes the dedicated real professionals to pause before extending themselves for the sake of a child's personal development. I have had teachers and coaches tell me that they are afraid to give a student or athlete a pat on the back or even a needed hug of encouragement for fear that it may be misinterpreted. I can not disagree with their concerns. Thanks to the child predator, this is a sad consequence of the world that we live in today.

Chapter 12

—

CASE EXAMPLE 9
"In Just Twenty Minutes..."

"*Lord, you know the hopes of the helpless. Surely you will hear their cries and comfort them. You will bring justice to the orphans and the oppressed, So mere people can no longer terrify them.*"

Psalm 10: 17-18 (NLT)

The suspect was a thirty-eight-year-old male who had befriended a group of single mothers. He first became friendly with the woman who lived with her five-year-old daughter in the other half of the duplex that he and his sister resided in. The front porch of the old dual-family house located on the west side of the city was shared by both families and allowed for casual conversations over the warm-weather months to evolve into a close friendship. When the single mother had car trouble and ensuing transportation problems, the suspect was all too ready to assist her. The suspect "loved kids" and enjoyed partaking in family-oriented activities with the mother and her young daughter. This endeared him both to the woman and her precocious little girl. The suspect attempted to date the woman, but eventually settled on just being good friends with her.

It was during this time that the suspect gained the unwavering trust of his neighbor, and he began watching her daughter when she was not at home. In essence, he became the girl's surrogate uncle. Through his close relationship with the woman, he was introduced to several of her girlfriends and became friendly with them as well. One of those women had a ten-year-old daughter whom the suspect took a special interest in. This mother was young and gravitated toward the suspect because he was always willing to lend a hand or provide much-needed transportation. As a result of these friendships, the suspect spent an exorbitant amount of time with both little girls and would even provide child care from time to time. Over the following year, the suspect enjoyed taking countless photographs of the girls, especially the younger one.

One winter evening, the suspect transported his neighbor, her daughter, and the ten-year-old to a mutual female friend's house in a suburban neighborhood. Once they arrived, the girls went down to the playroom in the basement with the friend's children while the adults remained upstairs in the kitchen and visited over coffee. Eventually, the suspect went down to the basement to "check on the kids." The suspect sat on the sofa and watched the children play. A short time later, one of the mothers went downstairs to check on things and returned upstairs. That was when the suspect made his move.

According to the ten-year-old girl, the six-year-old's pants kept falling down, exposing her bare buttocks. The suspect pulled out his digital camera and started taking snap-shots of the six-year-old girl's bare bottom. He even got her to bend over and pose for him several times. At some point, the suspect pulled down his own pants and exposed his erect penis to the children. He then placed the six-year-old vic-tim on his lap and covered himself and the little girl with a blanket so that the other children couldn't see what he was going to do. However, the older girl peeked under the blanket and observed that the young victim had her pants and panties completely off. She was sitting on the suspect's lap while the suspect rubbed his penis against her vaginal area and took photographs of the filthy act.

When the suspect was finished, he took pleasure in showing the older girl all of the photographs that he had taken while they were under the blanket. He instructed both girls not to tell anyone or "all of them" would get into trou-ble, and then the suspect would not be able to visit them any-more. The older girl deleted some of the photographs before giving the camera back to the suspect. The suspect eventu-ally left the residence, and both girls and the victim's mother stayed overnight. The next morning, the older girl told her little friend's mother what had happened in the basement the night before. The mother of the older girl was contacted, and then both mothers transported their daughters to the sheriff's substation in that town. After the report was made to a uni-formed deputy, the investigation was transferred to the Major Crimes Unit and it eventually landed on my desk.

I contacted both mothers and set up interviews with their daughters. The interviews occurred at the Bivona Child Advocacy Center, which provides a much friendlier environment for child victims than a police detective's office. From their testimony about the chronological order of events that night, we determined that this sexual assault had occurred within a twenty-minute time period right under the women's noses. I interviewed the six-year-old victim first, since the ten-year-old had already given the uniformed deputy a sworn statement. She confirmed the older girl's account. When I asked the little girl to describe what the suspect's erect penis looked like to her, she explained that "his pee-pee looked like a hot dog." This specific, gruesome testimony is required to substantiate that the suspect was sexually aroused and attempting to have intercourse with her. Out of the mouths of babes we gain some of the most damning corroborating evidence against a suspect. A young child would normally be incapable of providing such an anatomically correct description. The young victim also disclosed that she had touched the suspect's penis with her hand, and that the suspect had instructed the ten-year-old girl to take photographs of them with his digital camera.

At first, the ten-year-old denied this fact, but later she admitted that it was true. She hadn't shared that information with her mother or the police because she was afraid of getting into trouble. The photographs that she had deleted were the ones that she had taken. Her remorse for photographing the victimization of her young friend was what drove her to talk to the victim's mother right after waking up. Her young conscience was too tender to hide what she had seen and done. However, as many children do in these types of cases, she initially only told part of the story because she was ashamed and afraid of what people might think of her. I believe that the suspect's motive for instructing her to take the photographs was to manipulate her into having some culpability in what he had done. It was a way to control her. He led the ten-year-old to believe that if she told on him, she would get into trouble as well.

After interviewing the victims, I drafted a search warrant. Unlike television, most detectives write their own search warrants, which can be a time-consuming process. After a county court judge signed the search warrant, Investigator Tom Passmore and I drove to the suspect's residence in the city to attempt to interview him. It was a blustery, cold winter day, and I nearly fell on my back when I slipped on the icy porch steps leading up to the suspect's front door. No one answered the door, even though the suspect's vehicle was still parked in the driveway and covered by the recent snowfall. The six-year-old victim's mother had provided me the suspect's cell phone number, so after making our way back to our unmarked police vehicle I dialed it. No one answered. Investigator Passmore and I decided to park down the street from the suspect's residence and watch his vehicle. At that point, my cell phone rang. It was the suspect.

After I greeted the suspect and identified myself as a Sheriff's Investigator, I advised him of the allegations that were made against him. I didn't provide him with all the details and suggested that we meet in person to discuss the matter. The suspect stated that he already knew what the allegations were, and he advised that he had already contacted an attorney, who told him to not say anything to the police or the victims' families. To ease his concern, I casually told the suspect that he was not under arrest, so it was his choice whether or not to speak with us. I told him that I just wanted to hear his side of the situation. Ignoring his attorney's advice, the suspect agreed to speak with us later that afternoon. When I asked about his vehicle still being in the driveway, the suspect said that his boss had picked him up for work earlier that morning because he was having car trouble.

As planned, Investigator Passmore and I returned to the suspect's residence. He answered the door appearing as though he had just showered and changed into clean clothes. The suspect's sister and her teenage son voluntarily left the living room so that we could talk to him in private. He refused to accompany us to our office, preferring to be interviewed in the safety and comfort of his own home. The United States Constitution prohibits the police from forcefully removing a suspect from his residence without an arrest warrant. I believe that is a good thing. However, if the police have obtained an arrest warrant for their suspect in the State of New York, then by law, the suspect is not allowed to voluntarily waive his right to a lawyer without first speaking to one. Every lawyer that I have dealt with will initially tell their client not to talk with the police, so this is counterproductive for the investigator who is trying to find the truth. I firmly agree with the United States Constitution that everyone is entitled to legal representation upon their request when they are being questioned by the police. But I don't agree with the state rule that a suspect can't voluntarily waive their right to a lawyer just because an arrest warrant has been issued against them. This is very frustrating since police in most other states and the nation's capital are still allowed to interview the suspect without a lawyer if he voluntarily waives that right, even after they arrest him with an arrest warrant. This ruling has severely and unnecessarily hindered the police during the investigative process. This should concern the citizens of New York State. Criminals are being afforded a huge advantage that goes above and beyond what the United States Constitution requires.

Investigator Passmore and I did as we usually do— we attempted to interview the suspect in his own home and planned to apply for an arrest warrant afterward to remove him from the residence if he didn't go with us voluntarily. This is our usual process, but it is both a tactical and logistical nightmare that needlessly burns valuable time and resources. If a suspect chooses not to speak with the police and then refuses to go with detectives voluntarily, we have to stop the investigative process at that point to complete additional paperwork, contact a judge if court isn't in session (easier said than done), and then drive to the respective court and file the complaint for an arrest warrant. While the investigator is completing this task, at least two police officers have to remain with the suspect at his residence and detain him until the arrest warrant is in hand.

Sitting on the sofa next to the suspect, I advised him of his Miranda Warnings by reading them verbatim from the yellow rights waiver card that I carry in my wallet. Investigator Passmore sat in a large chair next to the television across the room. The suspect voluntarily waived his rights and agreed to talk with us. I began the conversation by recapping the allegations that were made against him. The suspect said that he was aware of the allegations, but he couldn't understand why both girls would be saying such things. He denied touching either of them. I then began asking him more pointed questions that required nothing more than a yes or no answer.

I asked the suspect if the six-year-old girl's pants kept falling down and exposing her buttocks and he answered, "Yes."

I asked him if he photographed the girls with his digital camera. He said that he did, but he denied taking photographs of the younger girl's naked buttocks. I asked him if I could look at the digital camera and he said yes. However, the camera was not in his possession because he had loaned it to his sister. *"How convenient,"* I thought. At my request, the suspect called his sister and allowed me to speak with her over the telephone. She confirmed that she did in fact use the camera over the weekend, but she had left it at a friend's house. Nothing is very easy in this business. At my gentle urging, the suspect's sister agreed to retrieve the camera so that we could examine it. Luckily for us, the woman didn't ask us why. I knew that the suspect was feeling confident because he had most likely deleted all of the photographs from the camera's memory. I still wanted a trained forensic examiner to attempt to retrieve anything that could be gleaned from the device, which was included on the search warrant. After we squared away the camera's whereabouts and agreed on its eventual surrender, I returned to the suspect's account of what had occurred in the basement. I asked him if the younger girl got under the blanket with him while they were seated on the sofa. The suspect said that she did, explaining that the little one sat on his lap because she was cold. I then asked him if their heads were under the blanket and he confirmed that they were. I asked the suspect if the ten-year-old girl got underneath the blanket with them for a period of time. He answered, "Yes."

Maintaining a probing style of questioning, I asked the suspect if the girls accidentally bumped into his penis while they were playing under the blanket. The suspect said, "They might have…I'm not sure." He certainly didn't close the door on us with this answer. I purposely characterized the question as if contact with his penis was accidental. This line of questioning gets us in the ballpark. Now it was time to pick away at his story as long as we could keep him cooperative. Sometimes conducting an interview is like creating a sculpture out of granite rock using a chisel and hammer. You methodically chip away at the crooked, crevassed boulder until the truth, or some semblance of the truth, begins to take form.

I asked the suspect if his penis ever got hard, for perhaps the girls might have felt it. He said that he didn't remember getting an erection while playing with them. I stared directly into his eyes and told him that something must have happened for the girls to focus their disclosures on his penis, but he insisted that nothing happened. I kept pressing. I told the suspect that I believed something happened and I suggested that maybe he had accidentally exposed his penis to the girls and now he was either ashamed or afraid to tell the truth. "Sometimes the truth lies in the middle," I offered.

I was attempting to downplay the suspect's culpability and provide him the opportunity to present himself to us in what he would perceive to be a better light. But he continued to deny that anything had happened, saying that as far as he was concerned, I was beating a dead horse. Looking back at him with softer eyes and lowering my tone of voice to nearly a whisper, I told the suspect that I believed he was holding back the truth, but his continued denials were a normal reaction for a person in his position. I told him that we all possess a natural instinct to not tell the truth when we get caught doing something wrong. It was a polite way of saying that I didn't believe him without actually saying that he was lying. No one likes to be called a liar, even when they are lying. Conveying empathy to a person who is lying usually works better than an approach that conveys a judgmental attitude. The interrogator can always escalate their tone and verbal aggressiveness later in the interrogation if needed.

I continued talking without seeking an immediate response from him. I was trying to offer him what he might perceive to be a legitimate excuse for why something "might" have occurred with the girls that he "never intended." I was hoping that a certain word or phrase would snare a thread of guilt in his conscience. If I could find that, I could gently tug on it until the fabric of his story unraveled.

"What would you be thinking if you were me?" I asked.

"I would think that I was lying," he answered.

"Are you ashamed or scared?" I asked.

"I'm scared," he answered.

"What are you afraid of?" I asked.

"What they do to people like me in prison," He answered. He was referring to his first bid in state prison for sexually molesting another little girl several years before.

Already knowing the answer to the question, I asked the suspect, "What'd you go to prison for?"

He said that he was wrongly accused of touching another young girl, but he decided to plead guilty to the charges anyway. Even though he didn't do anything to her, he wanted to spare the little girl from testifying in court.

"How old was that little girl?" I asked, trying not to laugh in his face and betray my disbelief of his incredulous statement.

"Six years old," he answered.

We were aware of this past conviction, which required him to serve four years in prison. It had occurred back in 1988. Because his criminal conviction occurred before January 1996, when New York State's version of Megan's Law became effective, he was not required to register as a sex offender. I honestly don't know why lawmakers didn't make the Sex Offender Registration Act retroactive, requiring convicted sex offenders within the past twenty years to register. I am sure that some lawyer would have argued that it would violate the ex-convict's constitutional rights if they were required to register. This legislative short-sightedness allowed this predator to fly under the radar screen and continue to freely have contact with children.

The suspect pretended that out of the goodness of his heart he pled guilty simply to spare the little girl, but the truth is that he was indicted on twenty separate counts of Sexual Abuse in the First Degree for repeatedly touching the penis of an eight-year-old boy and the vagina of a six-year-old girl. For reasons unknown to me, the suspect was allowed to plead guilty to only one count of Sexual Abuse in the First Degree, with a maximum sentence of four and one-half years in prison. Most likely, the two young victims were terrified of testifying and being cross-examined by the suspect's defense lawyer, leaving the prosecutor with no other choice but to plead the case out. That is the dilemma with these types of cases—victims refuse to testify or are incapable—and child predators count on it.

I asked the suspect how the other convicts in the prison learned about the crime that he had committed against the little girl (he never mentioned the little boy). He said that the prison guards told them.

At that point I pressed him for more of the truth. "Either you have an explanation as to why both girls would say that they observed your erect penis or, as far as I'm concerned, you molested them." I said. The suspect thought for a few moments while the three of us sat in silence. It was obvious that he was attempting to formulate some type of an answer that he felt would hurt him the least. He offered that right after the six-year-old's mother came down to the basement to check on things and returned upstairs, the victim came up behind him and pulled down his sweatpants, causing him to expose his erect penis to both girls. The suspect insisted that nothing else occurred.

"Was your penis erect when the girls looked at it?" "Yes," he responded. After a moment of silence, I asked the suspect if we could search his room and take a look at his computer. He said, "Yes, go ahead." I then asked the suspect if he would accompany us to our office so that we could take a written statement, but he refused.

"Why won't you go with us voluntarily?" I asked. "The last time I went with the police I ended up going to prison," the suspect said, sounding cagier than he did earlier.

I think he knew that the jig was up, but he wasn't going to go with us the easy way. I told him that was fine and that Investigator Passmore and I were leaving, but we would return shortly. We left the suspect in the care of a team of investigators who were executing the search warrant on the suspect's bedroom and computer. Investigator Passmore and I drove to the justice court in the town where the crime was committed to file a felony complaint and request an arrest warrant.

Once we had the arrest warrant in hand, we returned to the suspect's house and took him into custody. Just as he had feared, he was leaving his residence with the police and going back to jail. The suspect was charged with Rape in the First Degree; Sexual Abuse in the First Degree; Promoting and Possessing an Obscene Sexual Performance by a Child; Use of a Child in a Sexual Performance; and Endangering the Welfare of a Child. He was arraigned that night before the town justice who had issued the arrest warrant and was remanded to the Monroe County Jail in lieu of $25,000 cash bail or $50,000 bond.

The suspect's computer was now in our custody, but his digital camera was still at large somewhere between his sister and her friend. After we locked up the suspect, Sergeant Comanzo and I drove to the northwest part of the county to the sister's residence to retrieve the camera. I was pleasantly surprised when the suspect's sister did the right thing and voluntarily surrendered it to us. I was impressed that this woman had taken it upon herself to leave the comfort of her warm home on a frigid Rochester night to drive over to her friend's house to retrieve the camera for the police. She had several different options to choose from. She could have told her friend to lose the camera. She could have retrieved the camera and then lied to us about its whereabouts. Or she could have destroyed it. Some suspects' family members would have chosen one of those options to protect their loved one, no matter what the consequences. However, this woman chose to cooperate, and she should be recognized for doing the right thing. Soon you will understand why.

Assisting officers Investigator Kevin Garvey, Sergeant Comanzo, and Crime Scene Technician Deputy Dave Gutzmer conducted the search of the suspect's room and found numerous photographs of both girls and the suspect's personal diary. Most of the diary entries were love letters written by the suspect to the six-year-old victim as if she were an adult. Some of the photographs showed the victim posing in provocative positions and clothing that I believe the suspect had purchased for her.

The suspect's computer was also seized for forensic examination. Because the department's computer forensic technician had recently retired, we were lacking a trained expert to search it for corroborating evidence. As I have in the past, I looked outside of the department for a qualified examiner. I was able to solicit a longstanding friend of mine from the United States Secret Service, Special Agent Mike deStefano. Special Agent deStefano was an expert in this field, but normally he limited his forensic examinations to Secret Service counterfeit and fraud investigations. Despite his disdain of child pornography and child sex abuse cases, Mike agreed to help me out. And I thank God for that. Because of Mike's expertise and tenacity, he was able to retrieve the much-needed evidence despite the suspect's efforts to delete it. Mike was very disturbed by the images that he found. The quick-witted, razor-tongued agent with the gruff exterior but soft heart described in vivid detail what he felt should be done to the suspect. The vernacular that he used could not be printed in this book. In short, he feels that people like this should be unceremoniously executed in the cruelest and most unusual way possible and their remains should be tossed into dumpsters. You will empathize with the strong feelings of this now-retired thirty-year veteran agent as you learn that the images that memorialized the suspect's actions included a close-up photograph of the suspect's erect penis with her tiny little hand on it. He photographed his penis between her legs as he rubbed it against her vagina. He also photographed the girl with her beautiful little face near his erect penis with her tongue sticking out as if she was going to lick it. When I first laid eyes on these photographs I seethed with anger and disgust.

There are no boundaries to man's appetite for lust and sexual perversion. While I struggle with my own lustful thoughts and desires as most men do, I will never, ever understand how so many men can look upon young children as objects of sexual desire. In my opinion, this unfathomable evil is encouraged by demons, which are all too ready to enter into a man's heart when his deviate desires have opened a door to being seduced into committing such unconscionable acts.

The verbal admissions that the suspect made to us during the interview in his living room were suppressed after a pre-trial hearing. The judge ruled that the suspect's statements could not be used against him at trial because he had consulted with a lawyer about this investigation before we spoke with him and he was, therefore, unable to waive his right to counsel without actually having his attorney present. This type of ruling is exclusive to New York State and tragically it is very typical. I don't believe that any other state in the union would disallow the defendant's admissions to be used at his trial when he had been advised of his constitutional rights and voluntarily waived them while not in custody, and in the comfort of his own home, just because he had a brief conversation on the telephone with his lawyer beforehand. Remember, the suspect told us that he wanted to tell us his side of the story.

Because the suspect's statement was suppressed, it bolstered his confidence, making him reluctant to accept a plea bargain offer of twenty-five years incarceration. If he was convicted at trial, he would be looking at approximately forty years in prison. He was banking on the silence of his six-year-old victim. Many interviews with the child proved that she would not be able to testify at trial, which would seriously damage the case. The little girl could not speak of the abuse in an open and strange forum such as a courtroom as required. She could only whisper in her mother's ear, "His privates rubbed my privates." However, after the suspect's attorney observed the photographs that Special Agent deStephano recovered from the suspect's camera and computer, he was ready to negotiate a plea bargain. The suspect pled guilty to two counts of Sexual Abuse in the First Degree and he was sentenced to twenty years in prison. Special Agent Mike deStefano became the voice of this young victim. Had it not been for his hard work, the suspect might not have received even half that sentence.

Once again, this case demonstrates how single mothers are a child predator's favorite and most convenient target. The evil scheme of posing as their helpful and dependable friend ingratiated him to these unsuspecting women. This predator gained the trust of these women based upon their need of assistance. He then had unlimited access to the children that he targeted. As time went on, he photographed activities with the mothers and their children and chronicled his time and fantasies about these two girls in his fantasy book. He eventually put all of his energy into grooming the younger one to fulfill his evil desires. Based on the photographs that we seized from his room and my knowledge of these animals, there is no doubt in my mind that the suspect purchased sexually provocative clothing for both girls to play dress-up in. By doing this, he drew their sexuality out of them prematurely and transformed them into voluntary participants, willingly modeling the clothing for him. He controlled the victims and maintained their silence about this activity and the subsequent abuse by leading them to believe that they would get into trouble and not be allowed to see him anymore. He also frequently rewarded their silence by giving them gifts.

While I will not fault these mothers for what occurred to their daughters, I would question their judgment in allowing this thirty-eight-year old single man unlimited and unsupervised access to their daughters. They were targeted and manipulated by this animal once he determined their vulnerability. However, they did not hesitate to report the allegation to the police, which is much more than I can say for many other mothers in similar circumstances.

Last but not least, this case also epitomizes just how quickly the undetected child predator can strike. Without warning, he finally lunges to destroy and devour his prey. Within a twenty-minute time frame, he sexually assaulted one little girl in front of another and even brazenly memorialized the event on camera while one of their mothers was right upstairs visiting with two other women. I can only wonder how many times this scenario might have been carried out before with the six-year-old victim in private. If it were not for the bravery of her ten-year-old friend, this cunning serpent might still be free to keep offending children.

CHAPTER 13

—◊—

CASE EXAMPLE 10
TWO LEGACIES OF EVIL

*T*his last chapter offers two separate scenarios that portray the child predator operating in two different roles. In one we see a trusted authority figure; in the other, a "Peter Pan" complex. The predators' disguises are quite different, but the cases are similar in other aspects. Each left behind a legacy of evil, destroying many young boys' lives.

FIRST CASE

Monroe County Sheriff's Road Patrol Deputy Tyler Barrus was dispatched to an apartment complex in the northwest part of Monroe County for a suspicious adult male playing with seven- and eight-year-old boys. Two of the boys' mothers became suspicious after the man knocked on their doors and introduced himself as a "really nice guy," assuring them that he would never take their children anywhere without their permission. The man told the mothers that he thought their sons were "really cute" and that he just wanted to be their friends. He was showing up at the outdoor basketball court to play with young boys from the neighborhood. He would organize basketball shooting competitions in the format of the game known as "PIG," but he would use sexually-explicit slang words instead. He told the boys that he was very lonely and sad because he recently broke up with his girlfriend, and he invited them to go on bicycle rides and to accompany him down to the nearby creek.

Deputy Barrus, who served in the armed forces and at one time was assigned to guard the Oval Office during Ronald Reagan's presidency, possessed a knack for poking around and unearthing pertinent information during preliminary investigations. This skill, which exceeded the department's expectations, gained Deputy Barrus his promotion to the rank of Criminal Investigator and eventual assignment to the Major Crimes Unit. His canvass of the apartment complex revealed that most of the young boys had some type of contact with the suspect, but knew him only by his first name. Some of the boys were very defensive of the mystery man and reluctant to talk about him, yet most of the parents had no idea that he even existed. Deputy Barrus put the word out to other patrol officers in the area, which generated additional information over the following days.

Eventually, the suspect was positively identified. He was a thirty-nine-year-old white male who owned and operated a fishing lure business with his elderly parents. Deputy Barrus began interviewing numerous young boys who had had contact with the suspect. He was classified as a pedophile after it was reported that he showed a nine-year-old boy a pornographic magazine and invited the youth to follow him into the "magic forest" behind a local school to look for more discarded magazines. The suspect also asked the lad to accompany him back to his van to watch porn movies with him. The boy later revealed that the suspect offered to show the boy his penis and asked the boy to show him his.

A criminal investigator was assigned to assist Deputy Barrus after it became obvious that the suspect had some form of contact with numerous young males in the small village community. Monroe County Sheriff's Investigator Robert Connors assisted Deputy Barrus with many interviews of possible victims and witnesses. Investigator Connors, now retired, acquired the nickname of "Coonhound" because his investigative prowess was similar to that of a hound dog. He had the ability to sniff things out that most of us would never pick up on, and once he located the scent, there was no letting up until the criminal was in custody. On one occasion, Investigator Connors closed in on a fugitive who was hiding in a house. The home owner would not permit the police to enter. Being both tenacious and intuitive—and unpredictable Investigator Connors drove to a local fishing bait store and purchased a large box of live crickets. After issuing a final unheeded warning to exit the home voluntarily, Investigator Connors dumped the box of screaming insects into an open window and waited. Needless to say, the unorthodox tactic worked. The suspect came out shortly afterwards to escape the annoying swarm of varmints and Coonhound got his man. Whenever I worked a case with Investigator Connors, we not only solved the mystery and made an arrest, but we laughed a lot too. He possessed what I call "high entertainment value."

As the case moved forward, more young male victims began stepping out of the shadows of anonymity. Some of them were reluctant to talk with the police and even defended the suspect, describing him as a nice man and good friend. A total of thirty-one boys ranging from the age of eight to young teens acknowledged being sexually abused and/or sodomized by this animal. We learned that the suspect engaged everywhere that young boys might play: on the basketball courts, bike paths, their forts, and the local creek bed. He rode a mountain bike to meet them in the fields along the bike paths and creek bed. He took some of the boys fishing and gave them fishing lures. He stalked the apartment complex on foot, by bike and in his van, in search of his next potential victim. He even hiked up to their tree forts in the secluded wooded areas, a feat that most of us adults would never consider.

The suspect wasted no time in progressing to the seduction phase, trying to get his next victim in the mood for sex. He would first entice the boys with porn magazines and then invite them to his nearby camper to watch pornographic movies. The tactic worked for most, but not all of them. Some of those who rejected his maneuvers were forced to participate in sexual acts. They didn't report him because he made them afraid of him. The suspect would show each of the boys his loaded handgun and he even let some of them shoot the gun. This strategy served two purposes. For some, it was a lure into spending time alone with him, and to test whether they could keep a secret. For all of the boys, it was a control method. Every one of them feared that the suspect would shoot them if they told on him. This is most likely what allowed this predator to do so much damage before he was exposed.

This predator was bold. The balding thirty-something man had no problem approaching parents in the apartment complex and telling them how much he enjoyed their son's company. He would offer to take the boy fishing or to the sports card store. He would refer to other parents by name, which implied that they knew him to be of good character. To the unsuspecting parent, this personable, unassuming, man of short stature was harmless—nothing more than a young boy trapped in a man's body. Little did they know how ruthless and conniving he really was when alone with their child.

Eventually, the suspect was taken into custody and charged with multiple counts of sexual abuse and sodomy. Some of the offenses included elements of force and coercion. Represented by one of the top criminal lawyers in the Rochester area, the suspect eventually negotiated a plea agreement that allowed him to plead guilty to a lesser sentence. Most of the young male victims did not want to testify for fear of being exposed in a highly-publicized trial, so the District Attorney's Office reluctantly offered a prison sentence that maxed out at approximately twenty-eight years. While some would criticize a prosecutor for working out a plea agreement with such a monster, we do well to consider how we would feel if it was our child facing the strain of a years-long public trial and an even longer appeal process.

After the suspect was sentenced, the County Court judge decided to release him temporarily over the prosecutor's protest. This was to afford the suspect an opportunity to get his personal affairs in order and spend some time with his elderly parents. Just as the prosecutor had warned, the suspect jumped bail and never voluntarily returned to begin his prison sentence. He was deemed a fugitive and a media blitz ensued. The community was justifiably angry with the judge who unnecessarily released this convicted child molester who liked to arm himself with a loaded weapon. The victims and their families were terrified. This bad decision eventually cost the judge his position on the bench when it came time to renew his term. No child was safe while this desperate predator was on the run with nothing to lose.

The Monroe County Sheriff's Office launched a nationwide manhunt operation with the assistance of other local, state, and federal law enforcement agencies. The suspect was featured on the popular television show *America's Most Wanted*. Deputy Barrus was sent to the show's studio to field phone calls after it was aired. As a result of a phone tip, the suspect was apprehended in a small town forty-five minutes west of Rochester. Nearly four months after he went on the lam, he was located not too far from his home, just as Investigator Connors had always suspected. Shortly after he was in custody, the suspect confirmed to Investigator Connors that he had been hiding at his parent's residence for most of that time. Charges were never brought against the suspect's parents for harboring him, but he was charged with jumping bail and was immediately sent off to begin his prison sentence.

What started out as a routine "suspicious person" call from two concerned mothers mushroomed into a high-profile criminal investigation with an arrest and conviction of an armed and dangerous child predator. His reign of evil ended because of the intuition of two concerned mothers and excellent police work.

SECOND CASE

The suspect in the second case was a twenty-seven-year old full-time school sentry and coach employed by the Rochester City School District. He served as a deacon at his church and had been appointed to the Rochester Police Department Clergy Response Team. The team consists of selected ministers and pastors from local churches who respond to homicide scenes to comfort and counsel family members of the victims.

The gregarious suspect easily endeared himself to the students at the middle school where he worked. He particularly sought out young males who were lacking a father figure at home. The suspect would gain the trust of the boys' mothers by offering his time and attention to their sons to help groom them into productive young men. What struggling mother would not have welcomed assistance from such a man? He pledged to be their personal mentor, kept an eye on them at school, and steered them away from trouble. He was a deacon at his church and worked closely with the police department. Frankly, there was no logical reason not to accept this man's offer to be a positive influence in the midst of a mostly treacherous urban environment of drugs and violence.

On one occasion, the suspect showed up at the house of a single mother of five boys. He had become friendly with her two oldest boys at the school through his job. One of them was starting to get into some minor trouble, which concerned his mother. So when the suspect offered to mentor her sons, he was welcomed with open arms. Over the following seven years the suspect became a trusted friend of this very appreciative woman. From her vantage point and the community's, the suspect represented everything that any struggling parent of five boys could ask for.

Early in their friendship, the suspect was accused of inappropriate sexual contact with another young male, and for approximately eight months he was suspended from his job at the school. However, he was subsequently found not guilty due to the lack of physical evidence and uncorroborated testimony of the victim. After trial, the suspect was reinstated to his job and even assigned to the same school. The suspect led the mother to believe that his accuser was a disgruntled student bent on revenge.

The suspect eventually became an honorary member of the family. He developed a close relationship with the woman's youngest son, who was shy and timid. So impressed by this man and the positive role he appeared to be playing in her son's life, the victim's mother asked the suspect to become the boy's godfather. Over the years he showered the lad with gifts that included a cell phone, a YMCA membership, new school clothes every year, and spending money. He took the boy on overnight trips to Buffalo and paid for his plane ticket when he moved to Florida to live with his maternal grandmother. The boy's relationship with the suspect appeared to be a great blessing. But all of that changed with one phone call.

Shortly after his arrival in Florida, he disclosed nearly seven years of sexual molestation at the hands of his trusted mentor. Once out of the control of the suspect, the victim, now in his late teens, had time to digest what he had been subjected to. It was too much for him to bear, and he had an emotional meltdown. The telephone call to the victim's mother set off a chain reaction of shock and anger. The mother immediately called the suspect and confronted him with the allegations. Surprisingly, the suspect admitted to the abuse, saying, "I fell weak," and that he was now immersed in his own emotional turmoil. This could have been an attempt to appease the victim's mother and gain her sympathy so that she would not call the police. It didn't work; she filed a report with the Rochester Police Department.

Investigator Doug Boccardo, of the RPD Eastside Division Criminal Investigation Unit, was briefed by the patrol officer who took the initial report from the victim's mother. Investigator Boccardo has been an investigator as long as I have, and has dealt with just as much human carnage, if not more. His silver hair and light complexion are reminiscent of a scholarly school administrator. His features and sincere, friendly demeanor belie the skill and tenacity of one of the best in our profession. His sensitivity and dedication to seeking the truth are second to none. I have witnessed my colleague solve many big cases that would normally have remained in the unsolved file, passionately following through even when it took months or years to make the arrest.

Upon meeting the victim's distraught mother, Investigator Boccardo suggested that she make a second phone call to the suspect and allow the police to record their conversation. The victim's mother was successful in getting the suspect to admit that he molested her son "a couple of times." Even though the suspect minimized his criminal behavior—he had molested this young boy over 100 times—his admission weighed heavy on Lady Justice's scales of evidence. This turned out to be a crucial investigative tactic, because the suspect's recorded admissions became the cornerstone of the prosecution. As far as I am concerned, that type of admission is cleaner than any police-obtained confession. This was a voluntary discussion between the suspect and another civilian over the telephone. The usual legal issue of voluntariness connected to an admission or confession gained as a result of a police interview would not apply.

Shortly after the recorded control call, the victim's twin sister took it upon herself to confront the suspect. Investigator Boccardo and the victim's mother were unaware of her plan. She approached him at school while he was working. After quickly ushering her back outside so that no one could hear their conversation, the suspect told her that he could not talk to her about the allegations. She did not accept such a response, and continued to press him for an explanation. The young girl's line of questioning closely simulated that of an experienced interrogator. She asked the suspect if he was homosexual or bisexual. He responded, "No." She then confronted him about how he had attempted to stop her brother from dating a twenty-one year old girl by protesting to their mother that the victim wasn't mature enough for such a relationship. And yet, the suspect considered it okay for him to have anal sex with her brother. The suspect eventually relented and told her that he "fell weak," saying that it was a mistake. Attempting to gain her sympathy and rationalize his behavior, the suspect told her that he was abused by his uncle when he was a child. He attempted to downplay his actions by saying that it had occurred "only a couple of times" over the past year. He also offered that in his tortured state he hadn't slept or eaten in days. Understandably, the victim's sister showed no sympathy and reported her entire conversation to Investigator Boccardo. While this was unfolding as a very tragic scenario, from an investigative standpoint it was shaping up into a prosecutable case, with three verbal admissions by the suspect made apart from a police interrogation.

On the following morning Investigator Boccardo, with the assistance of his colleague, Investigator Tom Baccanti, responded to the suspect's school to conduct a non-custodial interview. The suspect nervously ushered them to the auditorium for privacy. While standing among the empty seats in the dim light of the school assembly room, Investigator Boccardo explained the purpose of the meeting. The suspect acknowledged that he was aware of the allegations, but denied any wrongdoing. He suggested that the victim had made them up because he was angry with him for expressing concern to the victim's mother about the victim's relationship with his girlfriend, who was a few years older than he was.

Investigator Boccardo asked the suspect about the most recent telephone conversation he had with the victim's mother. His depiction of the conversation was remarkably different than what Investigator Boccardo knew it to be. Investigator Boccardo opted not to share that the conversation had been recorded until the suspect was in custody. The purpose of this interview was to develop a rapport with the suspect and allow him the opportunity to respond candidly to the allegations in a non-adversarial setting. Many times the suspects are dishonest, which just offers more material for us to use against them in the future. If nothing else, it demonstrates that they are not only a child molester, but a liar as well. Investigator Boccardo closed the interview by thanking the suspect for his cooperation and time, and advised the suspect that he would get back in touch with him.

Because the victim was living in Florida and attending school, Investigator Boccardo had to interview him over the telephone. The emotionally-spent young man confirmed everything that was initially reported by his mother. Under the investigator's gentle questioning, the victim provided additional details.

Investigator Boccardo eventually arrested the suspect without incident. He invoked his right to counsel and refused to make any further statements to the police. After the suspect's incarceration, Investigator Boccardo continued with his investigation and took it upon himself to question the victim's older brothers about their personal relationship with the suspect. As a result, he learned that the suspect had molested each of the victim's older four brothers over the past decade as he "mentored" them through their adolescent years. One of the boys had once mentioned the abuse to their mother, but she quickly dismissed the statement as the ramblings of an overly-imaginative teenage boy, since none of the other boys had ever said anything. No one wants to believe that someone who possesses such good external qualities and has gained our trust would be capable of committing such reprehensible acts against children. It was a decision that she now greatly regrets.

A search warrant was executed on the suspect's personal vehicle, which had been impounded and repossessed by the bank during the investigation. Investigator Boccardo did not execute a search warrant on the suspect's residence because he learned that the suspect's family had cleaned the place out at the time of his arrest. But because the suspect's vehicle had not been at their disposal to remove potential evidence, it was deemed worth searching. Police found a Rochester Police Department identification card hanging on the rearview mirror of his vehicle. A jacket that was issued by the Rochester Police Department, bearing its patch and insignia, was found hanging in one of the rear windows. Both items were issued to the suspect when he joined the Rochester Police Department's Clergy Emergency Response Team. An empty handgun holster and a laptop computer carrying case were also found in the suspect's vehicle. The handgun and laptop were never found. The suspect never possessed a pistol permit, nor was it ever clearly established that he possessed a handgun. The empty holster could have served as a prop to lead his victims to believe that he possessed one. Most likely, the missing laptop contained child porn, since Investigator Boccardo received intelligence that the suspect spent a lot of time looking at it.

There is no doubt in our minds that the suspect purposely had the police symbols visible to present himself as a person of authority and trust in the community, and also to lure young boys into his vehicle. Child predators will use any program designed for doing good in the community to enable them to carry out their devious schemes.

The suspect's arrest received a large amount of media coverage, primarily because he was employed by the city school district and had used his official capacity to gain trust and access to his victims. The publicity prompted four additional male victims to come forward and testify how the suspect had molested them while he was their mentor. Investigator Boccardo met with each of those victims and introduced them to the prosecutor of the case, Monroe County Assistant District Attorney Kristina Karle. Most field investigators would have moved on after arresting the suspect for his crimes against the first victim, and they would be within their right to do so because of the volume of violent cases they handle on a daily basis. Investigator Boccardo continued to dig and escort additional victims to the grand jury. His investigation revealed that the suspect had molested a total of ten boys in various venues that included his church, the school, his apartment, and his vehicle. The suspect had even molested his own thirteen-year-old brother-in-law. Investigator Boccardo stayed in touch with each victim during the following months as they prepared for trial. He even took the time to bring one of the victims who had been raped by the suspect to the courtroom he would later testify in to allow him the opportunity to observe another trial in progress. This investigator's dedication, sensitivity to the victims and professionalism went above and beyond all expectations. According to Ms. Karle, Investigator Boccardo is considered the one most responsible for the successful prosecution of this case. He instilled confidence in each of the victims and gained their trust to openly talk about the suspects egregious and humiliating acts.

Nine of the ten male victims courageously walked into court and testified in a packed courtroom located on the fourth floor of the Hall of Justice. The boys and young men each shared their own tragic story as to what the suspect had done to them, attempted to do, or seduced them into doing.

As many child predators do, this suspect placed his confidence in believing that shame, embarrassment and fear of exposure would prevent these witnesses from testifying against him in a highly-publicized trial. Honestly, I don't know if I would have possessed the courage to do what they did if I were in their situation. It is my sincere hope that the process of openly confronting their abuser in a courtroom will help them recover from the emotional wreckage. Fortunately, their brave efforts were not in vain. The suspect was convicted of twenty-four counts of various degrees of crimes related to the molestation and rape of the nine boys. Being able to hear the suspect admitting to a victim's mother that he had molested her son during a recorded telephone conversation sealed this case and removed any reasonable doubt that the jury may have harbored. At his sentencing, the suspect was arrogant and without remorse, claiming that his conviction was the result of Assistant District Attorney Kristina Karle's Oscar-winning performance before the jurors. The judge disagreed with his criticism and sentenced him to twenty-nine to thirty-nine years in prison.

This case embodies many of the signature traits of a child predator operating in our midst while under the guise of an authoritative position in the community or trusted friend. Countless worried single mothers in our inner city neighborhoods are seeking real, solid male role models for their sons to follow after to keep them from succumbing to the violence that is perpetuated from the gang activity and drug trafficking. From an outward appearance, this suspect fit the bill as one of those much-needed role models. This well-crafted criminal investigation uncovered his crimes against children over a nine-year period. One can only imagine how many crimes this criminal committed against other unidentified young boys that he has yet to be held accountable for.

Coaches prepare their players for competition through the repetition of certain plays and drills, or "reps" as athletes call them. Through the case examples you have repeatedly observed how a child predator places themselves in your midst and patiently waits for you to become lax, which we all do. It was my mission to drill these foundational principles into your memory with the hope that it would build wisdom, but not paranoia. I am confident that whether your child is a preschooler, an elementary student, or an adolescent, when certain scenarios present themselves you will be able to recognize what an experienced police investigator or child protective worker would inevitably see as red flags." Our children are safest when we watch carefully for the undetected serpents among us.

SECTION III

—⟩⟩⟩—

THE VIOLENT SEX OFFENDER

SECTION III

—ᴎ—

INTRODUCTION

*W*hen a violent sex offender strikes, it sends a chill of reasonable fear throughout the community in which it occurred. Crimes where the victim was abducted and the perpetrator was not apprehended are particularly disturbing. Usually it will include a serious physical assault, torture or even the death of the victim. Adding to that tragedy, the murderer may hide the victim's body, never to be recovered.

Every long-standing police detective has worked on a handful of cases that have galvanized his soul. These are the cases that a detective will carry around until the end of his days, for they are embedded in his bones. Every major crime investigation is worth remembering, but most of them are replaced with others over the years. The following cases are two of about a dozen investigations that I have carried around over the past eighteen years as a Major Crimes Investigator and will most likely stay with me until my time on earth comes to an end. They demonstrate just how cold and calculating a violent sex offender can be when it comes to locating their next victim.

CHAPTER 14

—⟋⟍—

TREE JUMPER

"*Certainly there is no hunting like the hunting of man and those who have hunted armed men long enough and liked it, never really care for anything else thereafter.*"
Ernest Hemingway,
"On the Blue Water," *Esquire*, April 1936

During the winter and spring of 1992, several women in the greater Rochester area were raped in their apartments. Another woman disappeared from her apartment without a trace. Investigators from the Monroe County Sheriff's Office, Greece Police Department, and Gates Police Department teamed up to investigate and arrest the person or persons responsible.

Our first case was a burglary-rape that occurred in the Town of Henrietta. My partner Tom Vasile and I responded to the early morning call-out. A single mother of two was raped in her apartment by a stranger upon her return home from an evening out with her coworkers and friends. Her children were not home at the time. From law enforcement's point of view, these are some of the most vicious crimes committed against a person, and some of the most difficult to solve. A large percentage of rapes are committed by someone known by or at least familiar to the victim. These are easier cases to resolve by an arrest, as the positive identification of the perpetrator is not an issue. When the victim does not know her attacker, it is more challenging for law enforcement to prove. Until the perpetrator can be identified and apprehended, the victim bears an added trauma: she is forced to live with the knowledge that her assailant is still lurking about and could attack her again at any time.

In a prison environment, these types of rapists are branded with the moniker "tree jumper." Most convicts have family members of their own that they care about in the outside world. They worry about the safety of their mothers, sisters, daughters, or wives just as we do. They recognize that the tree jumper could very well attack one of their loved ones, for jumpers randomly choose victims that they do not know. Next to child molesters, rapists are the most hated criminals in a prison population, often suffering some form of retribution at the hands of other convicts.

The victim's apartment was located in a large complex on the south side of Monroe County, which is widely known for its large population of retail stores, restaurants, and one of the area's major shopping malls. This area borders the New York State Thruway, making it easily accessible to interstate-traveling, transient types. The victim had already been transported to the hospital by the time Tom Vasile and I arrived on scene. The patrol deputies and command officers at the crime scene advised us of the circumstances of the attack, which apparently lasted most of the night and early morning.

It appeared that the perpetrator was already in the apartment awaiting the victim's return. Hearing this fact made my mind drift to how afraid my wife is to enter our darkened home alone at night. That nightmarish thought turned into a horrible reality for this single working mother of two.

The apartment was very clean and well kept. The first responding deputy informed us that, according to the victim, when the perpetrator first attacked and blindfolded her, he wore a hockey goalie mask similar to the one worn by the Jason character in the *Friday the 13th* horror movies. We saw a pull cord from the window blinds in the living room lying on the floor of the victim's bedroom. It had been used to tie her hands to the headboard of her bed. Certain places in the apartment had been wiped clean by the perpetrator, and he had forced the victim to shower and wash her bedsheets after the attack. These chilling facts led us to conclude that the rapist had already done hard time in prison for sexual assault, and most likely had been convicted by trace evidence. It was obvious to Tom and me that we were after a genuine tree jumper who had perfected his sick game.

A canvass of the apartment building and surrounding buildings turned up nothing conclusive, just a report of a suspicious vehicle seen in the area a few days earlier. The description did not include a license plate number. Our preliminary investigation produced nothing more than a severely traumatized victim who was barely able to talk about the attack, and the realization that we had no evidence to work with and no leads to follow.

On Memorial Day weekend, Tom and I were called in from home early in the morning to the scene of another attack at an apartment complex in the Town of Penfield. This time there were two victims, a single mother and her teenage daughter. The mother was sitting up in bed watching the late news when her daughter arrived home after going out to dinner with her school friends. The daughter was excited about the upcoming school prom; they sat on her bed together and talked about those preparations that moms and daughters love to discuss. They shared an intimate moment that was meant to be a joyful memory in both of their lives for years to come. This precious memory was stolen by an evil criminal.

The daughter retired to her room for the night across the hall from her mother's bedroom, which was on the second floor of the two-story, townhouse-style apartment. The mother recalled sitting up in bed reading a book while *The Johnny Carson Show* played on the television when she noticed a large, masked figure standing in her bedroom doorway. Without saying a word, the intruder jumped onto her and began attacking her. I will spare you the gruesome details and simply share that this animal tied up the mother and her daughter in their respective bedrooms and sexually assaulted both of them. Each victim could hear the other being assaulted throughout this horrific night. Every time I think about this case it pierces my heart. I think of how my own daughters and wife bask in the safety and sanctity of our home, enjoying many special mother-daughter moments. The thought of this mother and daughter being violently attacked in what is supposed to be their personal haven and robbed of those cherished moments fills me with anger and hatred.

Once again, the perp did not leave us any clues to work with. A neighborhood canvass was fruitless and there was no physical evidence. We were left with nothing but our own seething anger and a burning desire to keep seeking answers. Since we had nothing tangible to further our investigations, Tom and I reached out to the other police agencies in the area. We soon learned that the Gates Police Department was investigating a rape that appeared to be similar in *modus operandi* (otherwise known as M.O.). The victim lived alone in an apartment complex and was attacked by an unknown intruder who spent most of the night sexually assaulting her. The perpetrator did not leave behind any workable evidence. The assailants in the Henrietta, Penfield and Gates attacks were all described as a Caucasian with a large build.

We also learned that the Greece Police Department was investigating the report of a missing young woman who lived alone in an apartment complex in their town. She was a young music teacher with a promising career and bright future ahead of her. Her vehicle was later found at the Greater Rochester International Airport. The investigation was a high-profile item in the media, receiving headline coverage for a sustained period of time. Much to their credit, the police in Greece were not showing their hand, which left the case open to much public speculation.

During their missing person investigation, the detectives from Greece had discovered that a man named Ed Laraby was employed at the apartment complex where the missing woman lived. Mr. Laraby, a Caucasian with red hair and a large build, was currently on parole for robbery. Back in 1983, he attacked a mother and her teenage daughter while they were walking on the canal path, a popular hiking and biking trail that runs along the historic and picturesque Erie

Canal. During the attack, Laraby wore one of those horrific-looking rubber Halloween masks, jumped out of the bushes, grabbed the woman's daughter and held a knife to her throat. Then he tied their hands together and robbed them. Further background investigation revealed that Laraby had been sent to prison after raping a fifteen-year-old girl and a seventeen-year-old girl in separate incidents in 1973. While wearing a ski mask, he kidnapped the fifteen-year-old at knife point, bound and gagged her, and then cut her clothes off with the knife. Laraby forced the seventeen-year-old into his vehicle as she was walking in a populated commercial area, and then drove her to a secluded area and raped her. Both crimes occurred in two of the more affluent eastside communities of Monroe County.

In 1980, Laraby's conviction was reversed on a legal technicality and he was released from prison. Shortly after his release, Laraby abducted another teenage girl at knife-point, tied her up and then forced her to commit oral sex on him. Incredulously, the judge released him after his arraignment. Laraby then attempted to escape to Canada, but he was arrested at the border. He later pled guilty to the attack and was sentenced to two to seven years of incarceration. Shortly after his re-incarceration, he was released yet again on a legal technicality that had nothing to do with his innocence or guilt. This left him free to continue to offend until he was arrested for the aforementioned attacks on the canal path in 1983.

Based upon his criminal history, M.O. and employment connection to the apartment complex of the missing woman, Ed Laraby was turning out to be a viable suspect.

Additional facts made him look even better: we had a perpetrator who was making his victims clean up after the sexual
assaults, indicative of a criminal who had been educated
about the legal importance of physical evidence; and while
the victims were unable to positively identify their masked
assailant, they described him as a large white male. Laraby
was big and he liked to use masks during his attacks.

Other graphic facts made him a likely suspect for
these crimes. The despicable things that the perp did to the
victims during these assaults were similar in the three cases
and appeared to have been learned from a prison environment. Anyone who has served hard time in prison knows all
too well that convicts are violently raped and sodomized by
other convicts. There are certain things that occur during
those sexual assaults that are specific to that particular environment. Consequently, many convicts adopt those behaviors
and continue them upon their release back into society. The
detective who frequently conducts investigations of reported
sexual assaults can recognize these very distinctive signa-
tures while debriefing a victim about the nature of the assault
and the assailant. Based on what we had learned about Ed
Laraby, he fit the bill in all aspects of these cases.

We had to come up with a plan on how we were going to investigate Mr. Laraby as a potential suspect and not
miss the opportunity to arrest him if it should arise. That was
much easier said than done. Mr. Laraby, as we knew from his
past, did not talk to the police. So picking him up for an interview was not a viable option. He would most likely invoke
his right to a lawyer and remain silent, and he would stop the
attacks since he would know that we were on to him. And

since none of the police agencies had any physical evidence to compare with a potential suspect, there was no way to corroborate our theory yet.

We were left with two options: set up surveillance on as many apartment complexes as possible in the area of Monroe County, which wasn't feasible based on the huge amount of manpower and resources that would be needed, or conduct a physical surveillance on Mr. Laraby. Following him around until he attacked his next victim was not an easy option either. Doing that without the suspect finding out is nearly impossible if you don't have a small army to do it with, and that wasn't going to happen. Nevertheless, with what we knew, we couldn't just sit around and do nothing. So each of the police departments designated a few investigators, and together we kept Mr. Laraby under surveillance during the evening hours.

Our team of seven investigators monitored the suspect seven days a week, from 8:00 PM until he went home for the night. He worked the B shift (3:00 PM to 11:00 PM) at a local machine shop on the west side of the city. We quickly learned that he liked to frequent several bars in the area, drinking for a few hours in violation of his parole, and then he would go out hunting for his next potential victim. On the nights that he didn't work, Mr. Laraby stayed close to home.

Laraby lived in a modest residential neighborhood in the Town of Greece, which is in the northwest area of Monroe County. A large Marriott Hotel housed a popular nightclub near his residence. Across the street from the club was a supermarket parking lot that proved to be a convenient location for many of the nightclub's patrons to hook up after the bar closed. Because the surveillance team staged in that parking lot when Laraby was at home, we obtained an uncensored insight into human behavior in the underworld of those looking for love in all of the wrong places. We wondered how they would feel if they knew that seven undercover cops were observing their every move.

During that particular summer, the Rochester area was blitzed with frequent and severe lightning storms, most of which occurred during the evening. The violent weather exacerbated my family's stress over my nighttime absences. My wife and young children were terrified and hardly slept a wink that summer. It didn't help that our house was struck by lightning twice during that time. Once, a large flame shot out of the wall light switch in our front foyer. The intense heat melted it, causing the house to reek of melted plastic and burning electrical wires. We even had to call the fire department to make sure that a fire wasn't smoldering in our walls.

For the first three weeks of surveillance, Laraby stuck to the same pattern. Because of all the media attention on the apartment complex rapes and added police patrols, he steered clear of those locations. Instead, he started driving around residential neighborhoods, peering into windows of single family dwellings. It was very stressful to watch such a criminal engage in this type of behavior, knowing what he was capable of doing to another human being. If we lost him or miscalculated his movements, he might have raped or even murdered a woman right under our noses. This was something that none of us wanted to have on our conscience.

By his movements and driving patterns, it appeared that Ed was getting restless and wanted some action. This, I believe, led him to the Lyell Ave area, which is one of several locations in the city where one can meet a prostitute who will take a ride with them. Sometime around 3:00 AM, near the end of our shift, Ed ended up pulling over and picking up a white female prostitute. He drove her to an industrial area on the west side of the city between Gates and Greece. We lost him and were unable to locate his truck for fifteen minutes. We were extremely dismayed, for that window of opportunity provided a criminal like Laraby enough time to choke someone and hastily dump their body. The fact that the woman was a prostitute did not make her life any less important. Her life hung in the balance, and we had to find him. Praise God, as I was driving down one of the streets in the area with all of the windows down, I heard a woman screaming. The road was very dark because there wasn't much traffic, nor were there many street lights. I stopped the car to listen. Then, out of the darkness, a young woman ran up to my car from behind one of the buildings, begging me to help her, screaming "He's trying to kill me!" Before I had time to respond, she jumped into the front passenger seat and yelled, "Get going! He's going to kill us!"

At this moment I observed a large figure running along the road in the dark up ahead of us. I was unable to grab my portable radio to call for back-up because the terrified woman had sat on it when she jumped into the car. Not wanting to lose sight of Ed running away, I gave chase by driving the car up next to him as he was running. I then hit the brakes hard just ahead of him and jumped out to meet him.

Since I was alone and it was dark, I drew my 9mm pistol on him, ordering him to stop. Ed stopped, but he appeared to be intoxicated. He started getting belligerent with me, making movements with his hands toward his waistband like he was trying to grab something. Since he was wearing an unbuttoned flannel shirt over a T-shirt, I couldn't see if anything was there. He turned halfway around like he was going to take off and then I noticed a bulge in the small of his back under the flannel shirt. This increased my sense of alarm. I ordered him to turn around, and I felt the instinctive movement of my finger starting to gently pull the hammer of my pistol back as Ed turned and faced me.

Ed then made a half-hearted attempt to get around the front of my car. Not wanting him to escape, but not having the legal authority to shoot him if he fled, I lunged and shoved him over the hood of my car. Being a big guy, Ed was hard to control once I had him on the hood. I had limited use of my strong hand, which was still holding my service weapon. Wrestling someone with a gun in one hand creates a grave risk for the policeman. A handgun is not loyal to its owner like a police dog: it will turn on you if it gets into the perpetrator's hands. Laraby was a heavy, strong guy with nothing to lose. Praise the Lord, a partner and friend, Glen Grana, arrived on the scene just as I was taking Ed down over the hood. Glen assisted me with gaining control and handcuffing him.

The victim had been screaming hysterically as she sat in the car while I was trying to get control of Ed, not realizing that we were the police until the event was over. After she finally calmed down, I informed her that we needed to talk to her. The prostitute, who identified herself as "Kim", was reluctant to cooperate, but she did share that Ed had driven her behind one of the buildings. After he parked the truck, they stepped out and sat on a picnic table to have sex. When Ed started to act abusive, Kim called the deal off and gave Ed his twelve dollars back. When she attempted to leave, Ed wrapped his big arm around her tiny neck and began choking her. Kim said that her feet were dangling in the air as she struggled to break loose. By the look of Ed's face and neck, Kim must have fought like a frenzied polecat during the attack. Ed then threw her violently to the ground. At this point she began pleading with him and he stopped the attack for a moment. That's when Kim made the move that saved her life: she got up and ran, screaming for help.

Typical of these incidents, the prostitute did not want to pursue criminal charges against her attacker. She demanded that we either release her or arrest her. We contacted Chuck Siragusa, who was the First Assistant to the Monroe County District Attorney at the time (he now serves as a federal judge in the U.S. District Court of Western New York). Unfortunately, he told us what we already knew—without the cooperation of the young prostitute, we had no case against Mr. Laraby. So we let her go. Now the question was, what should we do with Ed? And what type of explanation were we going to offer him as to why undercover police officers were there to rescue the young prostitute? We transported him to my office to afford me more time to think.

With a smirk on his lips and an overly friendly tone, Ed admitted meeting the prostitute for sex. He acknowledged that he had paid her, but claimed that she had tried to steal money from him while they were taking their pants off. Mr. Laraby's story wasn't far-fetched, for prostitutes are known to steal from their solicitors (also known as johns). I allowed him to believe that his slick buddy-buddy approach was softening me up. He then politely invoked his right to an attorney and refused to speak with us about the matter any further.

I told Mr. Laraby that we were operating a hooker detail along Lyell Ave. I also explained that while he had gotten caught in our web, since we were unable to catch them in the act, we were going to cut him some slack and let him go. He asked me if I was going to call his parole officer. I told him that I wouldn't, however he'd owe me a favor sometime in the future. I then supplied him with the information that he needed to retrieve his truck from the auto impound. Aside from the inconvenience and a stiff towing and storage fee, Mr. Laraby got away with attempted murder. Two members of the team, Glen Grana and Bob Trowbridge, drove Ed home and we called it a wrap for the night, which had already turned into morning.

Ed laid low for the next several days after he paid to get his truck out of the auto pound. We figured that he didn't have any money to go out drinking after work. So it made for any easy week, just hanging out and watching the rain pound on our windshields, listening to Dr. Ruth talk to sexually troubled people on late-night radio. We ate a lot of ice cream and other forbidden foods like pizza, burgers, hot dogs, and Buffalo-style chicken wings. What a life. While the rest of the world was sleeping, here we were, sitting in our undercover vehicles in a deserted parking lot in the middle of the night, watching ground-shaking thunderstorms blow in and out, eating junk food and listening to a seventy-year-old woman talk about sex and masturbation on the radio to stay awake. Only in police work.

Within a week or so, Ed was on the move again. He started leaving work at 11:00 PM and trolling the city night-club district in search of potential victims. Once again, we stalked the predator as he stalked his prey. Ed stayed away from the prostitutes, just as I had directed him. This time his travel appeared to be focused on the east side of the city and county. About six weeks into our surveillance detail, Ed made his move. We were in the downtown nightclub district, near a bar called "Heaven," which was a popular hangout for college students and younger adults. On weekend nights, the club crowd usually spilled over into the small side street and sidewalk. Ed would continually drive around a few blocks, lurking and looking, slowly moving in and out of traffic. He liked to park his truck and just watch his potential prey parade by, totally unaware of the danger that was just a few feet away. Ed's actions resembled that of a great white shark swimming among other species when he drove around this area. If some of these seductively-dressed young women had only known how close they were to a rapist and suspected murderer during those summer nights. Their physical appearance was like blood in the water to this creature.

We were afraid that Ed would just open his truck door and yank one of these unsuspecting young women into his truck and force her down onto the floor. This was a real concern because Ed's truck wasn't always in our sight. Being downtown, it was difficult to stay close to him without crossing his line of vision. While he didn't appear too concerned about whether he was being followed, Ed would get nervous if he observed the same vehicles and drivers showing up around him. It was a delicate balance to maintain—to stay loose enough to allow our target enough room to make his move, but close enough to not lose him without blowing our cover. I could only hope and pray that we would be right there when he pounced. Knowing that a kidnapping and violent assault could literally occur right under our noses was a serious concern for all of us. First, I give credit to God for our success in preventing such a tragedy from occurring. Secondly, I give credit to the members of the surveillance team for their skill and professionalism under extreme pressure, and not blowing our cover and the entire operation.

Ed picked out a potential victim, a petite young woman with long, curly blond hair, wearing skin-tight spandex pants and stiletto heels. She was walking away from the nightclub during the late evening hours. He continued to slowly drive around each block, circling and stalking her, as she continued eastbound on East Avenue. East Avenue is lined with ornate street lamps and beautiful old mansions with large manicured yards. It was once home to George Eastman, the founder of Eastman Kodak, and it continues to serve as home for many of the wealthy in our area. Incredibly, this petite young woman walked out of the downtown district by herself on the sidewalk that follows along historical East Avenue.

Laraby eventually parked his truck on one of the side streets that connects East Avenue with Park Avenue and started following his prey on foot. We watched him slowly gain ground on the unsuspecting woman as she continued walking eastbound. Once she was walking through a long stretch of darkness provided by some heavy foliage, Ed made his move. He ran up from behind her and wrapped his arm around her neck. The force of his attack lifted the victim's feet right off the ground and he pulled her into some shrubs adjacent to the sidewalk. At that point they were out of our sight. There were some large trees on the other side of the shrubs which provided plenty of concealment for the ongoing attack.

The stress we were experiencing at this moment was like nothing I had ever experienced. Here we had a vicious predator beginning to devour a victim right under our noses and we had to stand by just long enough to allow him the time to start tearing her clothes off to show his intent to sexually assault her. This victim was not just a decoy we were using to catch this monster; she was someone's child and loved one. As we prepared to close in and stop the attack, I started the "one-one-thousand count" to ten and was about halfway through it when Laraby bolted from the bushes, ran back to his truck, and drove off. I directed the team not to follow him. We could grab him anytime. Instead, we ran to assist the victim who had not reappeared from the shrubs. Once again, I was worried that something went terribly wrong and Laraby had seriously injured or killed her. It only takes a second to snap someone's neck or plunge a knife into their chest cavity.

By the time we reached the victim, she was back on her feet and attempting to make her way out of the foliage. Thank God, she didn't appear to be seriously injured, just shaken up. We immediately determined why Ed aborted his attack and ran like a bolt of lightning. This little blond bombshell in the tight spandex pants and high heels had five o'clock shadow growing on her face and an Adam's apple protruding from her throat. She was, in fact, a he. We could do nothing but laugh, wondering what went through Laraby's mind when he felt the man's beard stubble beneath his hand as he was forcefully pressing it over his mouth. I would have loved to see the expression on Ed's face at that moment.

Once again, God was on our side. Had we closed in on Laraby too quickly, we would have exposed our surveillance of him and blown the whole case. It was literally a matter of another two seconds. Once we made sure that our cross-dressing, alternative-lifestyle citizen was safely transported home, the team confirmed that Laraby drove directly to his residence after his failed attempt. I figured that if there was ever a time that Laraby would wonder if he should pack it in and go straight, this would have been it.

True to form, Ed laid low for another week or so before he started getting active again. We endured another several days of sitting around a deserted parking lot watching unsuspecting bar patrons from the Marriott Hotel hooking up in their cars to fornicate the night away in front of a half-dozen undercover cops. Instead of listening to Dr. Ruth on the radio, I managed to catch up on my recreational reading.

Sometime around the seventh week of our surveillance detail, Ed got his mojo back and was getting antsy. Once again, he started going out drinking and cruising after work. It was obvious that despite his two failed attempts that included a stern warning from the police to stay out of trouble, Ed couldn't control his desire to hunt and rape women. It was as if he were possessed by some evil demon that could only be satisfied by the violent act of rape.

Laraby would periodically park in a residential neighborhood and exit his truck. After hanging out around the truck for a few minutes, probably to see if he was being followed, he would walk around and peer into house windows. We figured that he was trying to find a female that was home alone. It was pretty wild to watch this monster hide in the bushes next to a house, staring into the window. Ed liked to choose houses that were surrounded with plenty of bushes and trees, for they served as great cover for him. For whatever reason, Laraby never attempted to enter one of those dwellings while he was under our surveillance. I am thankful for that. Had we been forced to go into a residence after him, it would have presented a very dangerous situation. He could have easily taken the victim hostage in a dark house that was unfamiliar to us. Also, if Laraby had entered someone's home while we were conducting a physical surveillance on him, it would have been a public relations disaster for the Monroe County Sheriff. How could we justify allowing Laraby to commit the crime of burglary in order to build a criminal case, instead of protecting the person that was inside the home? To prevent this PR nightmare, we would have had to grab Laraby just as he was in the process of breaking in. This would have allowed us to charge him with attempted burglary of a residence, which is considered a felony in New York State. Anything short of that would be a misdemeanor, and would not have accomplished our goal of locking this guy up for a long period of time.

So the pressure was on us to not prematurely close in on him and blow the case. We had to allow him the opportunity to start breaking in, but not allow him to gain entry into the home and take a potential hostage. The window of opportunity would only be open for a second or two to decide whether we should close in or not. It didn't help matters that we had to allow Laraby enough lead time so that he didn't observe us following him. The darkness, heavy rain, and the dark shadows of shrubs and trees made an already difficult surveillance task nearly impossible. The members of our team were extremely good at keeping their cool. If there was ever a time that we could have blown this case, it was during these very tense moments. Thanks to the competence and professionalism of my peers, and the grace of God, that did not happen.

After about nine nerve-wracking and wearisome weeks, our patience finally paid off. In the early morning of August 14th, 1992, Ed Laraby attacked again – and we were there to stop him. As he did many times in the past, Laraby was driving around and looking for potential prey after he got out of work the previous evening. The surveillance team lost Laraby at 11:35 PM in the area of Main and Broad Streets downtown. It wasn't until around 1:30 in the morning that we located his truck parked outside a saloon in East Rochester, which is approximately ten miles east of the city. These two hours out of our sight provided plenty of time to rape a victim and then go to a bar to revel in success and tie one on.

Laraby exited the bar at approximately 2:25 AM and got into his truck. He then drove to the Wegman's Supermarket on Fairport Road and went into the store. Ten minutes later Laraby went back to his truck and drove westbound on Monroe Avenue until he pulled into the parking lot of a fast-food restaurant. Laraby remained in his truck and turned the lights off. After sitting there for a moment, he continued driving westbound on Monroe Avenue. It was obvious to us that Ed was trying to figure out if he was being followed. His furtive behavior led us to believe that he was up to something.

Laraby continued westbound on Monroe Avenue well into the city, and then turned left onto Field Street, which is just east of the Interstate 490 junction with Monroe Avenue. In close proximity of that intersection was Grana's Restaurant, which was owned by one of the surveillance team members' uncles. I observed Laraby hawking two teenage females walking eastbound along Monroe Avenue in front of the restaurant, so I alerted the team that Laraby might be going around the block to do another drive-by. As suspected, Laraby turned back onto Monroe Avenue and drove by the two girls again as they continued walking eastbound on the sidewalk. Laraby then turned down a side street that was east of the female's location. He parked and continued the hunt on foot.

At first, Laraby walked eastbound on the sidewalk along Monroe Avenue, maintaining a position in front of the girls. It appeared that they didn't even notice that he was walking ahead of them. We figured that Laraby was looking for a place to hide himself, hoping that the girls would separate somewhere along the way. Moments later, Laraby did an about-face and began walking in a westbound direction directly toward the girls, who still appeared unaware of him. When Laraby met up with the girls on the sidewalk he continued walking right past them. Again, neither girl appeared to pay any attention as they passed. Laraby acted like a shark, greedily circling closer to its victim in anticipation of a fatal strike.

Just as we have seen numerous times on television shows that document the life and habits of various predators in the wild kingdom, Laraby did a second about-face and picked up his pace. He then broke into a short sprint toward his two unsuspecting victims and violently grabbed one from behind. Laraby wrapped one of his big arms around her neck and placed her in a choke hold. With his other hand he reached between the young woman's legs and grabbed her pubic area from behind. The force of the attack lifted the young woman's feet clear off the ground. Laraby then attempted to drag her backward, but the young woman fought back and was able to break free as Laraby stumbled. He let go and began running back to his truck—but it was too late. We closed in on Big Ed this time and took him down on the front lawn of a house on Monroe Ave. He put up a little bit of a fight, but he was no match for the likes of Investigators Bob Trowbridge, who reached him first, and Al Krause, affectionately known as "The Goon."

Because Laraby was combative even after he was handcuffed, we called for the city paddy wagon after the show-up was completed. (That is where the victim is given a chance to look at the suspect and tell the police if that was the person who attacked her.) It wasn't really necessary since we had at least six cops who witnessed the attack, but we did it anyway. It couldn't hurt our case. During the show-up, Laraby thrashed back and forth as Bob Trowbridge and I attempted to hold him still. Laraby kept saying, "just shoot me...just shoot me," repeatedly. Big Ed knew that he was going down. He had been caught fair and square in the middle of attacking another woman while attempting to kidnap and sexually assault her.

Upon its arrival, Laraby was placed inside the police wagon, where he was alone. He then proceeded to smash his face into a bloody pulp against the diamond-plated steel floor, yelling, "police brutality!" We didn't try to restrain him. In fact, we laughed at Laraby and photographed him during his tantrum to prove that we did not serve him any curb-side justice. The team members handled themselves like professionals and avoided any heavy-handed tactics with Laraby in spite of his antics. Eventually, Laraby ran out of gas and settled down. By the look of his face, he must have felt like someone hit him with a sledgehammer. We offered to take him to a hospital for treatment of his self-inflicted facial lacerations, but he refused, so we took him directly to jail. It was obvious that Laraby wanted his arrest mug shot to look as bad as it could so that he could accuse us of giving him a good old-fashioned police beating, but our photographs proved otherwise.

After we took detailed statements from our victim and her friend, we drove them home. I think it was about 7:00 AM when we finally called it a night. Because of how forcefully he grabbed the victim, we were able to charge Laraby with Sexual Abuse in the First Degree, which is a violent sex offense. Had Ed not grabbed her by the pubic area while he was choking and dragging her away, we would not have been able to charge him with a felony.

Monroe County Assistant District Attorney Ken Hyland was assigned to prosecute this case. Laraby retained

Mike Schiano as his defense attorney. As we were preparing for trial, Mr. Schiano advised Ken that Laraby wanted to work out a deal. Laraby offered to provide information regarding the whereabouts of the missing music teacher if the District Attorney's Office was willing to give him a lighter sentence. Laraby did not intend to confess to the kidnapping or murder of the young woman, but rather preface his information as secondhand. The Monroe County District Attorney's Office rejected Laraby's offer for the obvious reason that he was the leading suspect in that investigation. It was difficult to deny the young woman's family the ability to locate their daughter, but there was no way that we could give Ed Laraby a free pass for what we believed to be her murder. Fortunately, even without his "generous offer," the woman's body was located a few years later. It was discovered in a creek bed west of Rochester. That was consistent with the thoughts of a confidential informant close to Laraby and his family, who said that Ed liked to fish and had a small fishing boat. They had always thought that the young teacher's remains were buried somewhere near a body of water or at the bottom of a lake.

While Laraby was awaiting trial, we were alerted by the Monroe County Jail Bureau Command Staff that Laraby was planning to escape. He made the mistake of sharing his plan with another inmate who happened to be a trustee (someone who receives extra privileges for assisting the jail staff with duties in their cell block). The trustee told a deputy that Laraby planned to assault and overpower a female deputy and take her keys. Laraby expected to gain entry to one of the offices that has a window to the outside and then lower himself to the ground with some bedding tied together. This elevated his inmate status to high-risk. As a result, he was placed in a "box" and kept under twenty-four hour surveillance. He was accompanied by extra jail guards during his court appearances and wore shackles around his ankles.

When Laraby's trial finally started months later, the People of New York were very limited as to what they could present as evidence. Assistant District Attorney Ken Hyland was not allowed to demonstrate that the police had developed Ed Laraby as a suspect in connection to the apartment break-in rapes earlier that year. Nor could he share with the jury that the police spent nine weeks following Laraby, witnessing him stalk numerous potential victims and attack two other people. He also was not allowed to share that Laraby had previously been sent to prison after being convicted of raping and sodomizing other women. In other words, the case was presented as though we were a bunch of cops who, by chance, happened to be at the right place at the right time and observed this animal violently attack a young woman as she walked down the street with her friend. The court ruled that the aforementioned information would be prejudicial to the defendant and prevent him from receiving a fair trial.

New York State Supreme Court Justice Eugene Bergin presided over the trial. Justice Bergin was a solid judge and kept the trial on track. I testified at the trial along with some of the other members of the surveillance and arrest team. The case was presented to the twelve jurors and two alternate jurors without a hitch, and they convicted Laraby for Sexual Abuse in the First Degree. Before the jury was excused, Justice Bergin met with them along with the prosecutor to answer any questions or concerns they had. According to Ken Hyland, Justice Bergin took the opportunity to praise the jury for their decision to convict Laraby on what little evidence that was allowed to be presented. Justice Bergin advised the jury about Laraby's violent past and how the police had developed him as a suspect and had been following him for the entire summer. Justice Bergin closed his comments by telling the jury that they did Monroe County and New York State a great service by convicting him of this crime. Needless to say, Justice Bergin sentenced Ed Laraby as a triple-predicate violent felon (aka "three-time loser") and ordered him to serve twenty-five years in the custody of the New York State Department of Corrections.

Our command officers, Chief Anthony Ciaccia and Captain Cornelius Flood, contributed greatly to the success of this case by their patience and willingness to maintain faith in their detectives throughout the investigation and surveillance operation. Without it, this case would not have ended with a successful disposition. This type of aggressive police work is not for the weak of heart, and anything short of strong leadership makes it very difficult for any criminal investigator to be effective, no matter how good they are. The leaders who empower those who serve beneath them will always enjoy more success.

Several years later, I was contacted by a New York State Police Investigator stationed in Auburn. He advised me that Ed Laraby had suffered chest pains while in the Auburn State Prison. While he was being evaluated at the hospital, Laraby attacked the armed prison guard that was accompanying him. During the protracted physical struggle, Laraby wrapped a cord connected to his hospital bed around the neck of the much smaller prison guard and began to choke him out while reaching for his handgun. The prison guard was able to pull his service weapon and break free from his would-be killer's choke hold and thwart his attempted escape until the police arrived. State Police Investigator David Stebbins, who investigated the incident, advised that Laraby was arrested and subsequently tried and convicted of Attempted Murder in the First Degree and Attempted Escape. He was sentenced to an additional twenty-five years to life, to be served consecutively when his first life sentence runs out.

ADA Ken Hyland said that he was relieved to know that Laraby was not going to be eligible for parole until he was old enough to be back in diapers. Mr. Hyland has put many dangerous people in prison over the past two decades. While he is rarely intimidated by these thugs, he believes that Laraby is the only criminal that he ever prosecuted who would seek revenge after his release against those responsible for putting him in prison. Until I crossed paths with Ed Laraby, I had never seen evil up close and personal. And as of this writing, I have yet to encounter anyone as dangerous as this man. I have investigated and arrested numerous sick degenerate types who have committed unthinkable crimes against others, but I have never been amid such evil as when I was in the presence of Ed Laraby. This man is a predator of the female gender and an enemy of the human race.

I am often haunted by the memories from this investigation when my own daughters go out with their friends to the night club and coffee house districts in the Rochester area. I can't bear the thought of my daughters being so frightened while they are being violently attacked and facing a horrible death. From my professional experience, I know that parents of such victims are always haunted by what their child's last thoughts were when they met their untimely tragic demise. It is too much for any parent to bear.

As we scan the headlines and see reports of violent crimes, many shudder and wonder: *is there anything I can do to protect myself and my children? It seems so random, and I feel so helpless.* I would like to offer some practical suggestions of how we can reduce the risk of our loved ones becoming a tragic statistic. My two daughters are now young women attending college. I constantly preach certain things to them with the hope that it will give them a tactical advantage if they become someone's potential target. Many of these you will recognize as common sense, but some stem from my past experience as a police defensive tactics instructor as well as two decades worth of investigating violent crimes.

A rookie police officer doesn't take long to learn that they must always know what is going on around them, for it is a matter of daily survival. I have found that citizens who have survived a violent crime also become very aware of their surroundings. This is not a coincidence. Former victims have told me that their personal safety becomes their highest priority. They are acutely aware of their surroundings at all times. I tell my daughters the most important thing that they can do to protect themselves is to do the same. Just like the predator in the wild, the violent sex offender uses the element of surprise to gain control of their victim. They conduct surveillance, stalk, and sneak up on their unsuspecting target. They seek the victim who appears the most vulnerable. The one who is distracted and unaware fits the bill. She may be thinking about what she is going to purchase at the mall as she walks from her vehicle, or she is excited about getting home and trying on the new outfit that she just purchased as she exits the mall. Perhaps she is stressed out about a problem with her boyfriend or parents, deep in thought about how to handle it as she makes her way down the relatively safe street to her apartment. She is looking down, not noticing that someone is following her to her vehicle, ready to shove her inside and take her captive.

I constantly remind my daughters that they are more likely to be attacked by a violent sex offender in and around their own vehicle than anywhere else. He will either use his own vehicle as his platform to snatch the victim as she is entering or exiting her vehicle, or he will be on foot and force the victim into her own vehicle, overpower her, and then drive her to a secluded area to assault her. For this reason, I tell them to drive around a parking area and check it out before actually parking, and to pay close attention to what is going on in and around their vehicle as they approach it. I tell them to avoid parking too close to other parked vehicles, because sexual predators will hide between them. This rule applies to street parking as well as parking lots. And naturally I tell my daughters to always try to park their vehicles as close to a street or parking lot lamp as possible.

Sexual predators are very familiar with the behavioral patterns of their favorite prey, the unsuspecting female. They know where to find the lion's share of them: shopping malls and plazas, fitness center parking lots, nightclub parking lots, upscale city neighborhoods, college campuses, and apartment complexes with large parking lots. They will skulk around these venues to locate, target and stalk a potential victim. They will patiently wait for their target to unwittingly place herself in a vulnerable position, which usually results from her not paying attention to her surroundings. All of us are guilty of such distraction at some time or another; however an innocent distraction can prove to be a fatal error.

It should be noted that violent sexual offenders do not limit their activity to the darkness of night. A tragic example of this occurred fifteen years ago at a large shopping plaza in the Town of Pittsford, one of our upscale communities on the east side of the county. A beautiful female college student was abducted in the middle of a Saturday afternoon at the busy plaza. The victim was driven in her own vehicle to a secluded location in the city and brutally raped and murdered. In her terrified state, the victim managed to dial 911 on her cell phone and keep the line open. This was long before GPS was utilized in cell phone technology. So unfortunately, the frantic patrol units were unable to find the helpless young woman as her last horrific moments on this earth were overheard and recorded by the 911 operator. I could never bring myself to listen to the tape after learning that some of my close friends and colleagues in the Rochester Police Department Homicide Squad wept as they listened to it. The killer was eventually arrested and convicted at trial and is now serving a life sentence. But there exists no justice on this side of eternity that could avenge the horrific torment that she was forced to endure or replace the unfulfilled life of this precious child.

I urge my daughters to be on the ready when walking to their vehicle, keeping their head on a swivel while survey-ing their surroundings. I insist that they carry a small canister of pepper spray in their hand—not their purse—in case they are attacked. A good solid burst of pepper spray will stun the attacker just long enough to halt his attack for a mo-ment, which allows them the opportunity to break free and run for help. I have told my daughters that if they decide to fight off their attacker, they should not stop until they break free. In essence, I teach them to execute a counter-assault, like a cornered animal. Have you ever tried or seen someone attempt to take physical control of a wild animal? They are rarely successful if the animal is in a frenzy fighting for its life or freedom.

While some may not be comfortable with this stance, I believe that this is very essential in today's world. Rarely does anyone expect to become a victim of a violent sexual assault when they wake up in the morning. It helps to think and pray through what you would like your response to be if it should happen. Police officers are taught to visualize themselves responding to dangerous situations just as they were trained to do. When an actual high-stress event occurs, the officer who has done this will always respond more effi-ciently and safely. This is because it is as if he had responded to the situation, or one similar to it, hundreds of times. The mental rehearsals kept his mind sharp and prepared. I en-courage you to consider this type of exercise to make your-self prepared to survive an unexpected attack.

The decision to fight or submit to an attacker rests squarely on the victim. In the end, she should do whatever she thinks will keep her alive. No one, and I mean no one, is justified in passing judgment against any victim regarding this issue. If, God forbid, one of my daughters or wife were ever attacked, I would not dream of criticizing what they did or didn't do to prevent the assault. While I have taught my daughters how to fight off an assailant, the decision ultimately is theirs. If they survive the attack then they were successful, no matter what they did or did not do.

On another note, young women should refrain from drinking excessive amounts of alcohol and abusing drugs. Being intoxicated or under the influence of drugs drastically skews one's judgment, and women are very vulnerable to attack when they are in this condition. I have investigated far too many sexual assaults where the victim was mentally or physically incapacitated due to this element. High-school girls, college coeds and young professional women tend to fall victim to this type of crime. Nightclubs and bar districts, large festivals and college campus parties are usually congested with intoxicated young women looking for love in all of the wrong places. Violent sex offenders know that a victim who is intoxicated or under the influence of drugs usually can't remember much, if any, of the sexual assault. Even if the police are able to identify the assailant and make an arrest, the case is harder to prosecute.

Date rape drugs are a common tool of the violent sex offender today because it makes for a more cooperative victim and literally erases her memory of what occurred during the assault. Tell your daughters never to accept a beverage of any kind from anyone. I instruct my daughters to buy their own beverage. At the very least, they should watch it being opened, poured and prepared. They should never take their eyes off of it, even after it is in their possession. Law enforcement is seeing a huge spike in drug-induced rapes. Usually the victim's drink was spiked after they set it down, or they accepted a beverage from someone that they shouldn't have. I tell my daughters this simple rule: trust no one with your drinks, buy it yourself, and never let go of it.

Much to my chagrin, both of my daughters will be looking for their own apartment in the not-too-distant future. When that happens, I will be the kind of father that makes a thorough safety assessment of their new domicile. I will make sure that the windows can be secured and have pull-down shades so that peepers and sex offenders can't spy on them. Bolt locks on the doors and a planned escape route from their bedroom will be required. I will also check out the neighborhood and parking situation. After I have done everything humanly possible to make my daughters' dwelling safe and educate them about their personal safety, I will hand the situation over to God. I will pray that He assigns extra angels to watch over my daughters and to instill wisdom in them.

CHAPTER 15

—⁓—

THE DOUBLE INITIAL MURDERS

"*They lurk in ambush in the villages, waiting to murder innocent people. They are always searching for helpless victims. Like lions crouched in hiding, they pounce on the helpless and drag them away in nets. Their helpless victims are crushed; they fall beneath the strength of the wicked. The wicked think, 'God isn't watching us! He has closed his eyes and won't even see what we do!'*

Arise, O Lord! Punish the wicked, O God! Do not ignore the helpless! Why do the wicked get away with despising God? They think, 'God will never call us to account.' But you see the trouble and grief they cause. You take note of it and punish them.

The helpless put their trust in you. You defend the orphans. Break the arms of these wicked, evil people! Go after them until the last one is destroyed."

PSALM 10: 8-15 (NLT)

Within a two-year period three prepubescent females were kidnapped, raped, and strangled to death during the early 1970s in the Greater Rochester area. All three were kidnapped from their respective city neighborhoods and their bodies were discarded alongside roads in rural areas outside of the city. The victims were identified as Carmen Colon, Wanda Walkowicz and Michelle Maenza.

I can not share all of the facts of these cases because they remain unsolved. Certain information must remain confidential for the purpose of solving these brutal murders. The facts that I will share have already become public information over the years and have not proved to be detrimental to the investigation. My purpose for sharing these cases is to heighten parent's awareness about the predators that kidnap children and young women without warning. It is equally important to keep these cases alive and in the forefront of people's minds because they remain unsolved. When the deceased is a young child you can't help but take these cases to heart, especially when you have children of your own.

CARMEN COLON

Ten-year-old Carmen Colon resided at 72 Romeyn Street in the City of Rochester with her mother, Guillimina, and her stepfather, Miguel Colon. Carmen and her family were Puerto Rican. Miguel was also Carmen's paternal uncle; after Carmen's father abandoned the family, Miguel moved in with them.

On November 16th, 1971, Carmen went to visit her grandfather, Felix Colon, at his residence on 746 Brown St. At approximately 4:30 PM, Felix sent Carmen to Jax Leader

Drug Store, located on the corner of West Main Street and Genesee Street, known as "Bull's Head." This was because a stone statue of a bull's head was mounted on the upper level of the building that housed several of the shops on that corner. Even today, the statue still overlooks that intersection.

At approximately 7:00 PM, the Rochester Police Department was notified that Carmen did not return to her grandfather's residence or her home. A physical search of the southwest city neighborhood was conducted throughout the night, but Carmen was not located. A preliminary investigation did not produce any leads or witnesses to a possible abduction.

Two days later, Carmen's body was discovered in a field on Stearns Road in the Town of Riga, which is west of the city. Monroe County Medical Examiner Dr. John Edland conducted the autopsy. He found that Carmen was sexually assaulted and strangled to death. It was Dr. Edland's opinion that Carmen had been dead anywhere from one to one and-a-half days before she was found.

The lengthy follow-up investigation was both intense and exhaustive. One witness reported that they observed Carmen enter a vehicle at Bull's Head. Several other witnesses reported that they had observed a young girl matching Carmen's description running along the road on Expressway Route 490 in the Chili-Riga area. She was nude from the waist down as she was running away from a vehicle that was following her as it backed up along the shoulder. These sightings occurred on the evening that Carmen was reported missing. Descriptions of the vehicle varied. However, one of the descriptions matched the brand-new vehicle that Miguel

Colon had just purchased. Miguel was interviewed and his vehicle was searched. Investigators noted that the trunk appeared to have been washed down with a cleaning solution just before the search was conducted. Investigators contacted the auto dealer, who advised that the dealership did not wash the trunk prior to delivering the car to Miguel.

Mr. Colon left the area shortly after he realized that he had become a suspect. Detectives from the Monroe County Sheriff's Office were in hot pursuit, but remained a step behind him. They followed him to Puerto Rico, where he hid out in the jungle. The detectives requested the assistance of the local police. They searched the region that he was thought to be hiding in, but they were unable to locate him. At that time, the local police commander detained Miguel Colon's mother and put the word out that she would not be released from jail until Miguel returned to Rochester and cooperated with the authorities.

Several days after their return to Rochester, the detectives were advised that Miguel was on his way back to Rochester to cooperate. Upon his arrival, Miguel handed the detectives a note that requested them to call the police commander in Puerto Rico so that he would release Miguel's mother from jail. Miguel maintained his innocence throughout the aggressive, intense interrogation that followed. Detectives involved in the investigation felt strongly that he had abducted, raped and murdered Carmen, but there was insufficient evidence for a conviction at trial, according to Monroe County District Attorney Jack Lazarus.

On February 17th 1991, Miguel Colon shot himself to death after he assaulted Carmen's mother and her brother,

Juan Melendez, with the same gun. Investigator Tom Vasile and I interviewed Mrs. Colon and her brother at her residence. We hoped to hear potentially incriminating statements that he might have made over the years or a dying declaration of guilt. However, neither Mrs. Colon nor her brother offered any additional information. Miguel did not make any statements to them during the assault-suicide incident that suggested that he was guilty of raping and murdering Carmen. The Monroe County Sheriff's Office and the New York State Police remain the lead investigative agencies in this case.

WANDA WALKOWICZ

Eleven-year-old Wanda Walkowicz resided at 132 ½ Avenue D in the city of Rochester. She shared her home with her mother, Joyce; her ten-year-old sister, Rita; her two-year-old sister, Michelle; and Joyce's boyfriend, Peyton Raney. According to Wanda's mother, she was a street-smart little girl who was quite capable of taking care of herself and her sisters. I met with Wanda's mother a few times over the years before she passed away. She had always felt that Wanda must either have known her killer, or they wore a uniform or otherwise represented authority in the community. Based upon this aspect of Wanda's personality, it was believed that the killer might be a police officer, fireman, postman, teacher, or clergyman.

On April 2nd, 1973, at approximately 5:10 PM, Joyce gave Wanda a grocery list and sent her to the Hillside Deli, located at 213 Conkey Avenue. The small mom-and-pop store was a short walk away from the Walkowicz residence in the northeast quadrant of the city. Wanda was last seen at approximately 5:30 PM by four young play-mates and an adult in front of Public School No. 8 carrying a bag of groceries. After Wanda did not return home, her mother reported her missing to the Rochester Police Department at approximately 8:00 PM. An all-night search of the neighborhood proved futile. The following morning, a New York State Trooper on routine patrol discovered Wanda's body in the grass just off the approach ramp of the Irondequoit Bay rest area of NYS Route 104 in Webster.

Monroe County Medical Examiner Dr. John Edland also performed this autopsy. He found that Wanda had been sexually assaulted and strangled to death. Death was due to asphyxia due to strangulation. As with the other two cases presented here, the manner in which the victim was strangled and the condition in which the body was found is being kept confidential for the purpose of the ongoing criminal investigation.

Initially, several viable suspects were developed and interviewed, but eventually they were cleared after their alibis were corroborated. The follow-up investigation was exhaustive, but failed to locate and identify the person responsible for the kidnapping and murder of Wanda Walkowicz. It did not produce anyone who had witnessed her abduction, nor did anyone offer any information that would assist investigators in solving this case. The New York State Police and the Monroe County Sheriff's Office remain the lead agencies in this case.

MICHELLE MAENZA

Eleven-year-old Michelle Maenza resided at 25 Webster Crescent in the City of Rochester with her mother,

Carolyn, and two younger sisters. Her parents were separated. Michelle's father, Christopher, resided at 21 Hall Street in Rochester with Michelle's two brothers.

On November 26th, 1973, Michelle attended Public School No. 33 on Webster Avenue, where she was a fifth-grade student. Michelle reportedly left school at approximately 3:15 PM with a schoolmate and walked towards the Goodman Street Plaza. Michelle was last seen at approximately 3:30 PM by four friends as she was turning onto Ackerman Street from Webster Avenue. At approximately 5:40 PM, the Rochester Police Department was notified that Michelle failed to return home from school. Once again, the city's northeast neighborhood was searched all night with no result. No witnesses were located during the preliminary investigation.

Two days later, Michelle's body was discovered alongside Eddy Road in the Town of Macedon. Macedon is a rural community located in Wayne County, which is adjacent to the east border of Monroe County. The Wayne County Sheriff's Office served as the lead agency in the murder investigation and worked in conjunction with the Rochester Police Department, New York State Police, and the Monroe County Sheriff's Office, which were already embroiled in the protracted kidnapping-murder investigations of Carmen Colon and Wanda Walkowicz.

Monroe County Medical Examiner Dr. John Edland ruled the cause of death as asphyxia due to strangulation. Utilizing the most advanced forensic technology of that time period, a partial palm print was lifted from Michelle's neck. While there was no definitive proof that the palm

print belongs to the killer, comparisons were made with potential suspects who were unable to offer a substantiated alibi
for the date and time that Michelle was abducted.

During the long, thorough investigation a witness
told the police that at approximately 5:30 PM on the day that
Michelle disappeared, a 1966 light-colored Chevrolet was
parked in the vicinity where Michelle's body was found. The
vehicle was parked on the wrong side of the road and reported to be occupied by two persons. Investigators obtained
and scrutinized the list of 1966 light-colored Chevrolets registered in the Rochester area, but no workable leads were
developed. It is still unknown if the vehicle was connected
to this crime. There was also a possible sighting of Michelle
leaving the Goodman Street Plaza in a tan colored car with
a dent in the left side around the same time she disappeared.
But as of this writing, no suspects or witnesses to the abduction, rape or murder of Michelle Maenza have been found.
The Wayne County Sheriff's Office remains the lead investigative agency in this case.

These three horrible crimes rocked the Rochester
area and surrounding communities. Unlimited resources and
countless man-hours were dedicated to the ensuing investigations, but they proved fruitless. For several years afterwards,
citizens still lived in fear that another young girl was going
to be abducted and murdered.

There are some similarities in these cases: the victims' gender and age, the manner in which they were murdered and sexually assaulted. The fact that they were abducted while walking in their respective city neighborhoods and
their bodies were left in rural areas. An intriguing note is that

the victim's first and last names start with the same letter: CC, WW and MM. Furthermore, their bodies were discarded in townships that began with the same letter as their names. Carmen Colon was found in the area of Chili-Riga; Wanda Walkowicz was found in Webster; and Michelle Maenza was found in Macedon. Whether this is a mere coincidence or a contributing factor to the young girls' violent demise has yet to be determined, but this eerie fact is what prompted local media and police investigators to coin the phrase "double initial murders."

The original police detectives involved in these investigations considered all angles in their search for clues. They looked at school staff (each victim appeared to have some sort of learning disability), social services (all three girls came from broken homes and resided in poor city neighborhoods), and religious backgrounds (all three victims were from Catholic families). No stone was left unturned. Over the past three decades the murders have been investigated as cold case homicides by the respective agencies involved. Most recently, criminal investigators from the New York State Police, Monroe County Sheriff's Office, Rochester Police Department, and Wayne County Sheriff's Office have reunited and recommitted to pursue these investigations as a team.

Due to technical advances in the area of serology and DNA recovery and analysis, we have determined that much of the physical evidence that was recovered during the initial investigations can now be submitted for analysis. State Police Investigators Tom Crowley, Al Dombrowski and I have taken the role of coordinating the most recent stage of the cold case investigation. Sergeant Mark Mariano of the Rochester Police Department Major Crimes Unit has also assisted in this process. Our course of action has included reviewing the entire case file and police reports; interviewing many former police investigators who were involved either in the initial murder investigations or subsequent cold case investigations; re-interviewing persons with potential knowledge; and collecting DNA samples from past suspects and persons of interest for comparison with evidence collected from the crime scenes.

I have often been in touch with some of the retired detectives who worked these cases during the early years: RPD detectives Tony Cerretto, Louis J. Rotunno, Billy Barnes, Lenny Burriello, Sal Ruvio, Vito D'Ambrosia, and Lou "Bopper" Tacito; Monroe County Sheriff's Office detectives Nick DaRosa, Robert Russello and the late Don Clark; and retired New York State Police detective Ed Hooper. These former lawmen of a different era are living encyclopedias of the Rochester underworld over the past fifty years. I have enjoyed several pasta lunches with some of them over the years as we discussed the intricacies of these three murder cases at two of their favorite daytime hangouts, Antonetta's Italian Restaurant and Rocky's Italian Restaurant. Antonetta's, a worn old tavern with a large wrap-around front porch, is located on the corner of Jay Street and Dakota street in a neighborhood on the west side of the city that has seen better days. Rocky's stands alone in a non-descript building on the opposite end of Jay Street, where it intersects with Oak Street in an old industrial area on the outskirts of downtown Rochester. I have found these types of places in every city:

hole-in-the-wall joints that serve great food to members of every social strata. Both restaurants still get packed with politicians, lawyers, judges, cops, construction workers and corporate executives during the lunch hour. A lot of business is conducted by overfed patrons seated at one of the many tables adorned with red and white checkered tablecloths that are crammed into every space possible. Their paneled walls are covered with countless photographs of the rich and famous and special moments in history. The inexpensive food is served at a hectic pace by no-nonsense, fast-talking waitresses who call everyone by their first name—Honey.

It is in this electric atmosphere that I am schooled by these old-time detectives. I pick their brains for information not included in the case files. An opportunity to speak with a detective who investigated a murder when it was first reported is extremely valuable. I know from my own experience that a homicide detective's investigative reports generally don't include his thoughts and feelings about the cases that he didn't solve. However, those things remain in his heart for years, sometimes haunting him as unfinished business, long after he leaves the job. I seize every opportunity to speak with them about open murder cases. I make it a point to break bread with them when things slow down every now and then. A few of them have since passed away.

These guys didn't have the luxury of being able to rely on a computer database to retain their information. As a result, their minds are like steel traps—nothing has escaped them. They remember their cases and the criminals they pursued and arrested over the decades that they served. Some of them were policemen before the Supreme Court handed down the Miranda Rule, which requires that suspects in police custody be advised of their constitutional rights and waive them before they can be interrogated. Presently, I am the most senior investigator in my department, but even I still find it stimulating to talk about the old days with these men. They did things differently back then, but they got the job done, and still serve as a valuable resource.

While each of these retired detectives harbored their own thoughts regarding possible suspects in these investigations, three suspects have come up frequently over the past thirty years. Carmen Colon's uncle Miguel remained one of the two favorite suspects in her murder, although he was never charged because the prosecutor felt that there was not enough evidence to convict him at a trial. Retired Monroe County Sheriff Investigator Nick DaRosa, one of the detectives who pursued Mr. Colon in Puerto Rico, is one of those who still believes that Miguel raped and murdered his niece. The other favorite suspect was James Barber. Monroe County Sheriff Investigator Sergeant Robert Russello discovered that James had been arrested for molesting a young girl in the past, and he was wanted by authorities in another state for molesting another little girl. Sergeant Russello determined that Barber was drifting through Rochester and had social ties in Carmen's neighborhood when she was kidnapped and murdered. Barber left his job as an assistant chef at a local country club without any warning shortly after Carmen was found dead. Sergeant Russello stated that Barber left Rochester in a hurry, leaving behind everything he owned in his apartment. Sergeant Russello pursued Barber, but eventually lost his trail. Obviously, Barber did not want to be found. It is unknown whether he fled because of the sexual assault he was already wanted for, or if he fled because he was involved in Carmen's murder. Barber is not considered a suspect in the other two murders because he left the Rochester area shortly after Carmen's death. We recently determined that James Barber is now deceased and buried in another state.

Another potential suspect was Kenneth Bianchi, one of the infamous "Hillside Stranglers." Bianchi was born in Rochester, New York and was still living in Rochester when the double initial murders occurred. He eventually moved to Los Angeles and in partnership with his cousin, Angelo Buono, Jr., murdered ten women. However, it was determined that Bianchi was working and accounted for when Carmen, Wanda, and Michelle were abducted. He was also eventually eliminated by serological comparisons.

The most popular suspect was twenty-five-year-old Dennis Termini, a firefighter with the Rochester Fire Department. Several of the original police investigators consider him a top suspect in the murders of Wanda Walkowicz and Michelle Maenza. Unfortunately, detectives never got an opportunity to interview him. He committed suicide on the morning of January 1st, 1974 while patrol officers of the Rochester Police Department attempted to arrest him. An hour earlier, Termini had attempted to abduct a teenage girl at gunpoint shortly after she exited a hotel in the city, but the girl would not stop screaming and caught the attention of three witnesses in the area. Termini fled from the scene, but it wasn't enough to deter him from searching for another victim. His behavior was demonic, a predator totally out of control. That same morning Termini, armed with a .45 caliber semi-automatic pistol, attacked a second teenage girl from behind as she was walking alone in a neighborhood located in the northeast quadrant of the city. Termini shoved the pistol against the girl's side and forced her into a nearby residential garage and ordered her to undress. The victim was down to her underwear when Termini observed uniformed police officers pulling up in their cruisers. Leaving the victim behind, he exited the garage and began running through backyards as police officers gave chase. The chase ceased when Termini entered a vehicle parked in a driveway and locked the doors to avoid being apprehended. As the pursuing officer was waiting for back-up officers to arrive before attempting to take Termini into custody, he heard a single gunshot. Termini had fatally shot himself in the head.

After Termini's death, a team of detectives was assigned to investigate his background and formulate a time line of his life. Until the day of his death, Dennis Termini had been flying under law enforcement's radar. The Rochester Police Department had been investigating a number of reported rapes and had labeled the unidentified perpetrator as the "Garage Rapist" since some of the rapes had occurred in residential garages. This team determined that Termini was that rapist, suspected of attacking approximately fourteen female teenagers and young women during the same time period that Carmen Colon, Wanda Walkowicz, and Michelle Maenza had been murdered.

Detectives worked feverishly to determine if Termini could also be connected to any of the double initial murders. They were able to establish that Dennis stalked the same neighborhoods that the three murder victims had lived in.

Also, he did abduct at least one of his victims and drive her to a secluded area before raping her. Remarkably, detectives were able to place Termini in the area that Michelle was walking home when she disappeared. Independent witness testimony also placed a young girl matching Michelle's description in a vehicle that matched Termini's in a neighborhood adjacent to the one in which she was last seen walking. There is additional circumstantial evidence that may connect Termini to this young girl's disappearance; however I am not at liberty to discuss it at this time. I can say that it was compelling enough to convince a Monroe County Court Judge to sign a search warrant thirty-seven years after the crime, allowing us to exhume Dennis' body to retrieve a DNA sample for comparison against evidence recovered from the three crime scenes. All Investigator Crowley and I had to do was include the thirty-year-old findings of the original police detectives in our search warrant application. Ironically, we exhumed his remains thirty-three years to the day after his death; he was buried on January 4th, 1974 and was exhumed on January 4th, 2007. I did not realize this fact until I was showing the search warrant to the administrative staff of the cemetery that same morning.

It is more common for law enforcement to exhume a potential victim to determine cause of death when they suspect a covered-up homicide. Usually those procedures are conducted with a court order pursuant to the New York State Public Health Law and with the decedent's family's consent, so a warrant is not required. Understandably, most families would be against the exhumation of their loved one to investigate them for murder. And the New York State Public

Health Law does not include a provision for such cases. This is why we had to apply for a search warrant to search the grave site, casket, and physical remains of the suspected serial rapist.

Why did we do this thirty-seven years later? The technological advances in forensic serology, especially in the area of DNA research and comparison, have skyrocketed over the past ten years. When I first started working in the Major Crimes Unit, DNA comparison was still nothing more than a pipe dream. We were using blood types and secretor/ non-secretor comparisons as corroborating evidence in our physical crime investigations back then. Had the police detectives thirty years ago been armed with this type of forensic technology, there is no doubt in my mind that these cases would have been solved quickly. But now, time is our enemy. Witnesses and potential suspects leave the area or die. Physical evidence can get lost, mishandled, misplaced, and even corrupted. People's memories fade. The community forgets.

The exhumation and autopsy was conducted under the supervision and guidance of Monroe County Medical Examiner Dr. Caroline Dignan and her chief investigator, Robert Zerby. With the assistance of the cemetery personnel, the exhumation went quickly. Only an hour passed between the back hoe entering the soil and the casket being placed in the Medical Examiner's truck. It was then transported to the Medical Examiner's Office, where the casket was unsealed and opened. All of us had to wear special masks to prevent inhalation of the deadly spores that resulted from the nearly four decades of decomposition inside the casket. Within forty-five minutes of leaving the cemetery, Dr. Dignan positively identified the remains.

After Dr. Dignan and Chief Investigator Zerby retrieved the necessary bone and tissue samples, the corpse was placed into a brand-new casket since we had broken the original when we unsealed it. Monroe County appropriately paid the bill—fortunately, we obtained it at wholesale cost. I could not believe the mark-up price grieving families must pay for a casket. Mr. Termini was laid back to rest the following morning. His family was notified of the exhumation on the morning that we executed the warrant. I was relieved that both of his parents were deceased. The thought of having to tell someone that we were digging up their child was not something that I wanted to do. While we tried to execute the search warrant quietly, the local media still got wind of it a few weeks later. One news channel ran a special documentary on the investigation that included the exhumation. None of the principal investigators participated. I understand that reporters have a job to do, and I don't hold it against them when they are able to develop a story through their sources. However I was very grateful that we were able to complete our task and retrieve what we needed before it went public.

To maintain the integrity of the ongoing investigation, it would not be prudent to speculate on the results of the pending DNA analysis and comparisons. For reasons that I am not at liberty to mention, the results of those tests may take much longer than we first anticipated. Personally, based upon the numerous discussions that I have had with some of the original detectives of the investigations, I am not convinced that Dennis Termini is responsible for all three of these murders. However, he is a worthy suspect to pursue further since it was established that he was a serial rapist at the time of the murders. I mean no ill will towards his surviving family members, but I feel compelled to move these cases forward on behalf of the young victims and their families.

The story must cease here—for now. The investigation is still ongoing. Other potential suspects must be further considered, located, and interviewed if possible. More than likely, the end of this story will not be mine to tell. As the generation of police detectives before me tirelessly worked these cases and moved them forward, my generation has made our mark with the assistance of the technological advances in forensic science and moved these investigations closer to a disposition. The next generation of police detectives may very well be the ones to solve this tragic riddle and achieve some type of closure for the families of the three victims and the community in which they lived.

Intercessory prayer is very much needed to solve these three murder investigations. While it won't bring these young girls back to their families, it can offer them a much-needed explanation of what occurred to their precious child, and possibly even justice. Please pray for the respective police agencies to keep working these cases as a priority, and that the victims' families would be comforted in their loss and not lose hope. Also, please pray for those unidentified persons who possess a missing piece of this puzzle to come forward. No matter how big or complicated, every case is one phone call away from being solved. Please pray that we would receive that call.

SECTION IV

PREVENTIVE TOOLS, RESOURCES, AND CONCLUSION

CHAPTER 16

—⁄⁄⁄—

WHAT CAN YOU DO TO PREVENT YOUR CHILDREN FROM BEING SEDUCED AND MOLESTED?

"*P*ut on the whole armour of God, that ye may be able to stand against the wiles of the Devil."

EPHESIANS 6:11(KJV)

COMMUNICATE. COMMUNICATE. COMMUNICATE!

Because many of us must be employed outside of the home, we spend the majority of our day away from our children. Therefore we must make it a point to communicate with our children every day to learn what is going on in their lives and who they are having daily contact with. Our children are exposed to school staff, counselors, coaches, day-care providers, summer camp staff, and/or babysitters every day. Their social horizons have been expanded at a far too rapid pace. Many of us parents enjoyed a more relaxed childhood in the 1950s and 1960s when it was common to have our mothers home all day with us.

Like the faithful shepherd who checks each and every one of his sheep for parasites, diseases, and injuries, we must physically hold and hug our children and communicate with them every day. We need to reach out and make that connection and we must listen to them carefully. I constantly made the mistake of using the little time I was around the house to tell my children what I wanted them to do. I rarely took the time to ask them what was going on in their daily lives. Under the pressure of making a living and supporting a family, I would spend the time talking at my children rather than with them. Our two-way discussions were few and far between. Fortunately for our children, their mother did not make the same mistake. My wife always knew the who, what, when, where, and how of their daily lives. Through her patient guidance I eventually learned this very important principle. As I became more experienced in investigating sexual crimes against children, I realized just how important daily two-way conversations really are.

As soon as a child possesses the ability to carry on a conversation, there are two absolutely necessary questions that every parent or guardian should ask them every day: What bad things happened to you today? And, what good things happened to you today? Another way to phrase these questions is: Who treated you badly today? And, who was nice to you and made you feel special today? Even if your children were with you all day, still ask them these questions as a matter of routine. This way, from a young age they will be programmed to have this discussion with you. Based on the numerous interviews I have conducted with child victims and their parents, I believe it will prove invaluable to your efforts to keep them safe from predators who desire to seduce and abuse them. Remember that during the trust and courtship phases of the grooming process. The child is unaware of the real reason why the predator is treating them with such favor. There-fore, at this point in the relationship the child has no reason to hide anything from his or her parents. If the parents are communicating with their children daily about who they are interacting with and what they are doing with them, the child should still be willing to share everything. While any consci-entious parent would like to know what bad things happened or who may have mistreated them, I believe that the more important question to ask is, "What good things happened to you today?" My reason is simple. The child has not yet made a secret pact with a predator that comes with the seduc-tion phase, so they should be willing to share all of the great things this person is doing for them because they are happy and excited about it. Because the child's morals have yet to be compromised, they are most likely going to remain open and honest with their parents when questioned about their relationship with the undetected predator.

This is a significant time span that the parent must monitor aggressively. It is when the parent would find out from the child's own mouth if the child predator is spending more quality time or alone time with their child, or if their child is being taken to special places or being given special gifts by the predator. Most children in this situation will be very excited and happy about these special privileges and feel the need to talk about it as long as the child predator has not already told them not to. To an adult, it would be like winning the lottery. Attempting to contain good news like that would be difficult for even the most discreet person if someone asked them directly about it. The same goes for a child who is excited about the person who gives them special treatment. But we parents must remember to provide our children every opportunity to share such news with us. If you do, it will be hard for your children to contain their enthusiasm and remain silent.

As long as the child predator has not drawn your child into some questionable activity and made them feel that they have done something wrong that would get them into trouble, your child will usually share what is going on in their life with you. But you have to be persistent and consistent with your inquiries, and allow your children the time to talk to you. And you need to listen to them. I know that I am being redundant with this idea, but it is a critical part of protecting your child. It is one of the best ways to uncover a predator's diabolical scheme, so it can not be stressed enough.

If someone is giving your child gifts and special privileges, you need to know why. Be careful not to reprimand your child for accepting them, for it may shut them down and make them unwilling to tell you additional information that you really need to know. Remember, your child may be dealing with someone who is very manipulative and sinister. He or she was made to feel special by this person. It may very well be nothing. But then again, you may have uncovered a pattern of behavior that would normally not appear inappropriate which could have led to your child being seduced and abused. Stay calm, act happy for their good fortune, and then quietly explore what is going on by placing yourself between that person and your child. Make your presence known to them similar to the way the good shepherd places himself between his flock and the wolf. If he is a predator, eventually he will flee from you. But it may be too late if the predator has already begun to manipulate your child into lying about their relationship with him.

I advise all parents to not allow other adults to give your children gifts or special privileges unless they request your permission first and explain to you exactly why and what they are rewarding the child for. In particular, don't allow another adult to bestow your child with special privileges and gifts on a frequent basis. Whether they are a child predator or just a nice person, it sends the wrong message to your child. Left unchecked, it will eventually undermine your status as a parent. The child could become accustomed to such special treatment and seek it elsewhere. Parents have the tough job of disciplining where other adults can ignore bad behavior. To help counterbalance that, they should also be showering more positive attention on their children than anyone else. Generally, child predators will try to circumvent this rule. When confronted, they will apologize profusely, painting it as an innocent expression of affection. Don't buy it. Anyone who goes against your instructions about your child's upbringing needs to be cut out of your child's life.

DEBRIEFING AND GATHERING INTELLIGENCE: SHARING A MEAL

"Feed my lambs."

JOHN 21:15

Most cultures make sharing a meal a special occasion. Whether it is a holiday, a special celebration, a date, a family gathering, or a business luncheon, we share meals with people as an act of social acceptance and personal intimacy. It allows us to interchange our thoughts and feelings, as barriers to open and honest conversation melt away in a festive, inviting atmosphere. In the Bible we can see how God used the acts of animal sacrifice and sharing a meal to fellowship with His people around the temple. Jesus communed with His disciples over meals and dined with anyone who invited Him. Consuming food with another person has a way of putting us on the same social plane. For this reason Jesus was criticized by the Jewish priests for eating with the thieves, tax collectors and prostitutes in the community.

In the police detective world we employ a technique known as "debriefing and gathering intelligence." In essence, that is what we need to do as parents to learn about what goes on in our children's daily lives when they are not with us. I urge you to share a special meal with your children – not to gather intelligence for disciplinary action, but to assist you in keeping them safe. It should prove helpful to take your child out to a restaurant, for it will be much easier for them to open up to you in a neutral setting. Your authority as a parent is the greatest in the home; eating there may hinder your ability to make your child feel comfortable enough to speak openly about matters that they would consider more personal in nature. It doesn't have to be an expensive or fancy place. Most children and teenagers enjoy pizza, burgers, chicken wings, chicken fingers, tacos and ice cream. My daughters enjoyed going to cafés in the Park Avenue area of Rochester.

As a Major Crimes Investigator, I have shared a meal to obtain many confessions, whether it was a take-out order in the interrogation room or taking the perpetrator out to a restaurant. One criminal signed his voluntary confession to a violent crime with the joke that he was going to prison for a very long time because we ate Nick Tahou's garbage plates together in the interrogation room. Another criminal initially made it clear that he had nothing to say about his suspected involvement in a violent crime. I told him that I understood that he didn't want to speak with me about the crime, so I suggested that we just eat and relax before I started the paperwork for his pending arrest. It was quite remarkable. He insisted on telling me everything about his involvement in the crime after we shared a garbage plate and talked about our personal lives and families. He couldn't wait to bless me with his confession because of the camaraderie that we had shared over our plates of hot dogs, baked beans, fried potatoes and macaroni salad. When we finished eating and talking about our families he just looked at me and said, "Wheel in that typewriter, I'm gonna tell you what happened." When I testified in court about this event at the preliminary hearing a few days later, I observed the defense attorney shake his head in disbelief as if I was lying. Then I saw his client nodding his head and shrugging his shoulders, acknowledging to the court that I was telling the truth. And as I shared earlier, back in the late 1990s, I choked down a plate of linguini in red sauce while a child predator divulged the gruesome details of the kidnapping and murder of a four-year-old girl in his apartment complex over a plate of Chicken Parmesan. Yet just prior to sharing our meal, this perpetrator told me that he wasn't going to talk to me.

I have been a hostage negotiator for the Monroe County Sheriff's office for nearly twenty years. One of the things we always try to do during a hostage incident is to introduce food into the situation. Terrorists are familiar with this technique. They will appoint other people to bring food to their hostages and care for their basic needs, because they know that it is critical to not establish a personal relationship with them. That is also part of the reason why they place hoods over their hostages' heads and isolate them. Local and state law enforcement generally will encounter hostage situations resulting from violent domestic troubles, armed robberies or sexual assaults that have gone from bad to worse. These emotionally-charged standoffs between the perpetrators and the police will usually continue for several hours or even days. The need for food will usually arise; the experienced hostage negotiator will always be ready and willing to assist the hostage-taker in satisfying that need. In fact, I will continually remind the hostage-taker that they need to eat so that they will keep thinking straight during this time of intense stress. I will also suggest that it would be beneficial for them to feed and care for their hostages as well. When food is successfully introduced into a hostage situation it has a temporary calming effect on both the hostage-taker and the hostages. Personally, I like to send in all of the fixings for sandwiches. This would include different deli meats, breads, condiments and cheeses. It increases the possibility of positive interaction between the hostage-taker and his hostages. It requires them all to assist each other in preparing the meal before they eat it together. It is our hope that this activity would make it more difficult for the hostage-taker to harm or kill his hostages—especially if one of the hostages personally prepared a sandwich just the way their hostage-taker likes it. The process humanizes the hostages in the eyes of the hostage-taker, instilling them with a personal identity. Even in the most hostile environment, sharing a meal will break down social barriers. If this technique can work with hardened criminals and jacked-up hostage-takers who hate the police, it is certain to work between a loving parent and their child. Not only will you find out what is going on in their daily lives, but your relationship with your child will blossom and bless both of you.

I used this tactic with great success while raising my daughters through their teenage years. I would take them out to lunch separately to their favorite café. It was amazing how chatty they would become as we sipped our sodas or iced teas, awaiting our meal. By the time we were buttering our bread and starting our soup and salad, they would be revealing everything about themselves, their sister and their friends. It usually kept me a step ahead of them, and I truly believe that several tragedies were avoided because of these intimate meals with my daughters. I rarely had to break their confidence to accomplish these goals. Some of the information I gained from our lunch debriefings was passed onto other parents. We parents need to set our pride aside and begin to network with each other within our respective communities, sharing information about our children's daily activities. As time went on, my daughters knew exactly what I was doing with them, but they couldn't help themselves, just like many of those who knew that it was against their legal interest to speak with me about their involvement in a criminal incident.

On a more personal note, sharing meals with my youngest daughter over an entire summer changed the course of both her life and mine. She was going into the eleventh grade. She had done poorly in school the year before and was sneaking out of the house at night to party with her friends. She was going through a rebellious time, looking for acceptance in all of the wrong ways. We were at our wits' end, praying to the Lord for guidance and answers. About midway through that summer it came to me that our youngest loved when we prepared breakfast and lunch for her. She said that her food always tasted better when someone else made it for her. I guess that it made her feel special. I was working the 2PM-10PM shift that summer and my wife was working days. My oldest daughter had started working a part-time job, so I had several afternoons a week alone with my youngest. The Lord put it on my heart to eat lunch with her before I went into work. That was not an easy decision, since she was always grounded and grumpy most of the time that I was around. But she loved to eat home-cooked meals, and she did not like to eat alone. So I struck a deal with her. I said, "I will make you lunch and eat with you if you agree that we can read a couple of paragraphs in the Book of Matthew before each meal and then talk about it and apply it to our daily life as we eat together." I suggested that this would be good conversation material since all we had to talk about recently was her misbehavior. Surprisingly, she agreed. I prepared her favorite sandwiches – fried bologna, grilled cheese and soup, warm roast beef *au jus*, and submarine sandwiches. God had His hand all over this venture. Our first lunch was a huge success. The delicious food softened her heart and opened her mind. Suddenly God's Word started to resonate in her right before my eyes. For the first time, my spirited daughter absorbed the Word of God over her fried bologna. At the end of that first meal my daughter looked at me and said, "Daddy, that was awesome. I can't wait until tomorrow."

We went through the entire book of Matthew and communed over God's Word that summer. Shortly after that, she accepted Jesus as her Lord and Savior. She went on to score a nearly perfect GPA in both her junior and senior years in high school, and she became the captain of the varsity field hockey team for those two years. She has continued to do extremely well in college and works nearly full-time in addition to her studies.

The Lord has given us the blessed pleasure of enjoying good meals together. Now, I can't promise that fried bologna sandwiches will save your child's soul and solve all their problems; but if this technique softens hardened criminals enough to motivate them to talk to a police detective, then it will surely soften the hearts of your children to communicate more openly with you. Just keep at it, and don't give up.

NETWORK WITH OTHER PARENTS

Parents should work with each other and compare notes. Children, like adults, put their own spin on much of the information that they share. Unfortunately, our children are not always as honest as we need them to be. Usually that is because they are trying to prevent their parents from finding out something about their past or future participation in a questionable activity. So it would be fruitful for parents to set their pride aside and communicate with each other about what their children are sharing with them. This is an effective way to check the veracity of what your children are telling you, and this keeps them safe. A typical example is when a young teenage girl makes plans to meet the sexual predator she has been talking with over the Internet for the past two months. She lies to her parents, telling them that she is gong to stay overnight at a friend's house. Too many times in this scenario, for whatever reason, the parents never check with the friend's parents to confirm such arrangements, and the girl ends up raped or murdered. If parents make a habit of networking with each other, these types of situations can be prevented. Likewise, law enforcement agencies are much more effective in their fight against crime when they share information with each other rather than harboring secrets because of territorial pride, which is an unfortunate reality in many jurisdictions. If networking and sharing information works for the police, then it will be useful for parents as they attempt to protect and supervise their children. We hold back because we don't want to appear backward, paranoid or overprotective. We also are afraid of intimating that we don't trust our children. Satan's best weapon against man is man's own pride. Don't let it get in the way of protecting your children.

"HINDER" YOUR CHILDREN

Most of us are familiar with the picture of a first-century shepherd carrying a sheep or lamb over his shoulders as he is walking along with the rest of his flock. At first glance, the caption depicts a loving and caring Lord and

Savior. But few of us realize that the picture also represents our Lord's chastisement of the children that He loves. In the Bible studies I have attended over the years, I have learned that the animal we see being carried atop the shepherd's shoulders was a naughty little lamb. It was most likely guilty of wandering away from the rest of the flock. Most of us are familiar with the saying, "the grass always looks greener on the other side of the fence." This saying derives from the sheep that have developed the bad habit of walking the fence line, attempting to find an opening to the grassy field on the other side because they are not content with what the shepherd has already provided them with. Sound familiar? These misbehaving livestock are commonly referred to as "fence-walkers." The fence-walking sheep puts not only itself in danger, but the rest of the flock as well. When it is successful in breaching a border, the fence-walker puts itself at risk of getting lost and into the path of a watchful predator. The fence then becomes a trap to the unsuspecting sheep, who will rarely remember where the opening was when it needs to escape. It also is a barrier for the shepherd when he must rescue them from impending danger. In addition, the rebellious sheep may ultimately influence the rest of the flock to wander away from the shepherd into harm's way if its behavior remains unchecked.

The loving shepherd must chastise the animal and teach it not to wander away from the safety of the flock. To accomplish this goal the shepherd breaks one of the sheep's legs, which disables the animal from walking on its own. The shepherd must carry the injured sheep on his shoulders as he tends to the other members of his flock, only setting the animal down periodically to take care of its physical needs. The shepherd takes on the burden of this heavy, stinky, hairy animal with the hope that it will bond with him and come to realize how much it needs the shepherd for its survival. Without the shepherd voluntarily taking on the burden of carrying this rebellious sheep and personally tending to its needs, it would surely die. The sheep learns to rely on the shepherd and be content with what the shepherd provides for it. While this adds a great burden to the shepherd temporarily, this process of chastisement forges a new bond between him and the animal. When the sheep finally becomes healthy enough to walk on its own and is restored as a regular member of the flock, it tends to stay close to the shepherd because of the bond that formed between them. Hence, the dangerous habit of fence-walking is no longer an issue.

I believe that this is why God allows bad things to happen to all of us. He allows us to break our own legs. It is His hope that we will then call out to Him and allow Him to carry our burden as He heals us and tends to our needs, which teaches us how much we need Him for our spiritual survival. Parents should utilize this same model for teaching and disciplining their children. Now, I am not advocating breaking your child's arm or leg, or injuring them in any way. But we do need to hinder our children from participating in behavior that could place them in danger or wrongly influence other children. Like the Good Shepherd, we need to take on the burden of the rebellious child. Obviously, this is something that most of us parents do not enjoy doing. Sometimes we even attempt to avoid it. If you are a parent then you know that it is never convenient for us to punish or hinder our children, for when we do this we also punish and hinder ourselves—if we are doing it correctly. But like the shepherd who places the sheep that he purposely injured upon his shoulders, burdening himself for an extended period of time to allow the animal to heal and bond with him, we parents must assume the burden of our child's period of chastisement and use that time to bond with them, no matter how inconvenient it is to us.

We must not pass this responsibility on to someone else. If the shepherd handed off the sheep that he was hindering to another person, he would lose the opportunity to bond with that animal. Likewise, if a parent punishes their child by grounding them or restricting certain activities, but then passes off the responsibility of enforcing the punishment to another adult, they are losing an opportunity to bond with that child. That bond lessens the child's desire to take part in further detrimental behavior that would place them in harm's way. The greatest periods of personal growth for my children were when they were grounded and forced to spend time with my wife and me. We redeemed that time by reinforcing to our children how much they meant to us and how much we loved them. Like the sheep that chose to stay close to the shepherd when it was walking on its own again, we found that when our children were provided with their freedom again, they voluntarily chose to spend more time with us because of the bond that we had re-established with them during their time of chastisement.

It is important that punishment be dispensed fairly and consistently. The parent must use that time to interact with their child in a positive and appropriate manner. Without a doubt, the most difficult and challenging job that any of us will undertake in our lifetime is being a responsible parent who is consistent with their expectations and discipline. But the effort is well worth it.

THE INTERNET

"Be sober, be vigilant; because your adversary the Devil walks about like a roaring lion, seeking whom he may devour."

                              1 PETER 5:8

I was investigating crimes against children long before the Internet became part of our daily lives. When I began my career, it was still very much in the infant stages of its development and its use was limited to the corporate world. But as the Internet has evolved to its present state the frequency of crimes against children has increased astronomically, and its use is beyond our ability to regulate. No longer is your child safe in the confines of your home under your close supervision. The Internet is the predator's Trojan horse into what is supposed to be your fortress and sanctuary from the outside world. He is both invisible and insidious as your child willingly invites him in to his or her life via cyberspace. I have met child victims who communicated with their offender over the Internet right under their parents' noses. Because chat room language is cryptic and hard to decipher, it allows the child victim to become involved with, and eventually seduced, online by a predator. Many times the child will be lured out of the safety of their home to be sexually offended, or even kidnapped and murdered.

There is no possible way to accurately determine just how many encounters occur between a child and a predator over the Internet daily throughout this nation. While law enforcement is making a gallant effort to police cyberspace, it will be ill-equipped to even scratch the surface for many years to come. Therefore, every parent must shoulder the burden of monitoring their children's Internet activity. This task was made even more difficult within the past two to three years, since cell phones have been manufactured with the technology to access the Internet, and also to send and receive e-mail and text messages. Nearly every cell phone manufactured today also includes a camera or video and audio recording capabilities. While I understand that parents give their children cell phones in the hopes of keeping them safer, I view a cell phone in the hands of an unsupervised child or young teenager as a grave liability. A predator will use the cell phone to seduce and lure a child away from safety. When parents ask me my opinion on children and cell phones, I tell them to seriously consider not allowing their children to possess one until they are old enough to drive. It is my feeling that children should not be unsupervised until then. At that point, owning a cell phone would be a matter of safety in case they break down or get lost while driving alone. But until then, a cell phone would only increase their child's risk of crossing the path of a sexual predator. If you feel that your child needs one, I highly encourage you to buy one without Internet capability that you can limit to give and receive calls only from specific phone numbers. You should monitor your child's phone activity to make sure that they did not override your security controls.

If we depend on cell phones to keep our children safe, then we have a false sense of security. Whether we choose to believe it or not, our children will use it as a tool to deceive us and conceal their own mischievous behavior. Children will also resort to using their friends' computers and cell phones in order to carry out plans that they know their parents would never approve of, such as secretly meeting a stranger that they met on the Internet. This is why parents must be diligent and tenacious in order to monitor their adolescent's whereabouts and who they are with at all times. Let's face it, they are going to be naughty sheep and they should never be left unsupervised. It isn't about trust. It is about immaturity, ignorance, peer pressure, youthful adventure, temptation, and lust. Your young teen is in no capacity to deal with all of these elements of potential disaster on their own, nor should you be willing to allow them to fly solo too early.

I have labeled the children of today as the "Internet Generation" due to their highly advanced computer skills and propensity to seek out and use web sites such as YouTube and MySpace. Web sites such as these motivate and enable children to promote themselves to the rest of the world and provide personal biographical information for anyone to read. They also allow children to display seductive photographs of themselves and share their sexual fantasies. These web sites are feeding grounds for predators, arming them with all of the information they need to choose and pursue multiple potential victims. Jesus told us that in the last days men would acquire great knowledge and become lovers of themselves. He obviously foresaw the future. Satan is brilliantly orchestrating man's own lustful desires and the technological advances of today into an apocalyptic outcome.

Pre-teens and younger teenagers are the most common victims of those who roam cyberspace. These age groups are beginning to experience the development of their own sexuality, so they are curious and open for erotic conversation. The predator is all too ready to satisfy and enhance that child's curiosity. This leads the child to be secretive and lie to their parents about their newfound friend. I have found that most children will share this kind of activity with at least one close friend. Because it is exciting to them, they feel the need to tell someone about it. This is why I always try to interview the child victim's friends if they make themselves available. Many times the victim will share things about their experience with the predator with a close friend that they would not share with any adult, let alone the police.

Like many law enforcement agencies around the nation, the Monroe County Sheriff's office has dedicated an undercover deputy to play the role of a young teenager on the Internet. Similar to what has been demonstrated on network news television shows, the undercover deputy portrays himself as a twelve- or thirteen-year-old boy or girl seeking attention in order to proactively lure the predators away from other potential victims and into our snare. At times, the deputy may be playing the role on as many as four different computers simultaneously while sitting in his office. He educates himself on matters and language that are pertinent to either a teenage girl or teenage boy in order to appear authentic. Cyberspace predators are already becoming quite familiar with police tactics in this area.

I had the honor of being a member of the selection committee that interviewed candidates and selected the undercover deputies for this program, and I have made it a point to have follow-up discussions with them throughout their assignments. What these deputies have been exposed to and endured as a result of their conversations with these creeps is incredible. It is not uncommon for the undercover deputy to be viewing three or four separate computer monitors at the same time depicting different adult males exposing themselves and masturbating. The predator's intentionally have their webcams zoomed in on their groin areas, providing the undercover deputy with a full screen of erect male genitalia. Can you even imagine having to look at three or four computer screens depicting such filth at the same time, and then having to carry on a conversation with each predator as though you were a young teenager enjoying this activity? I think it is safe to assume that most of us would probably vomit, especially with the realization that millions of children are being exposed to this perverted evil every day in the sanctity of our own homes. Undercover deputies have been extremely successful in luring these deviants to a neutral location, where they are anticipating meeting a young teenage boy or girl for sex. You can imagine what an unpleasant surprise it is for them when they are met by a welcome committee of plainclothes police officers instead. Upon their arrest, some of these predators are found to be in possession of items such as rope, duct tape, sexual devices and lubricant. I credit these deputies for the program's success and for possessing incredible intestinal fortitude in such a challenging assignment.

For me, the Internet has added a new dimension of speculation in regard to what leads a man to possess images of children being molested or to fantasize about molesting young children. A recent case in the Rochester area serves as a perfect example of this issue. A doctor who was serving as the Director of Pediatric Emergency Medicine at a prestigious hospital was arrested and subsequently pled guilty for the possession of hundreds of child porn images on his computer. This man was considered to be both a leader and mentor in a highly-esteemed, honorable profession. I was not involved in the case, nor did I have an opportunity to speak with the doctor. Had I had the opportunity, these are some of the questions I would have asked him: What led a highly-educated, experienced and recognized doctor to amass child pornography? Did he have a sexual attraction to children from the time that he was a young man? If so, did that attraction in some perverted way influence him to become a pediatrician? Or, did his appetite for erotica and pornography place him on that slippery slope of iniquity and filth that eventually lured him into child porn sites? In other words, did he evolve into a pedophile as a result of his addiction to Internet porn, or had he always carried the dark secret of being sexually attracted to young children deep inside him, and the Internet porn sites simply cultivated this ugly sin?

Based on my professional experience, the Internet has become one of Satan's most important weapons against man's spiritual health. The Internet can be the Interstate of Iniquity, the Freeway of Filth and the Highway to Hell if a man allows himself to travel into the sexually perverted areas of cyberspace. Once a man gets hooked on pornography it is like being hooked on crack: he will constantly try to enhance his stimulation by increasing the shock value of the pornographic material that he is viewing. This is a dangerous existence on a very slippery and treacherous slope. It starts out with the standard pornography of naked women, and men and women having sex. In time the viewer needs something more graphic in nature for the same thrill effect, so he will move on to sexual sadism and more violent material. When that loses its luster he may even move on to homosexual material. I truly believe that when a man is at this phase, he unwittingly invites a demon to take over his life through the gateway of his lust. Eventually, his appetite becomes insatiable. He then moves on to "barely legal" teenager pornography, and at length he lands in the full-blown child pornography sites.

I have interviewed child predators who claimed that they were spawned as a result of their addiction to Internet pornography. Some of the predators I have interrogated over the years have told me that when they began viewing child pornography, they knew deep down in their heart that what they were doing was very wrong and against everything they believed in, but they had lost control of their lust at that point and were unable to stop. It should be noted that when a man is viewing any type of adult porn web sites, he is constantly being attacked by countless pop-ups that come across his screen, attempting to lure him to a different porn site. Some of these pop-ups are for child porn sites. Once Satan knows you're in the ball park, he invites you to the dugout and then eventually pulls you into his clubhouse.

CHAPTER 17

—∿—

COMMON RISK FACTORS
FOR SEXUAL ABUSE

" *There are only two kinds of people in the end: Those who say to God, 'Thy will be done,' and those to whom God says, in the end, 'Thy will be done.'* "

C.S. LEWIS

THE BREAKDOWN OF THE FAMILY INSTITUTION

There is a high correlation between the breakdown of the family institution and sexual abuse of our children. Single parenting has become very common in our society. Any single parent will tell you that it is no easy task to raise and protect their children, and yet make a living to support them as well. Many of the child victims I have met over the years were from broken families, lacking the proper parental supervision at the time of their victimization. If the shepherd continually leaves his flock unattended or improperly attended by the wrong person, the sheep will become vulnerable to the watchful predator. Some members of the flock will begin to wander away from the safety of the flock and into harm's way. Predatory animals of the African Serengeti Plain stalk at watering holes because their prey will eventually have to risk coming into the open to drink the life-sustaining water that can't be found elsewhere. Similarly, the child predator knows that children from broken homes will be exposed for the simple reason that the single parent can't always be there to protect their children if they are somewhere else working to support them. So the child predator will place himself in areas and situations where single parents and their children reside, play, and worship, hoping to take advantage of their vulnerability.

Dual-income families also face this vulnerability. When both parents are employed outside the home, their child is away from them for most of the daytime hours. It allows other adults to influence that child's personality and upbringing. The child becomes more open-minded to the other adult's ideas and attitudes, for the caregivers are play-ing a pseudo-parental role. In my personal opinion, children in these situations become more comfortable trusting other adults as the role of their own parents becomes less critical to their daily routine. The child is then more vulnerable to trusting the wrong adult, increasing the risk of being sexually offended. In addition, communication between parent and child is seriously reduced due to this separation. An over-worked and overtired parent will find it more difficult to de-velop a personal relationship with each of their children.

While some parents are fortunate to have their own parents provide childcare services, many must rely on pro-fessional daycare or a helpful friend or relative. This factor alone increases the risk of their child being targeted by a predator. Policies and protocols to protect children in day-care facilities are not always followed due to staff shortage, lack of training, or parents who challenge the rules. These circumstances make the facility vulnerable to a manipulative person with evil intentions. In the case of a helpful friend or relative, a parent can never really know what that person does or doesn't do, and whether they are providing a consistently safe environment for their child. Tragically, in some cases that person is the one offending the child. The parents are usually the last ones to know because they placed too much trust in these people. The most common factor I see in these types of cases is naiveté: it is hard to believe that someone in whom we have placed such great trust would expose our child to a predator or harm our child directly.

STEPFATHERS AND LIVE-IN BOYFRIENDS

Stepfathers and live-in boyfriends are frequent sexual offenders in an interfamilial setting. Obviously, not all stepfathers and live-in boyfriends are child predators, but I have arrested many predators who were operating in one of these roles. Based upon my experience, it is a correlation that cannot be ignored. Single mothers who expose their children to the men that they are dating increase the risk of their children becoming victims of sexual abuse. No matter how wonderful or genuine a male suitor appears, a mother should not expose her children to the man until he has withstood the test of time and a thorough spiritual scrutiny. Remember, these predators are wolves in sheep's clothing. They are master manipulators, and very engaging, crafty communicators. If a man desires to meet and spend time with your children, put a hedge of protection around them. Tell him that they are off limits for a very long time. This will clearly demonstrate that you are no one to mess with when it comes to your children. If he is an honorable man, he will not take offense to your protective attitude. Become suspicious if he takes issue with your strategy and accuses you of not trusting him enough. Tell him that you will not use your precious children as a means to demonstrate your trust. Become suspicious of his motivation if he brings up meeting your children again. Is he using his relationship with you just to gain access to them? He may tell you that he "loves children." While that might be true, he may love them for the wrong reasons. Become even more suspicious if he still tries to bring them into your activities together, such as buying them tickets to a function without your approval. Frankly, if you tell him that your children are off limits, then he should never bring them up again. Your suitor should be interested in you and you alone. Your children are your most precious possession and they should not be shared with just anyone. If any man has a problem with this philosophy, show him the door and close it behind him. I also offer this cardinal rule: When a single mother makes the decision to expose her children to a man she has come to know and trust, she should still never leave him alone with them. No ifs, ands or buts. This is the only absolute way to protect your children from this risk.

CHILDREN MOLESTING OTHER CHILDREN

The thought of a child sexually molesting another child is something that most of us never desire to even contemplate. Unfortunately, it occurs frequently, so every parent or guardian should be aware of the potential danger of this happening among their own children. Based on what I've seen and dealt with, I advise parents not to leave young children or pre-adolescent children under the sole care of pre-adolescent and teenage males. Whether you choose to acknowledge it or not, pre-teen and teenage boys can easily be characterized as raging hormones on two feet. Some of them will make tragic choices, using their younger siblings, cousins, or the neighbor's children as their personal sex objects to experiment on.

I don't know what makes certain children prone to this type of behavior or why. What I do know is that many of the tragic incidents I have investigated occurred without any warning signs. Therefore, I think it would be wise to err on the side of caution and not delegate any male youth as your children's caretaker in your absence. Unless you can read someone's mind, there is no way of knowing what level of sexual temptation that young male may be struggling with. So why risk it?

CHAPTER 18

—⟋⟍⟍—

PARENTS AND GUARDIANS: THE LORD'S SHEPHERDS

"*The LORD [is] my shepherd; I shall not want.
He maketh me to lie down in green pastures:
He leadeth me beside the still waters.
He restoreth my soul: He leadeth me
in the paths of righteousness for
His name's sake. Yea, though I walk
through the valley of the shadow of
death, I will fear no evil: for Thou
[art] with me; Thy rod and Thy staff
they comfort me. Thou preparest a
table before me in the presence of
mine enemies: Thou anointest my
head with oil; my cup runneth over.
Surely goodness and mercy shall
follow me all the days of my life:
and I will dwell in the house of
the LORD for ever.*"

*P*SALM 23 (KJV)

The Bible is loaded with countless pearls of wisdom that can be applied to raising our children. Most of us have been taught by our pastors that God gave us the Bible to serve as our manual for daily living and communing with Him. I know from my own personal experience that I walk in peace and joy throughout the day when I am reading, praying and meditating on God's Word. When I am self-absorbed in my own thoughts and ulterior motives, I tend to become very distracted and annoyed with the smallest and simplest problems of life. It is with good reason that we should strive every day to chew on some of God's Word, for it will steer both our hearts and our parenting habits in the right direction. It truly is our daily bread.

The twenty-third psalm is a remarkable Scripture because it can be applied to our lives in so many different ways. Authored by King David when he was a young shepherd, it identifies God as our Shepherd as He provides, protects, and cares for us unconditionally. The first part also reflects how King David cared for his flock while God prepared him to become Israel's next king. Most importantly, it speaks to us about Jesus, our Good Shepherd, and His perfect rule over those who trust in Him. It is for these reasons that I believe it can serve as a great example for parenting. I only wish that I had used it when my children were young.

Parents and guardians have been appointed to feed and care for God's children, both physically and spiritually (1 Timothy 5:8, Ephesians 6:4b). It is up to us to lay the right moral foundation and encourage them to cultivate a personal relationship with our Heavenly Father through Jesus Christ. It is wise for us to take a look at each verse of this psalm and consider how we should incorporate it into caring for our assigned flock of lambs.

The first verse, "The Lord is my Shepherd; I shall not want," can be translated into the belief that we, as parents, are the shepherds of our children. Parents are God's representatives and must uphold His expectations of how a child should be cared for. The King James word "want" equates to "lack" in our modern vernacular. It does not imply that every desire will be satisfied, but rather that every need will be met. While we are directed to lavish our children with unconditional love, I don't believe that God designed the family structure to be run as a democracy. A shepherd does not allow his sheep and lambs to take a vote on who, what, when, where or how he cares for them. He knows what they need, and he provides it for them.

Most children will always desire and ask for more of everything, for it is in our sin nature from birth. However, we must be careful in our response. If we give our children too much too fast, they will never be satisfied. They may develop into unruly adults who stumble into danger during their quest to attain more material possessions and satisfy their physical lusts. We also must constantly balance the rewards and rebukes, for too much of one or the other may send them in the wrong direction. In today's world, this is no easy task; nevertheless, it needs tending on a daily basis.

The second verse, "He maketh me to lie down in green pastures: He leadeth me beside the still waters," can be applied to providing a safe environment for our children to live in. The two important words in this verse are "makes" and "leads." Parents are responsible to provide a safe and harmonious environment for their children. Without the comfort of a secure home, a child will not be able to develop to their full potential and more than likely will suffer from anxiety or other emotional problems. Parents must lead their children away from the tumultuous waters which may cause them consternation or overwhelm them. Parents must lead their children to the quiet, still places every day. This could be in the form of reading with them without any distractions, or just talking to them quietly about their day.

If you bring your child to a calm, still place every day, they will learn to enjoy and appreciate the sense of tranquility that it brings them. Even if it is for a very short period of time, children will find comfort in the routine. Because you will come to represent peace and a safe refuge, eventually your children will look upon you as we look upon our Heavenly Father. As they mature, you should be bringing them into the presence of the Lord during these quiet sessions. This will enable them to make a seamless transformation from you to our Heavenly Father when they become old enough to understand the value of communing with Him daily. Those of us who walk with Him have experienced many wonderful times of peace, comfort and joy in His presence. It truly is a peace unlike any other (John 14:27). If we have often ushered our children into that place with us, they will become thirsty for it for themselves.

The third verse states: "He restoreth my soul: He leadeth me in the paths of righteousness for His name's sake." If a parent consistently follows the principles of the aforementioned verses, their child will find refreshment and restoration. Believe it or not, children—even teenagers—long to be inspired, led and counseled by the adults who love and care for them. There will be a plethora of potential paths that a child can take during their lifetime. With God's counsel, we must guide each of our children to the one that He has mapped out for them. We must set aside our own preconceived notions and assist our children in determining what gifts the Lord has bestowed upon them in order to bring glory to Him and allow them the greatest sense of fulfillment during their short time on this earth. We have our children for a certain number of years to train and inspire them into becoming good, productive citizens who will enjoy a personal relationship with their Creator. If we don't at least try to cultivate a personal relationship with them, then what will they have to draw from? What example have we provided them?

Even if our child ultimately rejects us and rebels when they are old enough to walk out, God will provide us with a sense of peace that we tried to do our best. While this outcome would obviously cause us great pain and sadness, God will comfort us beyond our natural understanding. We will have the confidence that we laid the proper foundation for our child to build upon when they decide for themselves if they will follow Jesus Christ. When they make that choice, they will look back and begin to reap the benefits of all of our efforts and loving guidance.

If I could do it all over again, I would speak more often with a quiet voice to my children when they were young and express myself gently during times of rebuke. I would never be a pushover, for it's not in my nature. I would exhibit more of a quiet strength in times of turmoil and I would not yell as much. I am sure that it would have saved my children and me a lot of unnecessary heartache, and they would have responded better. Now that my children are older and dealing with serious, life-altering issues at times, I try to be a person of restoration and gentle guidance. I don't always achieve this goal, but I try to adjust quickly to the way that God would deal with the issue. It boils down to having faith in Him and His timing, trusting that He works everything to the good for those who love Him.

The fourth verse proclaims: "Yea, though I walk through the valley of the shadow of death, I will fear no evil; for Thou art with me; Thy rod and Thy staff they comfort me." This encompasses a lot, for it talks of God comforting His children during trials and tribulations, which can include sickness and disease. Being with our children during the difficult times in their lives comes naturally to most parents. No one wants to see their child suffer, and most of us would do anything or sacrifice all that we possess to help our child.

The rod and staff are symbols of how the Good Shepherd tends to His flock just as the ancient shepherds tended to theirs. These tools represent defense against predators, direction, and discipline. I have come to call these the "three D's" of raising children. All three of these elements must be utilized every day. Being weak in one of them could lead to calamity and eventual destruction. No doubt, raising a child is the most difficult and challenging task that we could ever undertake. There will be no short cuts. Every child will present their own set of challenges. No matter what socio-economic plane we live in, raising a child is the great equalizer. While added finances might help, it certainly won't replace what is required to raise a child in a godly manner. God made it that way. Being a parent can be a lonely, thankless job if we don't seek God and follow His lead. Seeking His guidance, comfort and counsel will empower us to have confidence in what we are doing, even during the many times of difficulty.

All of our precious lambs are individuals. We must become intimately familiar with each and every one under our care. We must apply different strategies of managing them according to their individual personalities, not ours. Just look at the way that God dealt with His prophets or other notable characters in the Bible. While His message is always the same, God demonstrated it to different people in different ways. Jesus' earthly ministry was conducted mostly in the rural Galilean region of Israel, where farming and fishing were the main sources of income. He taught them by using parables that often spoke of agricultural matters so that they could easily understand His message. How well do you know each of your children? Can you recite their hopes and dreams? Do you know who their favorite friends are and what they are all about? Remember, Jesus knew all about everyone that He ministered to, just as He knows us today. We must follow His example and really get to know and understand each one of our children as the individuals that they really are, not the ones that we desire them to become.

A parent should know what particular methods of communication work most effectively with each child. For instance, my youngest daughter was the openly rebellious one. Our other two children were what I call passive resisters. They didn't rock the boat, but once they were out of the house, they would get into trouble while on the sneak. My youngest child would openly defy and challenge me in a very obnoxious manner, no matter who was around or where we were. She ate confrontation for breakfast every day and appeared to respond to my voice only when my veins were popping out of my neck. Her strong will is what defines her determination and the awesome success that she has enjoyed as a young adult. On the other hand, that strong will can be her downfall when it isn't being channeled in a positive direction. At times, she can be like a thoroughbred racehorse, thrashing and snorting in anticipation of its leap out of the starting gate. It was only after years of bashing my head against the wall that I finally came to the conclusion that I had to manage her in an entirely different manner than our two older children. Since that revelation, I have held her to a higher standard in some areas since she has been allowed to operate on a more independent basis. Unlike the rest of us who are quite content living on the ground, she has been allowed to cruise in her comfort zone 35,000 feet above sea level, soaring above the rest of us. As a result of this management adjustment, I have been blessed by not only her personal achievements, but her opening her heart to Jesus Christ and truly accepting Him as her Lord and Savior. Over the past several years, she has learned and lived by the Scripture that states: "To whom much is given, much is required." (Luke 12:48)

Direction and discipline should be applied with *agape* (unconditional) love, not anger or resentment toward our children. The cliché "different strokes for different folks" should be applied to raising our children as the individuals that God made them. The following story captures the essence of my relationship with our youngest daughter over the years. On one occasion during her tumultuous teens, she threatened to call the police on me if I touched her after I ordered her to her room. Now, other than a slap on her little bum when she was still in diapers, I have never laid a hand on either of my daughters. So where she got these thoughts of physical force is still a mystery to me. Knowing that I would never physically hurt her, my youngest daughter took great pleasure in pushing me to the edge with absolutely no fear. But this time I met her challenge with a calm and assertive voice. Knowing how ticklish she was, I told her that if she didn't retreat to her room and cool down, I was going to tickle her until she couldn't catch her breath. I then warned her that she would most likely lose control of her bodily functions at that point and would probably involuntarily pee and poop her pants while thrashing about on the living room floor. I then challenged her to call the police and try to report such an occurrence, and consider how ridiculous she would sound. I assured my daughter that both she and her attempted report would serve as one of the more memorable laughs of several roll calls at the police substation.

Seeing the intense conviction in my eyes, her entire demeanor changed. She could see that I wasn't kidding. My daughter knew that she had pushed me to the edge, and now I had a viable plan to cause her duress if she did not comply with my very reasonable demand that she go to her room to cool down. Although she was still spitting her venom at me the whole time, she eventually walked into her bedroom and closed the door.

The fifth verse states: "Thou preparest a table before me in the presence of mine enemies: Thou anointest my head with oil; my cup runneth over." God is preparing a banquet for when we join Him at His table in heaven. He anoints our head with oil to honor us as His special guest, and our cup is always full of His best wine. How do we apply this verse to raising our children? We embrace it and emulate its meaning by honoring our children and providing them with a spiritually bountiful life and unconditional love.

We have become a nation that places great value on material possessions. It is corrupting our children's priorities. Parents need to put more emphasis on having a personal relationship with God themselves, and set the right example for their children. I am not talking about drilling our children into religious submission through legalism and condemnation. When Jesus fellowshipped with the tax collectors, thieves and prostitutes, He didn't hit them over the head with dogmatic doctrine. Jesus simply loved and honored them, unconditionally. He put them first. We must follow suit and put our children before ourselves, every day. Our selfless care for them is our best witness. Lord knows, I have had my share of selfish days over the years where I did not think of my children before fulfilling my own desires. But if we string too many selfish days together over a protracted period, our children will be vulnerable to child predators because they will be thirsty for what we didn't give them. We live in a "me first" society. As a result, many parents will place the importance of their child's needs a little lower than some of their own. I am not implying that these parents don't love their children. We are all guilty of poor prioritization at times. Child predators are excellent students of human behavior and have learned to manipulate this parental lapse in good judgment. They depend on it: so beware.

Our children are our most valuable possession. Every day that they are in our care we must treat them accordingly, honoring them with abundant, self-sacrificing love and spiritual guidance. Some people would say that this approach is a little over the top, too protective, or too dangerous to the parent's own well-being. Not from where I sit and from what I've seen. The Good Shepherd doesn't take a day off from overseeing and protecting His flock, so why should we?

Verse six reflects a blessed hope and comfort: "Surely goodness and mercy shall follow me all the days of my life: and I will dwell in the house of the LORD forever." God bestows His overabundant love, mercy and grace on us, and it follows us throughout our entire life. Those of us who enjoy a personal relationship with our Heavenly Father through Jesus Christ are promised to dwell in His house now and forever. This doesn't mean that we will not suffer hardship and loss on this side of eternity. But it promises that He will comfort us beyond our own understanding during those difficult times as we prepare for life with Him in His kingdom.

I never knew what unconditional, *agape* love was until we had our first child. Then I got a glimpse of what God must feel for us as His children. No matter what our children do in life, they will always receive my mercy and grace. It will follow them wherever their life takes them, even if they abandon me. It doesn't make sense, nor do I understand it enough to put it into words. It just is. The important thing is that we communicate this God-breathed principle to our children. This doesn't mean that we have to accept our children becoming degenerates or criminals. God would never honor and bless that either. However, we must assure our children that we will always love them no matter what they do. They should know that they can return to the fold with a repentant, humble heart, just as the prodigal son did. As the Lord teaches us in His Word, we should hate the sin, but love the sinner. Godly, *agape* love will always prevail, no matter what the circumstances.

"But seek ye first the kingdom of God and His righteousness..."

"Finally, my brethren, be strong in the Lord, and in the power of His might.

Put on the whole armor of God that ye may be able to stand against the wiles of the Devil. For we wrestle not against flesh and blood, but against principalities, against powers, against rulers of darkness of this world, against spiritual wickedness in high places. Wherefore take unto you the whole armor of God that ye may be able to withstand the evil day, and having done all, to stand.

Stand therefore, having your loins girt about with truth, and having on the breastplate of righteousness; And your feet shod with preparation of the gospel of peace;

Above all, taking the shield of faith, wherewith ye shall be able to quench all the fiery darts of the wicked. And take the helmet of salvation, and the sword of the Spirit, which is the word of God; Praying always with all prayer and supplication in the Spirit, and watching thereunto with all perseverance and supplication for all saints."

CHAPTER 19

—⚇—

PROTECT YOUR CHILDREN
WITH PRAYER

*R*aising a child has never been more treacherous than it is right now, and it is only getting worse. I grew up during the tumultuous 1960s and 1970s, when the youth turned the social system of this country upside-down. But back then, the country was being built by the generation of World War II. It was far from perfect, but they laid a rock-solid foundation of wholesome morals and religious beliefs that were by and large based upon Biblical Christianity. As a result, God blessed this nation with an economy that was second to no other in the world. We became God's superpower.

While the past fifty years have seen unprecedented, incredible technological advances, the granite foundation built by our parents and grandparents has been reduced to shifting sand. Aside from being fleeced by greedy and unscrupulous high level executives, much of corporate America appears to be downsizing and outsourcing many traditional and manufacturing jobs to other countries. Additionally, we've become a population that places a distortedly high value in entertainment, pouring billions into the sports and gambling, pornography, and drug industries. Personal debt is off the charts. We have evolved into a nation of pleasure-seeking people, pursuing a "comfortable" lifestyle at the expense of our own eternal salvation.

This is the legacy that we are leaving our children. As a result, our children's own morals and values are being corrupted. Tragically, many of the people that they admire are nothing more than lovers of themselves, indifferent to the world around them. These so-called role models, whom we adults have placed on a pedestal and financially supported, are leading our children down the wide path of self-destruction. Satan, the master deceiver and manipulator, loves every bit of it.

Too many times I have lain in bed during the desolate night hours worrying about my children. I worry about their health, their personal safety, and their future. When they were younger, I would think about my own mortality, wondering how they would cope without me to love and protect them. I have often stated in exasperation that being a parent feels like I have been sentenced to a life of worrying. As parents, we know that many dangers, both physical and spiritual, surround our children. It is for this very reason that we should call upon God's Holy Spirit to protect our children, comfort us, and take away our needless worry. I have learned that replacing worry with prayer is not only good for my children's sake but it comforts me and gives me a sense of peace that is beyond my ability to attain on my own or from another human being. It fills that void in me that nothing else seems to fill.

Jesus instructed his apostles not to worry and stated that worrying doesn't help any situation (Matthew 6:27).

Easier said than done, but it is true. I can't think of one instance where worrying assisted me in resolving any issue, especially one involving my children. We must learn to surrender our worries, failures and lamentations to the Holy Spirit every day. This is especially true in the evening when the enemy likes to torment us as we try to rest. Jesus said, "Come to me, all you who labor and are heavy laden, and I will give you rest." (Matthew11:28 NKJV).

Some of the heaviest burdens that I have borne as an adult had to do with my children. The enemy will attack us through our children in an attempt to distract us and weaken our faith, and ultimately separate us from God. Therefore, we must pray unceasingly for strength, wisdom and comfort. While God does not require us to pray on our knees, I suggest that every parent take a knee at least once a day to pray for their children. A sincere act of respect and honor toward our Heavenly Father on behalf of our children demonstrates true humility. The Bible teaches us that "God resists the proud, but gives grace to the humble."(James 4:6b, NKJV) For our children's sake, all of us parents should pray fervently and daily before God. We will worry far less and sleep more soundly as a result.

Consider the Scripture from Colossians 1:9-11 (NLT) as a foundation of daily prayer for your children:

"So we have not stopped praying for you since we first heard about you. We ask God to give you complete knowledge of his will and to give you spiritual wisdom and understanding. Then the way you live will always honor and please the Lord, and your lives will produce every kind of good fruit. All the while, you will grow as you learn to know God better

and better. We also pray that you will be strengthened with all his glorious power so you will have all the endurance and patience you need. May you be filled with joy, always thanking the Father."

Build upon this in your own personal dialogue with God's Spirit. I have learned that prayer should not be regimented and redundant. It should be both personal and intimate. It should be as if you are talking to your best friend. Prayer is a two-way conversation, so allow time to be silent and just listen and feel His presence. Allow God's peace to enter and dwell in you.

For the skeptics who lack confidence in intercessory prayer, I suggest that you choose from the vast written commentary that exists in both secular and Christian book stores which cite true examples of the miracles produced by prayer. The list of available credible material out there is endless.

One of my favorite true stories is written by distinguished author and speaker Cheri Fuller:

The missionary rose and prepared to leave the campsite where he had spent the night en route to the city for medical supplies. He extinguished his small campfire, pulled on his canvas backpack, and hopped on his motorcycle to continue his ride through the African jungle. Every two weeks he made this two-day journey to collect money from a bank and purchase medicine and supplies for the small field hospital where he served. When he completed those errands, he hopped on his bike again for the two-day return trip.

When the missionary arrived in the city, he collected his money and medical supplies and was just about to leave for home when he saw two men fighting in the street. Since one of the men was seriously injured, the missionary stopped, treated him for his injuries, and shared the love of Christ with him. The missionary began his two-day trek home, stopping in the jungle again to camp overnight.

Two weeks later, as was his custom, the missionary again made the journey to the city. As he ran his various errands, a young man approached him—the same young man the missionary had ministered to during his previous trip. "I knew you carried medicine with you," the man said, "so my friends and I followed you to your campsite in the jungle after you helped me in the street. We planned to kill you and take all the money and drugs. But just as we were about to move in and attack you, we saw twenty-six armed guards surround and protect you."

"You must be mistaken," said the missionary. "I was all alone when I spent the night in the jungle. There were no guards or anyone else with me."

"But sir, I wasn't the only one who saw the guards. My five companions saw them, too. We counted them! There were twenty-six bodyguards, too many for us to handle. Their presence stopped us from killing you."

Months later, the missionary related this story to the congregation gathered at his home church in Michigan. As he spoke, one of the men listening stood up and interrupted him to ask the exact day the incident in the jungle had occurred. When the missionary identified the specific month and day of the week, the man told him "the rest of the story."

"On the exact night of your incident in Africa, it was morning here in Michigan, and I was on the golf course. I

was about to putt when I felt a strong urge to pray for you. The urge was so strong that I left the golf course and called some men of our church right here in this sanctuary to join me in praying for you. Would all you men who prayed with me that day stand up?"

The missionary wasn't concerned with who the men were; he was too busy counting them, one by one. Finally he reached the last one. There were twenty six-men—the exact number of "armed guards" the thwarted attackers had seen.[1]

If this true story does not boost your confidence in the Lord's desire to protect you and your children, then I have no words that will convince you. I suggest that you begin to simply ask God to help you believe in His existence and unconditional love for all of those who seek Him.

We need only look to the history of the Roman Empire to determine our pending fate as a nation. I believe that the only way to change our country's Titanic course for the sake of our children is to pray unceasingly for parental guidance and their salvation. There is no doubt in my mind that if we, as a nation of parents, repent from our own rebellion and sin and then call upon the Lord with a sincere and humble heart, He will answer (2 Chronicles 7:14). But we need to keep knocking on the Lord's door every day. Don't allow unclean spirits to convince you that you are not worthy or

---

1. Cheri Fuller, Author and Speaker, www.cherifuller.com.
Used by permission from her book WHEN FAMILIES PRAY, a
40-day (or week) devotional for parents & children. Published by
Multnomah/Waterbrook, Colorado Springs, CO.

good enough to ask the Lord for help. Jesus tells us in the Gospels that he came to cure those who are sick and in need of Him, not the self-proclaimed healthy people (Matthew 9:11-13). We are in the midst of a universal spiritual war. Prayer with a repentant heart is our best weapon. Jesus told us that where two or more are gathered in His name, He will be present (Matthew 18:20). Corporate or community prayer equates to a nuclear megaton-size spiritual bomb that will inflict great casualties against the Devil and his demonic army.

CHAPTER 20

—ⅶ—

QUICK REVIEW

*K*eep the following list in the forefront of your mind as you make decisions and monitor your children's activities. Be diligent in safeguarding your child from those inside their social circle using these principles, and you will automatically protect them from those outside the circle.

CAUTION FLAGS

1. OFFERS OF ASSISTANCE.

Be suspicious of people who manipulate their way into your life under the ruse of assisting you through a difficult time. Do they continue to offer assistance when it is no longer needed?

2. GREAT PERSONAL INVESTMENT.

Remember, the men that you trust most and display an obvious affection toward your children are the ones most likely to molest them. Have they made personal sacrifices, investing time and money to gain your trust? The child predator does this for the sole purpose of obtaining access to a child and eventually separating them from their parents.

3. SEEKING CONSTANT CONTACT.

Be leery of the person who is constantly seeking contact with your child because they "love children."

4. PROFESSIONALS SEEKING ALONE TIME WITH YOUR CHILD OUTSIDE OF THEIR NORMAL ROLE.

If your child is involved with a child-care professional, teacher, coach, mentor, or counselor in an extracurricular activity in a way that stretches beyond what they normally do for most children, stay on top of the situation and watch the relationship very closely. There are legitimate people in these professions who extend themselves beyond their professional role for the right reason. However, the predator will utilize this type of relationship to gain alone time with a child. Terminate the relationship if this person appears overly motivated to be alone with your child frequently.

5. TEENAGE BOYS PROVIDING CHILDCARE.

Stay away from allowing teenage boys to care for your children unattended, even if they are his younger siblings. They are not in control of their raging hormones and are influenced by today's sensual world via the Internet and other forms of media. If they are left alone with defenseless small children, they might decide to experiment on them.

6. MEN MAKING YOUR LIFE VERY CONVENIENT.

Be suspicious of any male who desires to be around your child and makes it convenient for you to enjoy time for yourself by offering to take the child.

7. POSSESSIVENESS.

Terminate your relationship with the person who becomes, or attempts to become, possessive of your child. This is definitely a red flag. Stay away from them.

8. SOLO TRAVEL.

Don't allow your child to travel alone with any male other than their own father. It doesn't matter how young or old they are or how much you trust them.

9. INTEREST IN PORNOGRAPHY.

If the child's father is a chronic voyeur of pornography, then do not allow him to be alone with them.

10. EXCESSIVE COMPLIMENTS.

Be suspicious of any male who tells you how attractive your child is—especially more than once.

11. FALSE SENSE OF SECURITY IN YOUR CHILD'S EDUCATION OR "STREET SMARTS."

Increasing a child's awareness of the danger that exists in this world is a good thing. However, the responsibility of keeping them safe falls directly on the shoulders of God's appointed shepherds, their parents. While safety information provided by schools is valuable, I believe that it may give some parents a false sense of security that their children are equipped to protect themselves from being tricked and seduced by a child predator. Children seek attention from those they look up to. This is what makes them so vulnerable. As they get older you will need to give them more freedom, but

don't stop protecting them, because they are still emotionally vulnerable. Asking a child of any age to not fall victim
to the cunning serpent is like asking a lamb to protect itself
from a wolf.

12. Computer and cell phone use.

Your child's activity on computers and cell phones must be
constantly monitored. Nothing good comes from easy access
and overuse of these devices.

13. Not Safe In Numbers

Unsupervised youths should not be considered safe in numbers. It is rather a potential for disaster, as the flock of sheep
is without their shepherd.

14. Inattentiveness to personal surroundings.

Teach your children and young adults to be constantly
aware of their surroundings, especially when getting in
and out of their vehicles and while using ATM machines.
Remind them that cell phone use will distract them from
paying attention.

15. Being careless with beverages.

Especially if they socialize at parties and nightclubs, teach
your children never to accept an open beverage from someone or let go of it after they observed it being poured and
served to them.

16. BEWARE OF SECLUDED WALKWAYS

Popular bike paths, hiking trails and canal paths can be treacherous areas for lone females to bike, jog and walk along. Serial offenders will frequent these locations for their next victim.

Be aware that the enemy wants parents to place more priorities ahead of their children, thereby placing them in a position where they must rely on other people and resources to care for them. As you have learned, the more time that your children are not under your supervision, the more likely they are to cross paths with a child predator. Daily communication with your children and constant parental supervision are the two most important components to keeping your children safe. Don't forget to pray for your children daily and begin to pray *with* your children as soon as they are capable of carrying on a conversation with you.

Parents who consistently practice these suggestions will significantly reduce the chances of their children being seduced and molested. If you are vulnerable in one of these areas, then do whatever it takes to close the gap. The safety of your children is at stake.

CHAPTER 21

—⁓—

POTENTIAL SIGNS OF A SEXUALLY MOLESTED CHILD

"A merry heart makes a cheerful countenance, but by sorrow of the heart the spirit is broken.

PROVERBS 15:13 (NKJV)

Frequently a child who has been sexually offended will display changes in their behavior long before they verbalize what had occurred. If they never disclose the abuse, they may never free themselves of the emotional burden and they will carry behavioral scars into adulthood. Many times parents of victims have observed one or more of these indicators, but understandably, they never suspected that it was the result of being sexually abused. Below is a list of indicators that I have seen over the years.

1. Your child displays unwarranted anger and hostility on a frequent basis.
2. Your child appears depressed and displays a low countenance.

3. Your child has become uncharacteristically anti-social.

4. Your child has lost their appetite, even for their favorite foods.

5. Your child no longer enjoys their normal daily routine and activities.

6. Your child uncharacteristically refuses to participate in extracurricular activities.

7. Your child verbalizes suicidal thoughts.

8. Your child suddenly avoids individuals that they were once close to.

9. Your child suddenly avoids certain parts of the residence.

10. Your child wants to move away from the neighborhood.

11. Your child suffers from nightmares and is reluctant to describe them.

12. Your child starts wetting their bed, but it has no medical cause.

13. Unexplainable irritation to their genital and/or rectum areas.

14. Complaint of pain in the genitals and/or rectum.

15. Suspicious marks around the genital areas or rectum.

16. Your young child becomes fixated with their own sexual parts and/or the sexual parts of others.

17. Your young child begins to act out or imitate sexual behavior.

I suggest that any parent who observes one of more of these changes seek the assistance of a pediatric therapist to explore the source of the problem. Hopefully, it will be something unrelated to sexual abuse. But if your child ends up disclosing abuse to the therapist, you have saved your child years of agony and provided law enforcement the opportunity to hold the perpetrator accountable and to protect your child and others from further abuse.

CHAPTER 22

—⟋⟍—

SAFETY TIPS FOR COMMUNITY ORGANIZATIONS

*I*f your children are involved in a church or community organization I urge you to check to see if a policy is in place to prevent children from being molested by an adult or older child. If a policy is in place, take a close look at it. Is it sufficient to keep your child safe? Is it being followed? Rather than criticizing the policy that may be lacking, I encourage you to take it upon yourself to be part of the solution. Attempt to improve the policy and ensure that it is being followed. Seek the assistance of other parents, set up a committee and work as a team. When it comes to the safety of your children, don't rely on others to address the weaknesses of the safety policy. Roll up your sleeves and work to implement a better one.

One of my co-presenters, Tom Corbett, oversees Child and Adult Protective Services as one of the top administrators of the Monroe County Department of Human Services. He recommends checking the following resources and organizations to get an idea of what your organization should implement:

1.   **Boy Scouts of America Youth Protection Policies**
These would be easily adaptable to any church or community organization. Search the Boy Scout website for the term "Youth Protection."

2.   **When Child Abuse comes to Church**
        by Bill Anderson.
This is an inexpensive, useful book based on the experience of a church that had a volunteer sexually abuse a child in a youth program. It was written quite a while ago, but contains great suggestions.

3.   **Reducing the Risk: Making Your Church Safe from Child Sexual Abuse** is a video training program for churches. This is reasonably priced at $50.00 and is used by many religious organizations.

4.   **Most insurance companies** that underwrite youth sport programs, community organizations and churches offer good information about abuse prevention policies in each of these settings.

I suggest that your organization review several of these polices and design one that works best for your organization's needs and the resources that you have to work with. As your organization changes in size and staff turns over, you should re-evaluate your policy and make the needed modifications to keep it effective. Remember, no policy will be effective without consistent adherence, enforcement and accountability. As you have observed in some of the case examples, the child predator will attempt to manipulate people to defeat whatever measures are in place.

If a child predator happens to be reprimanded, he will feign ignorance or offer that it was either bad judgment or an honest mistake. While everyone is entitled to make a mistake, depending on their infraction, you should either suspend that person for a sufficient period of time and then place them under close supervision upon their return, or terminate their participation. Anyone who breaks the policy repeatedly needs to be dealt with swiftly. Obviously, this should not be done in a public setting or with a mean spirit. The director of the program should explain to the offender in front of a witness that the organization has a strict policy with no exceptions when it comes to keeping children safe. We can never be too cautious when we are entrusted with other people's children.

CHAPTER 23

—⁓—

REPORTING AND INVESTIGATING CRIMES AGAINST CHILDREN

"*D*efend the poor and fatherless; Do justice to the afflicted and needy."

PSALM 82:3 (NKJV)

The two most appropriate ways to report suspected child abuse are to call 911 or your local or state child abuse hotline. The number is usually listed on the first page of the local phone book among the emergency phone numbers. Personally, I would call both the child abuse hotline and 911. If only the police are notified through 911, there is a chance that the child protective agency will not be notified to commence their own investigation, especially if the police officer who responds to the call does not believe that a crime was committed. Unfortunately, some of my most serious child abuse investigations were developed after the case was discarded by someone who was either inexperienced in these investigations or simply didn't believe the child.

Always call 911 if it is an emergency or an immediate safety issue. But if you are suspicious, or if a child makes a disclosure to you or someone you know, call the child abuse hotline first and speak to the people who specialize in these types of cases before you call 911. The hotline operators are professional child protective workers who can counsel the reporting person on how the investigation will commence and if 911 should be notified. Either way, the hotline will notify the child protective agency immediately. The child protective agency per their mandate will immediately respond to the complaint and they will work in conjunction with local law enforcement. If the reporting person desires to remain anonymous, the child abuse hotline will honor and facilitate that request and not identify them to law enforcement.

MANDATED REPORTING

New York State requires anyone who is state certified to work with children to report suspected child abuse. I believe that most states have similar statutes. Certified therapists, pediatricians, child psychologists and psychiatrists are among those under this mandate. Every suspected crime against a child needs to be thoroughly investigated by trained professionals, no matter how minor the complaint may appear. As you have learned by now, the initial disclosure of sexual or physical abuse in many cases turns out to be just the tip of the iceberg once an investigation begins to uncover the truth. Some of the most daunting and compelling cases I have worked resulted from what was initially considered a minor complaint.

The Bible clearly tells us to submit to the government and its laws. While I am all for repentance and forgiveness, I despise clergy members who feel that they are above the law in this area and think that this type of crime can be handled purely within the church. When a clergy member does not report suspected child abuse to the local authority or the child abuse hotline, he or she is not in compliance with the law and therefore is operating outside of God's Word. In my opinion, everyone who suspects or knows that a child has been molested, abused or neglected should report it to local law enforcement. I consider this a mandate from God.

INVESTIGATING REPORTED CASES OF CHILD SEXUAL ABUSE

THE MULTI-DISCIPLINARY TEAM ("MDT")

The Multi-Disciplinary Team is a nationally-recognized concept that we have adopted in Monroe County. The MDT in Monroe County is comprised of specially-trained, experienced professionals from law enforcement, Child Protective Services, the Strong Memorial Hospital REACH Program, the Monroe County District Attorney's Office, the United States Attorney's Office, Rape Crisis Center, and area mental health agencies. The main purpose of the MDT is to reduce the number of required investigatory contacts the child victim must endure during their time of crisis, and to enhance and streamline communication between all of the agencies involved. We work together as a unified team to investigate these types of crimes and meet the needs of the victims and their families.

I investigated crimes of child abuse long before the MDT concept was officially introduced to our jurisdiction. Frankly, it was a huge hassle for not only the victim and their parents, but also for all of the agencies involved. The young victims were required to tell their difficult and embarrassing story over and over to too many strangers in foreign surroundings. Before the MDT, investigating these cases worked more like an assembly line. Each agency representative would do their part and move the child and their parents on to the next stop of the investigative and prosecutorial process. Efforts were duplicated and much time was wasted as a result. Usually, my interaction with the other professionals was kept to a minimum, and I rarely kept track of my cases afterward. Needless to say, many victims and their families were overwhelmed and lost in the shuffle of a bureaucratic system of faceless people who rarely took ownership of the cases or followed them through.

Under the MDT model, the victim's need to repeat their story is dramatically reduced. Every reported case is investigated as a team and then tracked as it progresses from the initial report through its prosecution. We accomplish this by working the cases together through the entire process. The MDT meets every other week to update team members on each ongoing investigation and court case. If the victims had waived confidentiality, the victim advocate counselors will provide a report of how each victim and their families are coping through the legal process and after its conclusion. I consider this an important part of the MDT because it keeps us in tune with the human aspect of these cases. The news isn't always good, but many times it is, so it offers us a sense of hope that we are making a difference.

The MDT model has allowed members of each agency to understand the role of all of the other involved agencies. This understanding has transcended into a much more efficient effort. Since we all know what the other team members need to accomplish, we can work hard to assist one another in fulfilling our roles. Because I work with these professionals on a daily basis, I care about them accomplishing their goals, just as they care about mine. We coordinate interviews, medical examinations, and counseling sessions around each other's busy schedules so that everyone can do their job within the required amount of time. Unlike law enforcement, child protective service caseworkers are kept on a strict state-mandated time limit to complete their investigations and coordinate a safety plan for each child. Because I am now sensitive to their situation, I will do everything I can to help the child protective worker fulfill that requirement. In turn, they are careful to not interfere with my investigative strategy of pursuing the truth and arresting the suspect.

The MDT approach has dramatically improved the lines of communication between the police and the doctors who specialize in identifying and treating injuries sustained from physical and sexual abuse. While the doctors must maintain a certain amount of distance from law enforcement to remain unbiased and objective, it has been very beneficial for me to learn from these highly-skilled professionals. As a result of my frequent interaction with them, I have developed an eye for potential medical evidence and gained an understanding of how certain injuries occur under different circumstances. This type of communication and coordination between the MDT members is more valuable than I could ever express, for in the end the victims and their families are better served.

CHILD ADVOCACY CENTERS

Child advocacy centers are non-profit agencies that provide a specific off-site building in which the agencies involved in the MDT can work together. Monroe County is very fortunate to have the nationally-recognized Bivona Child Advocacy Center, which is currently located at 275 Lake Avenue in Rochester. The Bivona Center provides a state-of-the-art facility and support services to investigate reported crimes against children. It offers a warm, friendly environment for the children who visit the center. It houses the medical staff and facilities to conduct the forensic medical examinations and provide treatment for the children. One would think that they were in a pediatrician's office. It also houses child-and adolescent-friendly interview rooms that are equipped with mirrored windows to the adjacent observation rooms, as well as office space for the child protective workers, crisis counselors and support staff. Essentially, it is a one-stop venue that meets most of the needs of the victim and their families while allowing the investigative agencies to work under one roof as a unified team.

The Bivona Center is about three years old at the time of this writing. I view it as one of the most progressive and useful concepts to be introduced to the law enforcement community in Monroe County. Providing the MDT with a physical place for all of these disciplines to coexist in has enhanced our ability to fight this crime to no end. We hope to continue to build upon this solid foundation and expand the center's hours and services. The Bivona Center's Board of Directors, the Director, Mary Whittier, and her staff have already accomplished what no one else thought was possible.

I know that it will continue to grow and raise the bar for other advocacy centers in this part of the country to follow.

Child advocacy centers exist in many parts of the country. I would urge anyone who feels the call to support these generally privately-funded agencies in your area. Their needs are many and without question, their cause is very essential.

CHAPTER 24

—⚏—

DISCERNING THE VOICE
OF A CHILD

*I*f you are a registered voter, pay your taxes and have never been convicted of a felony, then you have a very good chance of pulling jury duty at least once in your life. If you ever have the opportunity to sit on a jury for a trial involving the alleged sexual abuse of a child, I ask that you give the child's voice serious consideration. Consider the courage it took for that child to disclose the abuse. Consider what the abuser told that child to keep him or her from telling anyone about the abuse. Consider how many times that child was required to tell their story to social workers, police investigators, medical personnel, prosecutors and the grand jury before they testified at the trial. Consider the emotional and mental stress that child had to endure during the entire investigative and prosecutorial process up until that point and during their testimony at a public trial.

If you believe that the child victim's testimony is truthful, then you are obligated to convict his or her abuser. Don't mistake confusion for untruthfulness. Defense attorneys will try to confuse the child victim with times and dates to create reasonable doubt in the juror's minds. Don't fall for it. Children possess a different concept of time than adults. Usually young children will connect the time of the abuse with a significant event such as a holiday, winter recess, spring break, or summer vacation. Even when other jurors want to vote "not guilty" and try to pressure you into following suit, if you believe the child, then hang in there and let the judge call a mistrial. The prosecutor will happily try the case again. Unfortunately, too many juries have believed the child but felt led to not convict on the grounds that there wasn't any physical evidence to corroborate the child's testimony. As you now know, most sexual abuse cases don't have physical evidence. They rely solely on the voice of a child.

While there are many cases I can cite as an example, the one that comes to mind is a case that was investigated by Investigator Daniel Gleason, one of my colleagues in the Rochester Police Department. (On a side note—Investigator Gleason and his former partner, Sergeant Mark Mariano, with the assistance of Monroe County District Attorney Michael Green, solved a string of morning rapes known nationally as the "School Girl Rapist" case.) In the example I am referring to, Investigator Gleason investigated a case where a male school teacher hooked up with a fourteen-year-old male over a telephone chat line and eventually cultivated a physical relationship with the boy that included both oral sex and anal sexual intercourse. During their relationship, the suspect took the victim to his classroom on more than one occasion when school wasn't in session. The suspect was subsequently arrested by Investigator Gleason.

Before trial, the suspect's attorney argued that the prosecution should not be allowed to tell the jury that the suspect was currently employed as a school teacher or that he brought the victim to his classroom, on the grounds that it would be prejudicial to the suspect for the jury to have that information. The prosecutor argued that the jury should be allowed to know about the defendant's profession because he brought the victim to his classroom on more than one occasion. The judge agreed with the defense and ruled that the defendant's professional position could not be introduced to the jury. According to Investigator Gleason, the defendant's unrelenting defense attorney kept the victim on the witness stand for three straight days. In the end, the jurors found the defendant not guilty, even though they believed the victim's testimony after the grueling and protracted cross examination.

The jurors rationalized their not guilty verdict by saying that they believed that the sex was consensual, despite the fact that the law clearly states the victim was not old enough to give his consent. The prosecutor questioned the jurors after they rendered their verdict. He asked them: if they had known that the defendant was a school teacher, would they have voted to convict? They said yes, they would not have condoned the sex between this young teen and this man if had they known that he was a school teacher, someone they would have normally trusted. Now, did their reasoning make sense to you? Whether this man was a teacher or not should not have mattered in their decision. They said that they believed the victim's testimony and knew that he was not old enough to give consent. According to the law, that was enough to put this child predator in prison. The prosecutor successfully proved his case, but the jury still chose to let him go free and return to his school. While the fact that he was a school teacher does make his crime even more despicable, it should not have had any bearing in determining his guilt or innocence.

This tragic type of rationalization occurs often in deliberation rooms. Now if a juror does not believe the testimony of the victim or a critical witness, then there is sufficient cause for reasonable doubt. However, if a juror believes a child victim's testimony to be truthful and accurate, then they are obligated to find the defendant guilty, regardless of the lack of physical evidence. Please bear in mind that not all testimony and evidence is brought before a jury. They are often suppressed due to legal motions filed and argued by the defense before the trial begins. Since you might not be hearing the whole story during the trial, it is absolutely essential that you convict the defendant if you believe the victim, no matter how young or close to legal adulthood they may be.

CHAPTER 25

—ɯ—

CONSEQUENCES OF ABUSE
IN OUR HOMES AND COMMUNITIES

*T*here is a high correlation between child sexual abuse and violence in our homes and communities. A remarkable example of this issue is the Biblical account of what occurred in the house of Israel's most revered king (2 Samuel 13). King David's son, Amnon, raped his half sister, Tamar, and he refused to admit his guilt and seek forgiveness. Bitter resentment festered within the family. King David's other son Absalom eventually killed Amnon in an act of revenge. This act of sexual assault ripped the house of David apart and ultimately divided his kingdom (2 Samuel 14-20). I believe that God shared this traumatic event with us to teach us that the sexual assault of a defenseless child should never be tolerated or ignored.

The Greater Rochester Area is populated by approximately one million people. For most of my career, this mid-sized city has held the dubious distinction of being one of the most violent cities in the entire state of New York, with the highest murder rate per capita. Ironically, the Greater Rochester Area was recently rated as the sixth-best place to reside in the United States. Looks can be deceiving. Many people don't realize that the Rochester area also possesses an above-average rate of child sexual abuse.

Ephesians 6:4 (NKJV) says: *"And you, fathers, do not provoke your children to wrath, but bring them up in the training and admonition of the Lord."* Many of the violent criminals that I have interrogated over the years were motivated by a deep-seated anger against everyone and everything. Generally, people who have been sexually abused as a child will suffer from emotional problems. Some victims never conquer their anger and become overly aggressive in certain social situations, which can lead to the commission of violent offenses against others. Others turn their anger inward and exhibit self-destructive behavior such as drug or alcohol abuse. I can't imagine anything that would provoke a child's wrath more than sexually abusing them. That rage doesn't always spark external violence, but its caustic effects permeate our society.

King David appeared to be too passive as a parent. His lack of authoritative action against Amnon for this heinous act triggered the violence that subsequently divided his family and kingdom. If we as parents and a community do not become more active in fighting this type of crime and holding the perpetrators accountable, our society will continue to become more violent and divided.

CHAPTER 26

—◊◊◊—

CLOSING ARGUMENT
BY KRISTINA KARLE,
MONROE COUNTY ASSISTANT DISTRICT ATTORNEY;
BUREAU CHIEF OF THE DOMESTIC VIOLENCE AND CHILD ABUSE
BUREAU, MONROE COUNTY DISTRICT ATTORNEY'S OFFICE

*H*e was her gymnastics coach. She was her mother. He was the sentry at their school. He was his youth pastor. He was a physician and her best friend's father. He was her mom's boyfriend. He was her uncle. She was his neighbor and babysitter. All were trusted. All were known to their victims. All used their positions of authority to gain access to their child victims and to sexually abuse them. All took something from these children that can never be given back.

Each of these cases I prosecuted, and in the process, I learned how these men and women get to our children. I learned how the abusers gain the trust of the child, and in most situations, they gain the trust of the child's family as well. Most people are scared that their child will be abducted at a bus stop and stolen by a complete stranger. But the reality is that most of our children are sexually abused by someone that they know, love and trust.

Sexual predators are everywhere: sitting in the pews of our churches, teaching our children, in line with us at the grocery store. They are coaches, doctors, teachers, brothers, sisters, mothers, and friends. They are trusted. They are loved. And often the abusers of our children are believed more than our child victims. They claim innocence, using their positions in the community and outward appearances to belittle the victims and rally people to disbelieve the children.

I will never forget a case involving a well-respected obstetrician/gynecologist in our community who sexually abused his daughter's best friend for years. After the media got hold of the case, the letters poured into my office. The doctor's friends, colleagues and patients criticized me for prosecuting this man. One woman wrote, "This doctor could never molest a child. He delivered my baby. I have known this man for years and he could never do such a thing." With each letter, I thought, "Why doesn't anyone support the victim? How come no one cares about the nine-year-old child who was sexually abused by an adult male? Why no letters for her?" After the respected doctor stated in open court that he was indeed guilty, the letters again came pouring in. For the child victim? No. Letters begging for mercy for the good doctor. "Please don't send him to jail. He will never re-offend," they pleaded. How could the same people who could not believe that their doctor and friend could commit such a heinous act now argue that he would never re-offend? The people that wrote the letters never knew this man in the first place. They did not know the man behind the degree. They did not know the man underneath the white jacket. The only person who truly knew the doctor was his nine-year-old victim–the child that he himself had in fact delivered nine years earlier.

Heidi* was seven years old when her uncle came to live with her. When her mother was at work, her uncle sexually abused her little body. He did unspeakable things to her. Fearing that it was she who would get in trouble, Heidi kept her uncle's secret for a very long time. When Heidi finally told, she had no clue what was in store for her. She simply wanted her uncle to stop doing bad things to her. She never expected that she would have to tell a male investigator what her uncle did. She would have to allow a doctor to examine her genitalia. She certainly never imagined that she would have to go into a courtroom and tell twelve complete strangers about her uncle removing her underwear and touching her privates– and that she would have to do it with her uncle, the perpetrator of her pain, staring at her the whole time that she testified.

I called seven-year-old Heidi as a witness at her uncle's trial. Something that happened next has left an indelible mark on my mind's eye. It was an indescribably heartbreaking moment. I turned my head and saw this little girl walk into the huge courtroom and start down what must have seemed to her the longest aisle that she had ever seen. She slowly stepped toward the witness stand. There was a slight hesitation to her stride, a barely noticeable shiver. A hint of someone walking in slow motion, and then her tiny body fell. I was hoping to reach her before she totally collapsed, but I was too slow. When I reached her trembling body, I scooped her up gently, but swiftly into my arms and carried her from the courtroom. I felt her tremble, her wildly beating heart. I felt her anguish.

* The victim's name has been changed.

Bravely, Heidi agreed to go back into the courtroom with me. I walked with her this time down that aisle, hand in hand. There on the floor, I saw tearstains where this courageous little witness had fallen. They were a testament to her broken heart, her broken childhood, and her courage to return and face her molester.

For me, more than any other moment, it shook my core. It said, "See, see the devastation that sexual abuse is causing our children." It begged the question: "How can our society sit back and do so little, while these molesters and rapists prey on our most precious children?" These abusers befriend the innocent; they groom them; they seduce them; and then they scare them into silence. The abusers hope that the courage of Heidi does not exist.

He was a renowned gymnastics coach. Future gymnastic hopefuls sought him out, but he was looking for something else: a victim. One of the girls that he coached became just that. She looked up to him. She admired him. She wanted so badly to become a successful gymnast–to compete and to win. As such, this child spent as much time with her mentor and coach as she could. When her mom and dad dropped her off at practice, they believed that she was in the safe hands of someone who would protect her. This man, this coach, had become like family. Little did they know that behind the closed doors of the gym, this man was sexually abusing their daughter.

At first she felt special to have time alone with him, but that time alone quickly changed to a time of seduction. After the coach's victim disclosed the sexual abuse, her parents felt absolute betrayal and guilt for trusting this man with their precious daughter. This betrayal filled them with questions. How could someone who did so much for their daughter be responsible for her sexual abuse? How come they did not see it coming? How could they have been so blind to his evil purpose? Why did this have to happen to their daughter?

Trusted coaches do abuse, but unfortunately, so do parents. Kathy* is fifteen years old. Kathy was raped by her mother's boyfriend. Even more disturbing is the fact that Kathy's mother watched her boyfriend rape her daughter. Kathy's mother even encouraged her boyfriend to rape her daughter. Kathy's mother lay next to her daughter, holding that precious child's hand as Kathy was being raped, saying "Kathy, it's okay–Mom is here."

After testifying before a grand jury, I walked out of the courtroom with Kathy. This broken child looked at me and tears filled her eyes. She whispered, "What they did to me was wrong, wasn't it?" Until that moment Kathy did not fully understand how wrong it was–that this unnatural act was not normal, and it was okay to be filled with hurt and pain. Kathy didn't understand this because the woman that she called "Mother" had given this forty-two-year-old man her blessing to rape her own daughter. I remember holding Kathy as she wept. Tears of pain. Tears of loss. Like the tearstains that I had seen on a courtroom floor, Kathy's tears stained my lapel. Another tiny testament to the horror of sexual abuse.

---

* The victim's name has been changed.

He was a school sentry, a minister, a basketball coach, a youth mentor, and he became a dear and trusted friend of the victims' mother. The sentry came into her life in April 2000 after one of her sons got into trouble for setting a car on fire. A single mother of five sons and a daughter: she needed help. She had a son bound for life on the streets, and he had no father figure until this man appeared on her doorstep. This mother told me that she would never forget that day. She opened the door to his knocking, and there he stood in his school sentry uniform. He offered to help, and she gladly accepted. After all, he was also a minister, a youth mentor, a basketball coach, and he was responsible for security at her son's school. How could she not trust him?

Over the years, he spent time with all five of her boys. Taking them to the movies. Taking them bowling and to ride go-carts. He also spent time with her. They prayed together and they read Scriptures together. They often sat around and sang hymns together. On Thanksgiving, he said the blessing at her family's table. She broke bread with the man who molested each and every one of her five boys. "I handed my boys to him on a silver platter," she told me with tears in her eyes. "I trusted him."

These are just a handful of cases that I have prosecuted in the last few years. There are so many more stories to tell of children who have been hurt for a lifetime. Every six minutes a child is sexually abused. It happens behind the closed doors of homes in the suburbs and the inner city, behind the closed doors of churches, schools, and daycare centers. Our society must stop being blind to the suffering of our most innocent, vulnerable victims. We can't keep choosing to pretend that it's not happening or be too disturbed by the subject to act.

Stop and imagine what a child must think when her stepfather tells her, "I am going to show you what it is like to be with a boy," and then rubs his penis on her vagina. Or when a father tells his biological daughter, "It's time to be nice," right before he puts his mouth on her vagina and has sex with her. This is disturbing, and it should shock you. But you should not be shocked that this actually happening to our children *every day*. Please stop being blind to our children's pain and suffering.

Holocaust survivor Elie Weisel has devoted his life to ending human suffering. He once said, "There may be times when we are powerless to prevent injustice, but there must never be a time when we fail to protest." Don't deny that this is happening to our children. Don't tell yourself it is too horrible to think about. I beg each and every single one of you–please–let's band together and start protesting the atrocities that are perpetrated against our precious children every day. Don't wait for someone else to do it. Don't leave it to the justice system alone. Hear their voices and believe. Hear their voices and act. Hear their voices and help heal their wounds.

"... *Children* are a heritage from the Lord."

PSALM 127:3 (NKJV)

SECTION V

—⁕—

CONCLUSION

Fun in the pool, two years.

Kali at six months,
not happy about winter hat.

Kali with Boo-Boo Baby.

Easter photo at one and a half.

May 1994, almost five.
Last photo.

CHAPTER 27

—◊◊—

A MOTHER'S TESTIMONY
BY JUDY GIFFORD-TOSH
MOTHER OF KALI ANN POULTON
SEPTEMBER 20, 1989 – MAY 23, 1994

*T*O MY PRECIOUS ANGEL KALI,

It is September 20th, 1989 at 9:00 AM, and I wake up feeling a little different than I had for the last nine months. After going through my natural childbirth classes, I believe that I am in labor and you are about to enter the world. I did not know if you were going to be a girl or a boy because I wanted to be surprised, but I knew that I had already fallen in love with you. I had much anticipation and excitement, realizing that my life was about to change forever.

Exactly at 9:50 PM you made your entrance into the world as a seven-pound, nine-ounce baby girl, and I named you Kali Ann. After two days at the hospital I took you home, realizing that this precious, frail, innocent little angel was mine, and I was now officially a mother. I would hold you and stare at you with such amazement that I had created you and carried you under my heart for nine months.

As you know, my relationship with your father was anything but good or stable. Your father came from a very dysfunctional family without a lot of love. I believe that your father loved you the best way that he knew how, but it was not enough for me.

I knew when I got pregnant that I was going to be a single mother, and I had come to terms with that. I now had a purpose and direction for my life, which was being your mother. After a rocky relationship with your father, I took you and moved out. I loved you too much to let you grow up in an environment that was unhealthy for both of us.

Right before your third birthday, we moved to Gleason Circle with the hope of a new beginning. There were times when things were tough and money was tight, but our love for each other always helped us survive. Your father had made a statement once that I really did not have a life. What he never understood was that *you* were my life, Kali.

We were planning to move to Virginia so that you could grow up near your relatives and start kindergarten in September 1994. I was excited to have you near your grandmother, aunts, uncles, and cousins. Your Aunt Wendy, my sister, spoiled you beyond belief. She was so excited about you being born because you had made her an aunt. Because she worked at The Disney Store, you were constantly dressed in Disney clothes and smothered with Disney stuffed animals and toys. Thanks to her, we were planning a trip to Walt Disney in June. You were very excited to meet all of your favorite Disney characters. Unfortunately, that trip would never come.

In March 1994, you and I met a man that would change our lives forever. The man that we knew as Mark had a little boy that you enjoyed playing with at the playground. But he was not who either of us thought that he was. Mark often commented on how pretty you were, but we were used to hearing that because you were such a beautiful little girl. At one point Mark made Mommy feel uncomfortable because of something he had said. From that point on, I went out of my way to avoid him when you and I were outside together. He made me feel uncomfortable, as he appeared to have an unusual attraction to you that a grown man should not have toward a four-year-old child. Later I learned that Mark could tell by my actions that I did not want him near you, even though I never told him that.

After work on May 23rd, 1994, Mommy picked you up from daycare and we went home. I was working a part-time job on top of my full-time job so that we could save money to go to Disney World. I had just started delivering magazines at a nearby apartment complex. I had to put them in order by apartment number and then you and I would deliver them. You liked going up to the mailboxes and dropping the magazines into them. You were a very good helper; it was the kind of job that you and I could do together.

That night I made dinner and started putting the magazines in order. You wanted to go outside to play. You were a little unsettled and kept asking me to let you go out and ride your Big Wheel. I really wanted you to stay inside until I was done; then we would go deliver the magazines and then off to McDonald's to play in the outside play area just as I had promised. After you pleaded and begged to go out, I finally gave in.

I gave you your Big Wheel with strict instructions to stay in front of our apartment on the sidewalk until we were ready to go. It would only take me about five minutes to finish. After those minutes passed, I looked out front and did not see you. I called your name, Kali, and kept calling your name because I did not see you. I got very scared because I could not find you–or your Big Wheel. I ran up and down the sidewalks within the complex, screaming your name at the top of my lungs, hoping to find you.

Because I could not find you and I was scared to death, I called 911. The police and fire department came, and the search for a missing little girl named Kali began. The day after you disappeared, the police department assigned detectives Patrick Crough and Tom Passmore to us. In the days and months that followed, I spent endless hours with them. We looked at Big Wheel pieces and clothes that had been located; I took polygraph tests and a voice analysis test. I was even hypnotized with hope of remembering something about the night you went missing. I was willing to do everything and anything to find you.

That day would seem to never end. It turned into twenty-seven months of just not knowing where you were and if you were okay or not. You being missing consumed my life. I did anything and everything possible to find you. We made posters for storefronts and cars. We made truck posters and gave them away at truck stops and the Thruway; we mailed them around the country. We went on *America's Most Wanted* and all of the talk shows numerous times telling your story. A satellite was even named after you before it was sent into space to bring attention to the fact that you were a missing child. You were registered with all of the missing children agencies around the country with the hope that just one person might recognize you. The help from everyone in the community and around the country was beyond belief, and for that I am forever grateful.

I was willing to do everything and anything to help find you. Because of the lack of evidence, what normally happens is that the police will look at the parents. Kali, because I was the last person that supposedly had seen you, the police looked mostly at me. I remember one of the first questions that Patrick asked me when he arrived at my house the day after you went missing: had there been anyone that had recently moved in or out of the apartment complex that showered you with gifts or unusual attention? At first, I said no. Then I thought about the question more and gave him Mark Christie's name. I was already at the point where I was avoiding him because of what he had said that had made me uncomfortable.

I came to trust Pat and Tom as they helped me survive the first months that you were missing. They were my heroes, and I knew that they wanted to find you as much as I did. More importantly, they believed me and trusted me when most of law enforcement did not, which made my relationship with them very difficult.

Kali, I could not imagine my life without you, and I desperately wanted you back at any cost. I wanted to believe that someone took you to keep you and love you. At least I had hope with believing that: I had hope that someday I would hear your voice, see your face, and feel your embrace again. I hated thinking that someone else was caring for you, but at the same time believing that gave me some peace, because it meant that you were alive. I could not even begin to imagine that someone could harm my precious little four-year-old daughter. "How could one human being do this to another?" I asked myself a million times. I was unable to understand that. And I could not understand how I was still living. The night that you went missing, it felt like someone had ripped my heart out and was holding it, still beating, in their hand. How could I still be standing or breathing? Why was I still alive, how could I be?

Your beautiful face was spread around the country in a desperate attempt to find you. No one wanted you back more than me, but so many people wanted to be the one to bring you home to me. During the time that you were missing, Mommy met a man named Floyd. Floyd was a single father of two daughters. His reason for helping me was that he could not imagine having his children missing, not knowing where they were. I could not understand how he could get involved with Mommy. I had a missing daughter and my life was a nightmare. "Why is he so persistent when I constantly push him away?" I would ask myself. I did not have time for a relationship. You were missing and you were my focus. Besides, I did not have a heart left to feel anything. Your Aunt Wendy believes that I was not meant to know the truth about you when you first disappeared because there was nothing more important in my life than you; without you, there was no reason for me to be alive. A year after meeting Floyd, your Mommy and he started a relationship. Two years later, we got married. I was amazed that a man that never met you seemed to love you almost as much as I did.

The world knew what Kali Ann looked like, but they did not know who you really were. They did not know that you loved Barney, were scared of clowns, and that you desperately wanted to learn to read. Remember, Kali, how Mommy read you books day after day to the point where you remembered every word? Often at night when I was tired I would skip a word here and there, but you would let me know that I had missed a word. I remember catching you one day in your room reading a book to your baby dolls that you had lined up on the bed. What made me smile was that after reading the page to them, you would turn the book toward them and show them the picture like they did with you at pre-school. That was a precious moment for me. Unfortunately, I never had the chance to tell you that.

I am sure you remember your favorite doll–Boo-Boo Baby. My friend Suzanne loved you very much and was happy that she got to know and love you, unlike most of the world. She gave you a soft-bodied doll for Christmas after you turned two. You loved that doll very much and dragged it everywhere with you. I remember picking you up from day-care one day, noticing that your doll's eyes looked crossed. Later I learned that a child at daycare had done that to your doll. That really did not seem to bother you that much. After some time I noticed a crack in your doll's face. I knew that it was going to eventually break away, and she would have a hole in her face. Eventually that day came where your baby doll was literally loved to pieces. Your daycare provider stated that you were very upset by that and seemed to be dis-interested in your baby now. So I sat with you and told you that your baby now had a boo-boo, and she actually needed *more* loving because of that. I told you that when you had a boo-boo, I would patch you up and give you extra loving, and you needed to do the same for your baby. It was amazing to watch you then love that doll more than you ever had. She never had a name prior to that happening— you just called her Baby. But from that point on, her name was Boo-Boo Baby. I loved that you loved her that way. You were such a little mother to all of your dolls. It gave me some comfort to see you love your dolls the way that I loved you.

After twenty-seven months of not knowing anything about what happened to you, the man that you knew as Mark confessed to taking your life and hiding your body somewhere where no one would have ever found you. After getting this news, I became paralyzed. The little bit of life that I still had inside me just died. This was the man that I told the police I believed was somehow involved, but that had been pushed aside because they were too focused on me.

Kali, as your mother, it is my job to protect you and keep you from harm. It breaks my heart that I somehow failed you as your mother, Kali, and I will have to live with that for the rest of my life. I can't imagine the fear that you must have experienced, having someone that you knew hurt you so badly. I constantly "what if" myself. What if I had never moved to Gleason Estates? Would this have happened? What if I had not let you out that night? Would this have still happened? Did Mark have you pegged as his next victim, looking for any opportunity to get to you at some point in time? There are so many things that we will never know the answers to. Only God above holds those answers. But one thing that I do know is that Mark heard me calling for you that night that you were missing; and I know that if he heard me calling your name Kali, then you heard me calling your name. You knew that I was trying to find you and save you from whatever was about to happen.

Kali, I refuse to let your death be in vain. I must make a difference in someone else's life. I sit on a board of a missing child group to help other parents of missing children during the most heartbreaking time of their lives. I am also now helping to be part of a book about child abuse that teaches parents how to recognize the signs. My doing that somehow brings me closer to you.

I know that you have given me many signs over the years, Kali, that you are here. At first I did not know how to recognize those signs, but now I embrace them when I get them. I believe that I will be reunited with you again someday. I remember a pastor once telling me that you did not belong to me. I was quite upset with that. I said, "I am her mother, I gave birth to her – she is mine." He stated that you were given to me to love and be your mother for whatever time that God allowed me to have you. Kali, it was way too short of a time. I had such visions and dreams for you that will never come to be, but I am truly grateful that I had you for almost five years. You taught me so much about life and about undying love that I will carry forever.

I am going to end my letter to you the way we ended every day when I tucked you into bed at night. I would ask you "How much does Mommy love?" And you would reply, "Around the world and back again." Please know, Kali, that I did go around the world and back again to bring you home to me, because I loved you that much.

With endless
Love,
Mommy

Kali, nine months, with Mommy.

CHAPTER 28

—⁓⁓—

A CALLING...
A MISSION FIELD...
A MINISTRY...

"Jesus wept."

JOHN 11:35 (KJV)

I can't help but think that Jesus weeps for those little ones who fall into the hands of a child predator. I also believe that Jesus weeps over the despair and hopelessness that we experience as a community because of the crimes that are committed against our children. We know from the Bible that God especially hates the sin of adultery because it destroys families and communities (Malachi 2:14-16, 1 Corinthians 12:26a). If this is true, can you imagine how much more God hates sexual abuse, considering the destruction it causes in the life of a child? As parents and as a community, we must do everything that we possibly can to fight this evil and eradicate it.

In December 2005, United States Attorney General Alberto Gonzales addressed 1500 local, state, and federal law enforcement officials at a conference in Washington

D.C., stating that crimes against children was second only to terrorism on his agency's agenda. While I would not argue with this prioritization, I believe that Satan desires us to stay preoccupied with our borders and threats from outside so that he can continue to quietly devour our children and destroy us as a nation from within. Through our own sexual deviate behavior and liberalism, Satan has been able to deploy the Internet to increase child abuse and exploitation to a pandemic level. Child predators are one of the most important components of his sinister scheme against fallen man. If we seriously reduce, or even eradicate, that component, we significantly hinder the forces of evil. Granted, the Bible teaches us that evil will not be eliminated from the world until Jesus' return. However, until that happens we must continue to be proactive with this effort on behalf of our children.

If there is any chance of eradicating the population of child predators, we will need to fight this battle on the spiritual front as well as the physical front. Every parent should pray for their children daily. Every church and Bible study group should pray for each child that they are connected to. Designate prayer warriors every week to take on this assignment. Because the Bible tells us that we wrestle not against flesh and blood, but against principalities (Ephesians 6:12), the spiritual aspect of this battle is more important than any other aspect. Jesus taught us to seek the kingdom of God first (Matthew 6:33). If we seek Him first, then we have His blessing and His power to do all things that He ordains for us to do. The Bible teaches that the weapons of our warfare are not carnal (2 Corinthians 10:3, 4). As believers, we have a weapon that is more powerful than any earthly program alone. It would be foolish not to use it against an evil that is clearly spiritual in nature.

Please take note that this request for prayer does not come from a pastor, minister, church elder, deacon, or Bible teacher, but a cynical and callused police detective who has made a living operating in the destructive wake of the Evil One and his minions. While humanists will tell us that good exists in every person, I have learned otherwise throughout my law enforcement career: I have learned that every person has an enormous amount of evil in them. While many from a human perspective will also possess a certain amount of good, every person is capable of pondering and committing evil. Long before I picked up the Bible, I discovered that every man and woman possesses a dark side, fueled by pride, selfishness, jealousy and lust. Some of us do a remarkable job of suppressing these and are able to function as decent people, even though we battle the desires daily. When we attempt to fulfill these desires, it is never enough. Whether it is a desire for power, wealth, fame, or sex, it is never quenched. This lack of fulfillment eventually gives way to criminal behavior for some. They have lost complete control and placed themselves in bondage to that particular sin. That is when they usually end up on law enforcement's radar screen.

While prayer is the best action any person can take against the crime of child sexual abuse, God has equipped and called some of us into the battle that exists in the physical realm. We in the church body need to recognize the issues of child sexual abuse, physical abuse, and neglect as a mission field that needs tending. Sexual abuse is a topic that most churches choose not to openly speak of or concern themselves with. It is the elephant in the room that no one wants to openly acknowledge and then address. Pastors, ministers and other members of the clergy need to unify and appoint some leadership to minister to those families who are victimized by this crime. I understand that not every clergy member will be able to stomach this issue, just as all law enforcement officers cannot. It is important for the clergy to appoint those who possess the spiritual strength to minister to those who fall victim.

Additionally, members of the clergy should recognize a profession dedicated to battling this evil as a worthwhile calling for the young adults in their flock to consider. God has blessed certain individuals with specific spiritual gifts that would make them very effective in dealing with one of the most difficult issues facing mankind. They should encourage those who appear to have these spiritual gifts to consider careers in law enforcement, social work, child protective work, counseling, forensic interviewing of reported child victims, forensic evidence investigation, and medical positions related to identifying and treating the injuries of abused children. All of these professions need competent, motivated people that are dedicated to seeking the truth in all reported cases of child abuse. This kind of work is not for the faint-hearted, nor is it for those who become overly emotional when discussing the topic of child sexual abuse. One must be passionate about this work without being overcome and hindered by such passion. I can not think of a better group of people to recruit from than those in the Body of Christ. Attempting to enter this overwhelming battle without the rock-solid spiritual foundation of Jesus Christ would be similar to the young shepherd and future king, David, attempting to fight the giant warrior Goliath with the useless armor of King Saul, the defunct King of Israel.

I was raised as a Catholic and attended an all-boy Catholic high school run by Jesuit priests. But I lived outside of God's will and was always in search of the true meaning of life. Even though I wasn't walking with the Lord at that time, He still blessed me with a wonderful family and a successful career. He used me to expose many horrific crimes and bring the perpetrators to justice, in spite of my own wicked and selfish heart. It was my own exhaustive search for an answer to why people do such horrible things to each other that led me to read the Bible and begin to learn the answer of this haunting question. Under the guidance of God's Holy Sprit, I gained both wisdom and comfort surrounding this difficult issue, which I once considered virtually unattainable.

I consider myself a member of the modern-day Roman guard, working for a twenty-first century Rome and enforcing its laws. But since I accepted Jesus Christ into my heart and asked Him to forgive me of my sins, I am now a converted soldier who openly works for God, according to His will. After I started walking with the Lord approximately eight years ago, I immediately thought that He would desire me to retire from my police job and begin a new life of service, away from the filth of society and the ranks of the Roman guard, where sin and temptation run rampant. But every time I started to prepare myself to make the separation, something would tug on my heart to not follow through with it.

Finally, I came to the realization that I had to surrender the issue to the Lord to decide and stop telling myself what I thought He wanted me to do. This was not easy for a person such as me, but by His grace, I was able to let go of it. The Lord eventually spoke to my heart after I waited on Him for several weeks and just focused on Him rather than on my future. The Lord told me in His quiet voice that He had blessed me with the gifts that made me successful in my profession, even when I wasn't walking with Him. So why would He want me to quit the job that He had appointed me to do now that I had accepted Him into my heart and daily life? In essence, God told me to continue working in the same capacity, but now to do it under His influence and direction, and watch how much more He would bless me. Without any reservation, I can honestly say that God has blessed me beyond belief since I accepted and embraced Him in my life and started doing my job for the sole purpose of glorifying Him. I feel so privileged.

As a temple of the Holy Spirit, I now view my job as a ministry. I know that God has placed me in this role for a reason, so I look to Him daily for guidance and strength. Despite the heart-wrenching challenges, God allows me plenty of rest and restores me to face the next wave of evil and its destructive wake. Having investigated many horrible crimes over the years, I can say that there is nothing more emotionally challenging than investigating a reported crime against a young child. However, I never feel a better sense of purpose than when I am working on behalf of a reported child victim. They are the helpless ones. I feel close to God when I am working one of these cases, even when I am anguishing over my inability to bring the perpetrator to justice. God provides me with an inner peace beyond my understanding that enables me to be patient and have confidence in Him to unfold the truth in His own time.

Like the young King David, there comes a time when we must act on our faith in Christ and have the courage to step out in front of the rest of God's army and take on the enemy that no one else desires to. I challenge all church leaders to answer the call in both the spiritual and physical realms. If anyone in Christian leadership desires to explore this challenge, please contact me and I will be happy to pray and brainstorm with you for direction in how you and your fellowship can enter this very important battle and mission field.

CHAPTER 29

—⁓—

ASK JESUS FOR HELP

"*Again, I observed all the oppression that takes place under the sun. I saw the tears of the oppressed, with no one to comfort them. The oppressors have great power, and their victims are helpless. So I concluded that the dead are better off than the living. But most fortunate of all are those who are not yet born. For they have not seen all the evil that is done under the sun.*"

ECCLESIASTES 4:1-3 (NLT)

When I read this passage I can not help but think about children who are forced to endure being molested over a span of time long enough to darken their soul and leave them hopeless. The person who is supposed to comfort and protect them is so often the very one who oppresses and offends them. These predators have misused their God-appointed authority and have fed on them like ravenous wolves. As these children are being devoured and their tears fall with no one to wipe them away, it is no wonder that they long for death and envy those who were never born.

If you experienced this type of crime as a child, then I have no doubt that you can relate to the aforementioned passage. Please look to Matthew 18:6, which assures us that God will unleash his wrath upon the one who offended you if they have not truly repented and sought God's forgiveness. Jesus Christ made it very clear that it would be better for these people to have a large millstone tied around their neck and be thrown into the deep sea than to face God's wrath for such an offense. God also said, "...I will take revenge. I will pay them back..." in Hebrews 10:30 NKJV. I urge you to pass this burden on to Jesus to carry and ask Him to comfort you beyond all understanding, for we will never understand why certain people resort to such evil.

If the phrase "comfort beyond all understanding" is a new concept to you then please consider the following. When we were young we were unable to understand why our parents did not allow us to have our own way in certain situations. Even when our parents were patient enough to explain why, there were times when we were unable to comprehend what they were trying to teach us. Additionally, we were too young to fully comprehend why our parents loved, protected, and comforted us. We just automatically sought refuge from them during our time of need. We possessed a strong faith and expectation that the adults who cared for us would provide comfort and protection. If you are a responsible parent then you understand this.

Jesus teaches us to look upon God as our Heavenly Father and approach Him as a child approaches a loving parent. I suggest that you not attempt to understand why bad things occur in our lives. We do not have the capacity to understand the answers to these questions on this side of eternity. Just take comfort in the knowledge that God loves us and desires that we approach Him as one of His beloved children. We inherited the capacity from Him to love our children unconditionally no matter how they behave, even when we are insanely angry with them. Take comfort in knowing that God loves us in the same way, but in an even more perfect and superior way than we are capable of loving our own children. Seek His love through our Lord and Savior, Jesus Christ and you will be comforted beyond your ability to understand why. He loves us so abundantly, so we can experience great peace and joy during our times of tribulation. Just accept it as a child would accept a gift.

"Come unto Me, all ye that labor and are heavy laden, and I will give you rest. Take My yoke upon you, and learn of Me; for I am meek and lowly in heart; and ye shall find rest unto your souls. For My yoke is easy, and My burden is light."

MATTHEW 11:28-30 (KJV)

Matthew 5:44 instructs: "pray for those who spitefully use you and persecute you." If you are still living under the emotional and spiritual bondage from past molestation, I urge you to pray for the person who hurt you. As difficult as that is to believe, it will bring you peace beyond all understanding. The Devil would rather have us walking around absorbed in our own pain; he would never want you to forgive the one who molested you. This is one of the many ways that spiritual warfare works. The Devil uses this crime to destroy a child's sprit. He wants them to harbor life-long pain and hatred for the abuser, for he knows that God will not bless that and can not commune with a person who carries around such malice in their heart. For our own sake, we must stop focusing on our own hurt. Ask the Lord to heal your heart, help you forgive the person who abused you, and repent from your own sinful ways. In return, the Lord will then heal and restore you. But we must truly surrender our anger and hatred to Him. Keep asking Him every day to take negative thoughts away from you and He will. Sooner or later, you will begin to feel the transformation from despair to inner peace and strengthened faith. This is the personal miracle that God offers everyone who sincerely asks for it. I have no doubt that this experience will demonstrate God's unlimited power to you. Having faith in Jesus Christ will eventually remove the restraints of emotional bondage that resulted from being victimized as a child.

PLEASE READ AND MEDITATE

ON THE FOLLOWING SCRIPTURES (NLT):

"For God loved the world in this way: He gave His One and Only Son, so that everyone who believes in Him will not perish but have eternal life. For God did not send His Son into the world that He might condemn the world, but that the world might be saved through Him. Anyone who believes in Him is not condemned, but anyone who does not believe is condemned, because he has not believed in the one and only son of God. This, then, is the judgment: the light has come into the world, and people loved the darkness rather than the light because their deeds were evil. For everyone who practices wicked things hates the light and avoids it, so that

his deeds may not be exposed. But anyone who lives by the truth comes to the light, so that his works may be shown to be accomplished by God."

JOHN 3:16-21

"The Father, in fact, judges no one but has given all judgment to the Son, so that all people will honor the Son just as they honor the Father. Anyone who does not honor the Son does not honor the Father who sent Him."

JOHN 5:22-23

"I am the way, the truth, and the life. No one comes to the Father except through Me."

JOHN 14:6

"I assure you: The one who believes in Me will also do the works that I do. And he will do even greater works than these, because I am going to the Father. What ever you ask in My name, I will do it so that the Father may be glorified in the Son. If you ask Me anything in My name, I will do it."

JOHN 14:12-14

"If anyone loves Me, he will keep My word. My Father will love him, and We will come to him and make Our home with him. The one who doesn't love Me will not keep My words. The word that you hear is not Mine but is from the Father

*who sent Me. I have spoken these things to you while I re-
main with you. But the Counselor, the Holy Spirit—the Father will send Him in My name—will teach you all things
and remind you of everything I have told you."*

JOHN 14: 23-26

IF YOU DESIRE A PERSONAL RELATIONSHIP WITH OUR
LORD IN HEAVEN, JESUS CHRIST, THEN PRAY THIS
PRAYER WITH A SINCERE HEART:

*"Dear Jesus, I come before You as a sinner and ask
that You forgive me of my sins. I know that You voluntarily
died on the cross for me and shed Your blood to wash away
my sin so that I may enter the Kingdom of Heaven to reside with You and our Heavenly Father. Please come into my
heart, Jesus. Please wash, replenish, and overflow me with
the waters of Your Holy Spirit from this day forward, so that
I may do Your will and not my own. Amen."*

Congratulations and welcome to God's family and
the Kingdom of Heaven! Does this mean that you will be on
Easy Street from this point on? No. In fact, Satan will probably dispatch one of his minions to bring a spiritual attack
upon you, for he is upset that you took such a great step of
faith. But rest assured, you have joined the winning team in
this raging spiritual battle. Just keep your focus on Jesus and
He will lead you out through the trials that fill our daily lives
just as He will carry us through the valley of the shadow of
death to enter into His eternal rest.

Remember to "talk" with our Heavenly Father every day through our Intercessor, Jesus. Get your hands on a Bible and start reading it daily—even if it is just a verse or two. If that is all that you are able to read but you choose to ponder it all day long, it will nourish your soul incredibly. If the language of the King James translation is too difficult to understand, then visit a Christian book store and ask for assistance to help you find a translation that you are comfortable with and can understand.

Also, seek out other people who pursue a personal relationship with God through Christ. God blesses those who congregate to worship Him. The fellowship will bless you and bring you comfort. Jesus said that where two or three are gathered in His name, He will be present (Matthew 18:20). Remember, God works through every one of His followers— including you—when they surrender their lives to Him. God will bless you through other believers and He will bless them while working through you. This is the gift of community worship, otherwise known as "church."

> *"Trust in the Lord with all your heart,*
> *and do not lean on your own understanding.*
> *In all your ways acknowledge Him,*
> *and He will make your paths straight."*
>
> **PROVERBS 3:5-6 (NIV)**

ACKNOWLEDGEMENTS

—◊—

THIS BOOK WOULD NOT
HAVE BEEN POSSIBLE IF NOT FOR:

Monroe County Sheriff Patrick O'Flynn appointing me to work with the Faith Alliance Group of pastors and ministers in the Greater Rochester Area in bringing their message against child abuse to the community and his continual support of the Child Abuse Network (C.A.N.) Program; Dr. John Walker, who is the founder of C.A.N. and the most dedicated and passionate person in the cause. This book is the result of his persuasion to convert my verbal presentation about child predators to written form. Dr. Walker is truly a man of God who I have come to admire, respect and love dearly.

This book would not be possible if the following members of my church had not put in long hours of hard work without any form of compensation in this temporal world. They include my editor (who wishes to remain anonymous) for her generosity, dedication, and insight. Her willingness to take on this project inspired me to continue when I was ready to give up. Thanks to Rob Kellogg, for designing and setting up our website, MillstoneJustice.org and overseeing it to assist in the distribution of this book; Cherie Wood for donating her professional skills as book layout and graphic designer to prepare the book for print and designing its cover; also, Steve Pettis for designing the illustrations that are depicted throughout the book.

I would like to take this opportunity to recognize and thank my accountants, Mike and Francis Cudlipp, for setting up and overseeing our non-profit organization, Millstone Justice Children's Advocacy, at no cost to me or the organization to fund this project. If you are familiar with the paperwork, man hours, and fees associated with this process then you know how generous a gift this was and will continue to be.

God inspired and used these folks as His vessels to deliver this message to you. Their benevolent service has truly humbled me, and serves as a stellar example of what it is to make a sacrifice without contention or expectation of notoriety.

I would like to thank notable author and speaker Cheri Fuller for allowing me the privilege of using her story of the missionary as an excellent example of how daily fervent prayer protects us and those we love. Also, I would like to thank those individuals who took the time out of their busy lives to read and critique my manuscript at some point during the process of creation and transformation into what it is today. You know who you are.

Above all others, I thank the most important people in my life: my wife, Suzanne, and our three children, Jason Allen, Jessica Lee, and Cassidy Hope, for their unwavering love and support, encouragement, and prayers over the two years this project took to complete.

Finally, and most importantly, this book would not be possible if not for God's unfailing love, grace, and mercy, and a lifetime of countless undeserved blessings that He has bestowed upon a wretch like me.

I *am* forever
in His debt.

ABOUT

—⟨⟨⟩—

THE AUTHOR

Patrick Crough has been employed with the Monroe County Sheriff's Office since 1983. He served as a deputy sheriff in the Parks and Marine Unit and on the Road Patrol until December 1987. In January 1988 he was transferred to the Criminal Investigation Division where he worked as a plainclothes deputy in the Violent Warrant Squad and as an undercover officer in the Vice Squad and Narcotics Unit. In January 1990, he was assigned to the Zone B substation CID evening squad as an acting investigator, where he supported the road patrol by investigating serious felonies. He was later promoted to the rank of Criminal Investigator and transferred to the Major Crimes Unit in January 1991. He currently serves in that unit as the most senior investigator.

Investigator Crough and his colleagues in the Major Crimes Unit investigate murders and other reported homicides, suspicious deaths, physical assaults that result in serious physical injury, sexual assaults, crimes against children, police-involved shootings, and conduct covert, special investigations per the authority of the Monroe County Sheriff.

During the late 1990s Investigator Crough was assigned to a federal violent crime task force and served as an undercover agent in a firearms suppressions unit that proactively targeted convicted felons and violent criminals who trafficked and sold illegal firearms in Western New York.

Investigator Crough has served on the Monroe County Sheriff Hostage Rescue Team since 1989 as a hostage negotiator, and currently serves as the commander of that specialized team.

Investigator Crough resides in the Rochester, New York area with his wife, Suzanne, and two daughters, Jessica Lee and Cassidy Hope. Patrick and Suzanne also enjoy the company of their two grandchildren, Christopher Allen and Caitlin Rose. They are both gifts from God as a result of the union of their son, Jason Allen, and his wife, Sarah.

Investigator Patrick Crough with former Monroe County Sheriff Andrew P. Meloni, whom the author gratefully calls "the man who provided me with the opportunity of a lifetime when he hired me and promoted me to the rank of Criminal Investigator seven years later."